The Egyptian Gods

An Illustrated Introduction

Matthew Leigh Embleton

Copyright ©2025 Matthew Leigh Embleton. All rights reserved.

The Egyptian Gods

Introduction	5
Timeline of Egyptian Religion	9
Locations	11
Symbols and Objects	16
The Ogdoad: The Eight Gods of Hermopolis	25
The Ennead: The Nine Gods of Heliopolis	27
The Theban Triad	28
The Memphite Triad	29
The Elephantine Triad	30
The Abydos Triad	31
The Four Sons of Horus	32
The 42 Judges of Ma'at	33
Aker: Guardian of the Horizons	36
Amun: The Hidden One and Supreme Creator	38
Amunet: The Invisible One and Primordial Mother	40
Anput: Goddess of the Embalming and the Dead	42
Anubis: God of the Afterlife	44
Anuket: Fertility Goddess of the Nile	46
Apis: The Sacred Bull of Memphis	48
Aten: The Sun Disk	50
Atum: The Primordial Creator	52
Bastet: Leonine Warrior and Feline Protector	54
Bat: Goddess of the Cosmos and Fertility	56
Bennu: God of Creation and Resurrection	58
Bes: The Household Protector	60
Geb: God of the Earth, and Father of Snakes	62
Hapi: The Flooder of the Nile	64
Hathor: Goddess of the Sky, and the Afterlife	66
Hauhet: Primordial Goddess of Infinity	68
Heh: Primordial God of Infinity	70
Heqet: Goddess of Fertility and Regeneration	72
Heru-ur: God of the Sky, Sun and Moon	74
Hesat: The Milk Goddess	76
Horus: God of the Sun and the Sky	78
Imentet: Goddess of the Afterlife	80
Imhotep: God of Wisdom and Medicine	82
Isis: Goddess of Magic, Protection, and Healing	84
Kauket: Primordial Goddess of Darkness	86
Kek: Primordial God of Darkness	88
Khepri: Scarab-Headed God of the Morning Sun	90
Khnum: The Divine Potter	92
Khonsu: God of the Moon	94
Maahes: The Lion-Headed Warrior and Protector	96
Ma'at: Goddess of Truth, Justice, and Order	98
Menhit: Goddess of War and Protection	100
Min: God of Fertility	102
Montu: God of War and the Sun	104
Mut: Goddess of Motherhood and the Sky	106
Naunet: Priordial Goddess of the Waters	108
Nefertem: The Healing God of the Lotus Flower	110

Neith: Goddess of War, Hunting, and Weaving 112
Nekhbet: Ancient Winged Mother and Protector 114
Neper: God of Grain 116
Nephthys: Goddess of Mourning and Lamentation 118
Nepit: Goddess of Grain 120
Nu: God of the Primordial Waters 122
Nut: The Sky Goddess 124
Onuris: God of War 126
Osiris: God of the Afterlife and Resurrection 128
Pakhet: Goddess of Hunting, War, and Protection 130
Ptah: God of Craft, Architecture, and Metalwork 132
Ra: The Sun God 134
Renenutet: Goddess of Grain and Nourishment 136
Satis: Fertility Goddess of the Nile 138
Sekhmet: Goddess of War and Medicine 140
Serket: The Scorpion Goddess of Healing 142
Set: God of Chaos, Storms, and Violence 144
Shu: God of the Air 146
Sobek: The Crocodile God of the Nile 148
Tatenen: God of the Primordial Mound 150
Tefnut: Goddess of Moisture, Rain, and Humidity 152
Thoth: God of Wisdom, Science, and Magic 154
Wadjet: Cobra Goddess and Protector 156
Wosret: Goddess of Power and Protection 158
Summary of Names in Hieroglyphs 160
Source Texts for Egyptian Mythology 164

Cover: An Ancient Egyptian Temple of the Imagination
Source: AI generated by the author

Acknowledgments

I have long been fascinated by languages and history, and I am very grateful to the special people in my life who have supported and encouraged me in my work. Thank you for believing in me. You know who you are.

Introduction

The Egyptian gods are the key players in Egyptian mythology, an ancient collection of narratives that evolved over thousands of years to explain the origins of the forces of nature around us, their impact on our lives, the nature of humankind itself, what it means to be human, our relationship with the earth and the cosmos, and our sense of place within it.

If we include all of the major gods, minor gods, spirits, demi-gods, mythical creatures, etc. from all of the different traditions across the ancient Egyptian world, we would be looking at about five hundred, and if all of them were included in this book, it would be so thick that you would have to ask Montu, Horus, Set, and Bes to hold each corner of it for you, so this is an illustrated introduction to sixty two of them.

In ancient Egypt, the gods were not just figures of worship, they were central to most aspects of daily life. As ancient Egyptian civilisation declined and foreign powers took hold, the prominence of these gods waned but was never entirely forgotten. Egyptian culture spread through trade, conquest, and cultural exchange. During the Ptolemaic dynasty, Egyptian and Greek culture and mythology was fused together, resulting in the philosophical and spiritual tradition of Hermeticism, the foundation of Esotericism, Alchemy, Astrology, Magic, Occultism, and modern spiritual movements.

Egyptian gods and goddesses like Isis, Osiris, Horus, Anubis, and Serapis, were worshipped outside of Egypt across the Mediterranean, Greece, Asia Minor, and across the Roman Empire as far away as Gaul, Germany, and Britain. In later centuries, particularly during the 19th century, archaeological discoveries sparked the imagination, and interest in ancient Egyptian religion and mythology surged once more. In modern times, the gods of ancient Egypt continue to capture the imagination. They appear in literature, films, television, video games, fashion, and fine art. Characters inspired by Egyptian mythology can be found in everything from graphic novels to Hollywood blockbusters.

This book is designed to be a useful introduction and an opening reference to the subject, for readers who are interested in mythology, history, deities, and the ancient Egyptians, and who would like to know more.

Who are the 'main' gods in ancient Egyptian mythology?

There isn't one single pantheon of Egyptian gods as such, not like the Greek or Roman gods, where in popular consciousness there seems to be a clear 'top 12', i.e. 'The Olympians'. Different gods emerged from local folk beliefs, merged with some, replaced others, and evolved and grew stronger over time, but in this case... over so much *more* time. When we talk about the Egyptian gods, we're talking about over 3,700 years of history, events, peoples, and beliefs. As cities and dynasties rose in prominence, so too did their local gods, sometimes rising to national importance and beyond. Perhaps one way of beginning to answer the above question, is to look at the family trees of the gods and compare them with the Greek and Roman traditions.

The Ogdoad, the eight gods (four divine male-female couples) worshipped at Hermopolis represent the primordial forces of creation that came together to create the cosmos. They are loosely comparable to the Primordial Gods of Greece and Rome:

Nu and Naunet	The Primordial Waters
Heh and Hauhet	Infinity and Endlessness
Kek and Kauket	Darkness
Amun and Amunet	Hiddenness, Air, or Invisibility

The Ennead, the nine gods worshipped at Heliopolis represent the created world and divine order. They are loosely comparable to the Titans of Greece and Rome:

Atum	The Creator
Shu	The Air
Tefnut	Moisture
Geb	The Earth
Nut	The Sky
Osiris	The Dead
Isis	Magic
Set	Chaos
Nephthys	Mourning

The following gods could be loosely equated with the Olympians of Greece and Rome:

Egyptian	Greek / Roman Equivalent	Description
Horus or Amun-Ra	Zeus / Jupiter	Kingship, sky god, divine authority. Horus is the divine ruler on earth. Amun-Ra is the supreme creator and sun god.
Ra or Horus	Apollo / Apollo	Sun god, order, healing, protector of truth. Ra as solar deity. Horus as avenger / protector.
Neith or Seshat	Athena / Minerva	Wisdom, warfare, weaving. Neith is a creator goddess, patron of war and crafts. Seshat is goddess of writing and wisdom.
Set	Ares / Mars	God of war and chaos. Set embodies destructive force and violence.
Hathor	Aphrodite / Venus	Goddess of love, beauty, pleasure, motherhood.
Thoth or Anubis	Hermes / Mercury	Thoth: god of wisdom, writing, mediation. Anubis: guide of souls (psychopomp). Hermes / Mercury combines both roles.
Osiris	Hades / Pluto	Ruler of the underworld, judge of the dead.
Isis	Hera / Juno	Wife / sister of chief god, protector of marriage, motherhood, royalty. Isis is also a magical healer and mother figure.
Bastet or Sekhmet	Artemis / Diana	Protector, huntress. Bastet = protective, feline goddess. Sekhmet = warrior goddess, hunter.

Egyptian	Greek / Roman Equivalent	Description
Ptah	Hephaestus / Vulcan	God of craftsmen, creation, builders, artisans.
Renenutet or Isis	Demeter / Ceres	Agricultural and fertility goddesses. Isis has fertility and motherhood aspects. Renenutet watches over crops.
Bes or Hathor	Dionysus / Bacchus	Music, pleasure, revelry, protection. Bes is a joyful, protective god. Hathor is linked to music, dance, and intoxication.
Nephthys	Hestia / Vesta	Goddess of the hearth, home, and inner life. Nephthys is a guardian and mourner, associated with protection of the household and death rituals.

Generally speaking, the most prominent, widely worshipped, and influential Egyptian gods are:

Ra	The sun god, a creator god, and king of the gods.
Osiris	God of the afterlife, resurrection, and the dead.
Isis	Goddess of magic, motherhood, and healing.
Horus	The sky god, protector of the pharaoh, and god of kingship.
Set	God of chaos, storms, desert, and violence.
Anubis	God of mummification, embalming, and the dead.
Thoth	God of writing, knowledge, science, magic, wisdom, and the moon.
Ma'at	Goddess of balance, cosmic order, justice, and truth.
Amun	A creator god who later merged with Ra as Amun-Ra.
Hathor	Goddess of love, music, motherhood, and joy.
Bastet	A cat goddess of home, fertility, and protection.
Sekhmet	A lioness goddess of war and healing.

What roles do the Egyptian gods play in daily life and religion?

The Egyptian gods are central to daily life, religion, and world view in ancient Egypt. They are protectors and providers, maintainers of *ma'at* (cosmic order), governors of agricultural cycles and seasons, and guides in the afterlife. Their temples are not only religious centres, they are hubs of activity, employing many people (artisans, priests, scribes, farmers, etc.) and bringing people together from all walks of life.

What is the story of Osiris, Isis, and Horus?

The story of Osiris, Isis, and Horus is a story about death, rebirth, and rightful kingship. Osiris, a just king, is murdered by his jealous brother Set, who seals him in a coffin and later dismembers his body. Osiris's wife Isis recovers and magically reassembles his body, conceiving their son Horus in the process. Osiris becomes ruler of the underworld, while Isis hides Horus until he grows strong enough to challenge Set. After a long struggle, Horus defeats Set and is declared the rightful king of Egypt. The story symbolises the cycle of life and death, the triumph of order over chaos, and the divine role of the pharaoh as Horus on earth.

What do ancient Egyptians believe about the afterlife and the gods' role in it?

The ancient Egyptians believe the afterlife is a continuation of life, but in a perfected, eternal form known as the Field of Reeds, a paradise where the soul can live forever in peace, provided certain conditions are met. The gods play a crucial role in this journey.

To reach the afterlife, the deceased have to pass through a judgment process. The heart (seen as the seat of the soul) is weighed against the Feather of Ma'at. If the heart is light and pure, the soul is granted eternal life. If it is heavy with sin, it is devoured by Ammit, a fearsome creature, ending the soul's existence. The god Osiris, ruler of the underworld, presides over this judgment. Anubis, god of embalming and protector of the dead, guides souls and performs the weighing. Thoth, god of wisdom, records the outcome. Isis and other protective deities also aid the deceased on their journey.

Proper burial, preservation of the body through mummification, and magical texts like the Book of the Dead are essential to help the soul navigate dangers, recite protective spells, and gain the gods' favour. The afterlife is a sacred journey guided and judged by the gods, and the goal is to achieve a harmonious, eternal existence by living a life in line with *ma'at* (cosmic order).

Were pharaohs considered gods?

Pharaohs were often considered living gods. They were the mediators between the gods and human beings. They were responsible for maintaining and upholding *ma'at*, and guarding against *isfet* (chaos, injustice, violence, and falsehood). Pharaohs were also associated with Horus in life and Osiris in death.

Were any of the pharaohs women?

There are at least seven female pharaohs who ruled in their own right, not just as queen consorts or regents.

Merneith (1st Dynasty, c. 3000 BCE) is possibly the earliest female ruler of Egypt. Some evidence suggests she ruled as pharaoh, though this is debated.

Sobekneferu (12th Dynasty, c. 1806-1802 BCE) is the first confirmed female pharaoh with full royal titles. She ruled after the death of her brother, Amenemhat IV.

Hatshepsut (18th Dynasty, c. 1479-1458 BCE) is one of the most successful and famous female pharaohs. She took on the full powers of a pharaoh and even depicted herself as male in statues.

Nefertiti (possibly co-regent or ruler as Neferneferuaten, 18th Dynasty) is the wife of Akhenaten. She may have ruled briefly under the name Neferneferuaten, but her status as pharaoh is debated.

Tawosret (19th Dynasty, c. 1188-1186 BCE) was the last ruler of the 19th Dynasty. She ruled Egypt independently after the death of her husband and stepson.

Cleopatra VII (Ptolemaic Dynasty, 51-30 BCE) was the last active pharaoh of ancient Egypt. She ruled alongside her brothers and son, but wielded considerable power on her own.

Arsinoe II or III (Ptolemaic Dynasty, debated) held regal power, but it is debated whether or not she was officially a pharaoh.

Timeline of Egyptian Religion

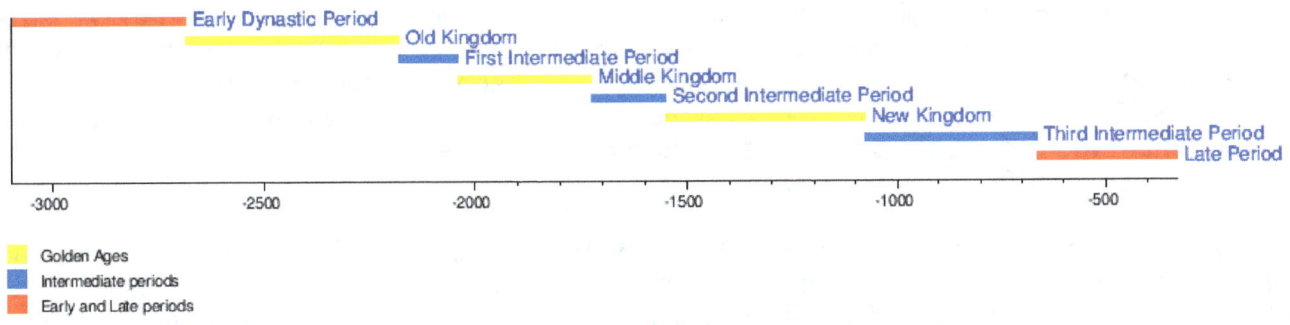

Wikipedia Creative Commons, Public Domain

The Pre-Dynastic Period (before c. 3100 BCE): People believe in the forces of nature as powerful spirits. They worship the sun, animals, the River Nile, and other natural elements as sacred and life-giving. Different gods start to become important in different areas. During this time, people begin making burials more detailed, which shows they are starting to believe in the idea of life after death, with the underworld as the journey and the afterlife as the destination. These early ideas help shape the more complex beliefs and gods of ancient Egypt later on.

The Early Dynastic Period (c. 3100–2686 BCE): With the unification of Upper and Lower Egypt, a more centralised form of religious practice begins to take shape. The idea of divine kingship appears where the pharaoh is seen as a living god on Earth, and as a representative of the god Horus. Religion becomes more closely linked to the government, helping to strengthen the pharaoh's power and keep the country united. Although local gods remain important, there is a move to include them in a wider, national religious system.

The Old Kingdom (c. 2686–2181 BCE): The sun god Ra becomes the most important god in Egypt. Pharaohs are closely linked to Ra and people believe that after they die, they travel to the heavens to join him. This time is known for building the great pyramids, which are huge tombs showing how important the afterlife is in their religion. The oldest religious writings, the Pyramid Texts, are written on the walls inside these royal tombs. These texts help guide the dead pharaohs on their journey through the afterlife, showing that they are gods and connected to the universe.

The First Intermediate Period (c. 2181–2055 BCE): After the central government falls, religious power spreads out and becomes less controlled by one ruler. Local gods become more important. Without a strong central government, temples and religious groups in different areas play a bigger role in people's religious lives. Even though old beliefs continue, religious practices vary a lot from one place to another.

The Middle Kingdom (c. 2055–1650 BCE): Egypt becomes united again, and religion becomes more central and welcoming to everyone. The worship of Osiris grows to include all people, not just the pharaohs. This shows that everyone in Egypt can hope for eternal life. The Coffin Texts, which come after the earlier Pyramid Texts, are written on the coffins of ordinary people. Religious practices become more personal, and people still worship local gods, but all within a more connected system of beliefs.

The Second Intermediate Period (c. 1650–1550 BCE): Egypt is divided into smaller dynasties for a second time. The Hyksos people of West Asia migrate into the north of Egypt, establishing the 15th Dynasty and ruling from Avaris in the Nile Delta. They bring new religious ideas with them, new gods, rituals, customs, etc. Local gods and traditional religious groups still play a big part in everyday life. Even with foreign rulers, the main parts of Egyptian religion stay the same.

The New Kingdom (c. 1550–1069 BCE): Egyptian religion and power are at their strongest. Amun-Ra becomes the most important god, a fusion of the Theban god Amun and the sun god Ra. Many large temples are built, especially in Thebes which becomes the religious capital. During the Amarna Period, the pharaoh Akhenaten introduces monotheism, the worship of just one god, Aten, the sun disk. Akhenaten closes the old temples and attempts to stop people worshipping other gods. After he dies, his son Tutankhaten reopens the old temples and restores the worship of multiple gods, including Amun who becomes important again. The Book of the Dead, a set of prayers and spells to help people in the afterlife, becomes popular during this time.

The Third Intermediate Period (c. 1069–664 BCE): Egypt is divided into smaller kingdoms, and political instability follows. Religious practices mostly stay the same. The priests of Amun, especially in Thebes, become very powerful and sometimes challenge the pharaohs. Foreign rulers like the Libyans and Nubians learn Egyptian religion and mix it with their own beliefs. Even though the government becomes weaker, temples stay very important, and people keep worshipping the traditional gods.

The Late Period (c. 664–332 BCE): In the Late Period, Egypt brings back many old religious traditions but also mixes them with ideas from other countries. Egyptian gods like Isis become popular abroad, and they are connected to foreign gods. Animal worship grows strong, especially for animals like the Apis bull and the ibis, which is special to the god Thoth. Religion becomes more focused on magic, with more use of oracles, amulets, and protective spells.

The Ptolemaic Period (332–30 BCE): The Ptolemaic Period begins when Alexander the Great takes over Egypt. During this time, Greek and Egyptian religious traditions mix together. The Ptolemies, a Greek ruling family from Macedonia, call themselves pharaohs and support Egyptian religion. They build large temples like the ones at Edfu and Philae Island, using traditional Egyptian styles. One of the biggest religious changes is the creation of the god Serapis, who combines parts of Osiris, the Apis bull, and Greco-Roman gods like Zeus (Jupiter) and Hades (Pluto). The worship of Isis becomes more and more popular, and her cult spreads outside Egypt to Greece, Rome, and beyond.

The Roman Period (30 BCE – c. 395 CE): The old religious temples and traditions still continue, but they become less powerful in politics. People still strongly worship Isis and Osiris, and their cults become important in Roman religion too. Temples stay open with help from the Roman emperors, and Egyptian priests keep working in their local areas. But from the 2nd century CE, Christianity spreads quickly across Egypt. Tensions grow between Christians and people who follow the old gods. By the end of Roman rule, Christian emperors begin to limit and then stop the traditional Egyptian religious practices.

The Byzantine Period (c. 395–642 CE): Christianity is now the official religion of the empire, and the old pagan temples slowly close down. The ancient priesthoods come to an end. The famous Temple of Isis at Philae Island, one of the last places of old religious worship, is closed around 537 CE by Emperor Justinian. By this time, the old Egyptian religion with many gods mostly disappears. However, parts of Egyptian religious ideas, symbols, and language stay alive in Coptic Christianity, Egypt's native form of Christianity. It takes some things from the old religion and changes them into new Christian traditions in worship and art.

The Egyptian Gods   *An Illustrated Introduction*

Locations

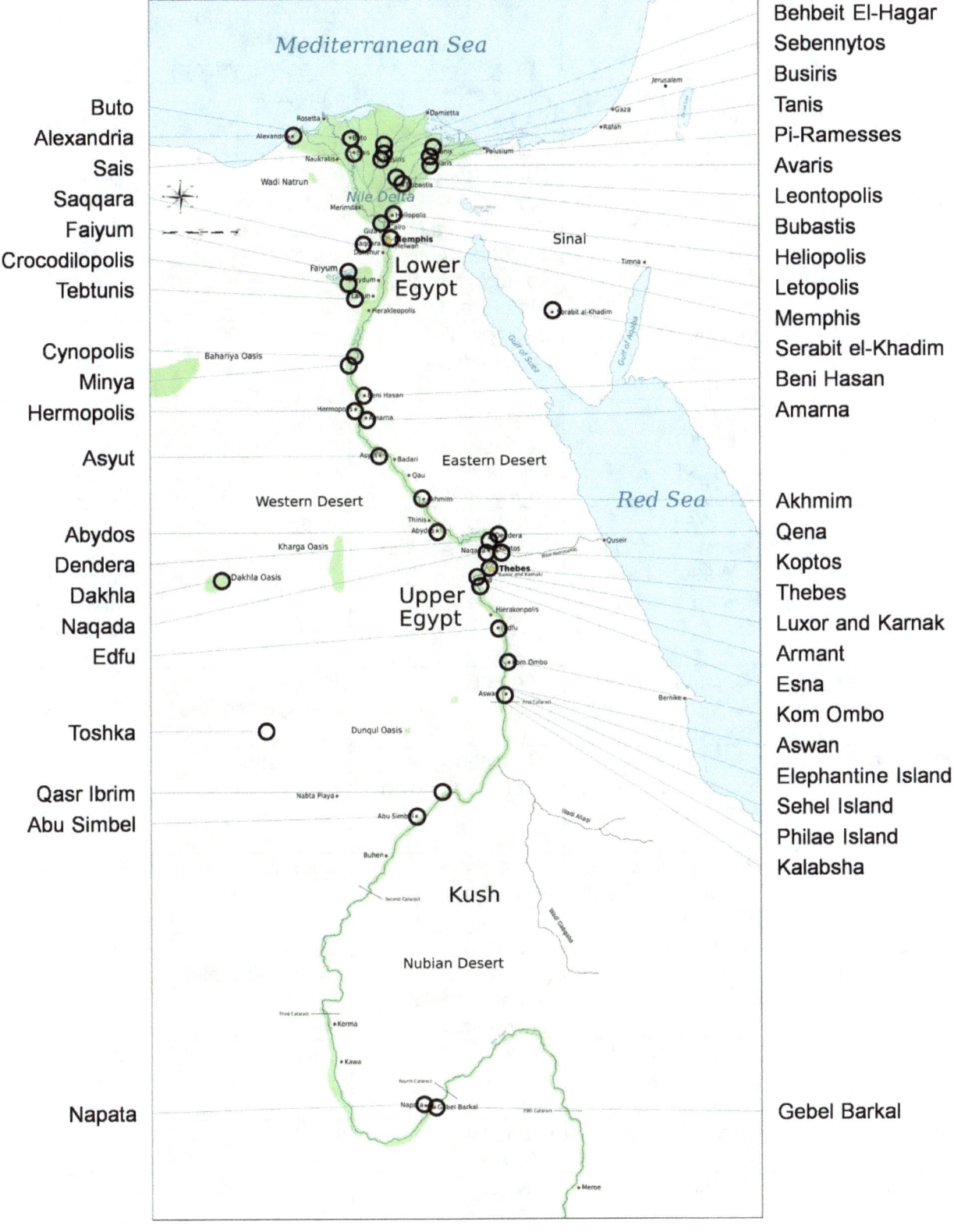

Buto
Alexandria
Sais
Saqqara
Faiyum
Crocodilopolis
Tebtunis

Cynopolis
Minya
Hermopolis

Asyut

Abydos
Dendera
Dakhla
Naqada
Edfu

Toshka

Qasr Ibrim
Abu Simbel

Napata

Behbeit El-Hagar
Sebennytos
Busiris
Tanis
Pi-Ramesses
Avaris
Leontopolis
Bubastis
Heliopolis
Letopolis
Memphis
Serabit el-Khadim
Beni Hasan
Amarna

Akhmim
Qena
Koptos
Thebes
Luxor and Karnak
Armant
Esna
Kom Ombo
Aswan
Elephantine Island
Sehel Island
Philae Island
Kalabsha

Gebel Barkal

The Egyptian Gods — An Illustrated Introduction

Name	Ancient Egyptian	Greek	Roman	Modern Arabic
Abu Simbel	*Abw* or *Ibsambul*	Abousimbel (Ἀβούσιμβελ)	Abu Simbel (no special Latinised name, known by Greek/Egyptian)	Abu Simbil (أبو سمبل)
Abydos	*Abdu* or *Abdju* (ꜥbdw)	Abydos (Ἄβυδος)	Abydos	Abdus (أبيدوس) or Abidos
Akhmim	*Ipu* or *Khmin* (Jpu, Xmìn)	Panopolis (Πανόπολις)	Panopolis	Akhmim (أخميم)
Amarna	*Akhetaten* (ꜣḫt-ꜥtn, "Horizon of the Aten")	Akhetaten (used mostly Egyptian, Greek sources mention Akhetaten)	Akhetaten (rarely used, mostly Egyptian)	Amarna (عمارنة)
Armant	*Iuny* or *Hermonthis* (Jwny)	Hermonthis (Ἑρμώνθης)	Hermonthis	Armant (أرمنت)
Aswan	*Swenett* (Stw-nṯt)	Syene (Συήνη)	Syene	Aswan (أسوان)
Asyut	*Zawty* or *Zawet* (Zꜣw.tj)	Lycopolis (Λυκόπολις)	Lycopolis	Asyut (أسيوط)
Avaris	*Hut-Weser* (ḥwt-wsr, "House of Weser", the Hyksos capital)	Auaris or Avaris (Αὔαρις / Ἄβαρίς)	Avaris	Hawara (هَوارة) (nearby modern village; Avaris itself is Tell el-Dab'a – تل الدابة)
Behbeit El-Hagar	*Behbit* or *Per-Hebit* (uncertain)	Behbeit (Βηβεῖτ)	Behbeit (no specific Latin name)	Behbeit el-Hagar (بهبيط الحجر)
Beni Hasan	(No specific ancient city name; near *Menat Khufu*)	(No distinct Greek city name known)	(No distinct Roman name recorded)	Beni Hasan (بني حسن)
Bubastis	*Per-Bast* or *Bastet* (pr-bstt, "House of Bastet")	Bubastis (Βουβαστίς)	Bubastis	Bubastis (بو بسطس)
Busiris (Aphroditopolis)	*Per-Usir* (pr-ꜥsr, "House of Osiris")	Busiris (Βούσιρις) / Aphroditopolis (Ἀφροδιτόπολις)	Busiris (Aphroditopolis)	Busiris (بوسيريس)
Buto	*Per-Wadjet* or *Urt* (pr-wḏꜣt, "House of Wadjet")	Buto (Βουτώ)	Buto	Buto (بطو)
Coptos	*Gebtu* or *Kebtu* (Gb.t)	Coptos (Κόπτος)	Coptos	Qift (قفط)
Crocodilopolis	*Shedet* (Šd.t), city of Sobek	Arsinoe (Ἀρσινόη) (named after Arsinoe II, often for Crocodilopolis)	Crocodilopolis or Arsinoe	Shedet (شديت) or Kom Ombo area name

Name	Ancient Egyptian	Greek	Roman	Modern Arabic
Cynopolis	*Saka* (city of dogs)	Cynopolis (Κυνόπολις)	Cynopolis	Saka (ساكا) or sometimes lost as a place name
Dakhla	(No well-known ancient name, part of the *Dikallah* oasis region)	(Known as part of the Dakhla Oasis; no separate Greek name)	(No Roman name recorded, part of Oasis region)	Al-Dakhla (الداخلة)
Dendera	*Iunet* (wn.t)	Denderah (Δενδέρα)	Dendera	Dandarah (دندرة)
Edfu	*Djeba* or *Behdet* (ḏbꜣt)	Apollonopolis Magna (Ἀπολλωνόπολις ἡ μεγάλη)	Apollinopolis Magna	Idfu (إدفو)
Elephantine Island	*Abw* (ꜥbw)	Elephantine (Ἐλεφάντινη)	Elephantine	Elfantina (الفنتين) or Elephantine Island
Esna	*Iunet* (wn.t) or Latopolis?	Latopolis (Λατόπολις)	Latopolis	Esna (إسنا)
Faiyum	*Shedet* or *Shed* (Šd.t) or "the Lake of the Crocodile"	Arsinoe (Ἀρσινόη) (Faiyum region)	Arsinoe	Al-Fayyum (الفيوم)
Gebel Barkal	*Napata* (Npt) or *Barkal* (site associated with Kushites)	Napata (Νάπατα) (Kushite city)	Napata (Kushite city)	Jabal Barkal (جبل بركل)
Heliopolis	*Iunu* or *On* (jwnw)	Heliopolis (Ἡλιόπολις)	Heliopolis	Ayn Shams (عين شمس) — modern Arabic name for Heliopolis area
Hermopolis	*Khmun* or *Khemenu* (ḫmnw)	Hermopolis Magna (Ἑρμώνπολις ἡ μεγάλη)	Hermopolis Magna	El Ashmunein (الأشمونين)
Kalabsha	(No known ancient Egyptian name; Nubian site)	(No Greek name recorded, Nubian site)	(No known Latin name)	Kalabsha (كلابشة)
Karnak	*Ipet-sut* (jp.t-swt, "The Most Select of Places")	(Greek sources used "Thebes" or local names; Karnak per se not renamed)	(No specific Latin name, part of Thebes region)	Karnak (كرنك)
Kom Ombo	*Nubt* (city of Sobek and Horus)	Ombos (Ὄμβος)	Ombos	Kom Ombo (كم أمبو)
Leontopolis	*Taremu* or *Taronuot* (t3-rnwt)	Leontopolis (Λεοντόπολις)	Leontopolis	Tell al-Muqdam (تل المقدام) or known by Greek name

The Egyptian Gods   An Illustrated Introduction

Name	Ancient Egyptian	Greek	Roman	Modern Arabic
Letopolis	*Khem* (ḫm, "City of the Fish Goddess")	(Usually kept as Letopolis or transliterated)	Letopolis	Letopolis (لتوبوليس) (rare usage, mostly Greek name)
Luxor	*Waset* (wꜣs.t)	Thebes (Θῆβαι)	Thebae	Al-Uqsur (الأقصر)
Minya	*Men'at Khufu* or *Mnut* (mnw.t)	Men'at Khufu (Greek name not widely used or unknown)	(No widely used Roman name)	Al-Minya (المنيا)
Naqada	*Nekhen* or *Nekheb* (depending on exact site)	Nekhen (Greek sometimes Nekhen or early forms)	(No clear Roman name; possibly Nekhen in earlier periods)	Naqada (نقادة)
Philae Island	*Pilak* or *P'lai* (site of Isis temple)	Philae (Φίλαι)	Philae	Fayla (فيلا) or Philae (فيلاي)
Pi-Ramesses	*Per-Ramesses* (pr-Rꜥ-ms-s, "House of Ramesses")	Pi-Ramesses (Πι-Ραμεσσες) (often kept Egyptian)	Per-Ramesses (often kept Egyptian)	Bir Mas (بر مس) (modern name near site)
Qasr Ibrim	(No specific ancient Egyptian city name, Nubian site)	(No Greek name known)	(No Roman name known)	Qasr Ibrim (قصر إبريم)
Qena	*Qinai* or *Qin* (uncertain)	(Greek name unknown or unrecorded)	(No known Roman name)	Qena (قنا)
Sais	*Sais* or *Zau* (z3w)	Saïs (Σαΐς)	Saïs	Saïs (سايس) or Saïs (mostly Greek name retained)
Saqqara	*Sqqara* or *Sekhem* (related to Memphis necropolis)	(No distinct Greek name, part of Memphis necropolis)	Saqqara	Saqqara (سقارة)
Sebennytos	*Tjebnutjer* (ṯb-nṯr, "The Place of the God")	Sebennytos (Σεβέννυτος)	Sebennytos	Sebennytos (سبيننطس) or nearby modern town
Sehel Island	*Sahil* or *Sehel* (site near Elephantine)	(No Greek name recorded)	(No Roman name known)	Jazirat Sehel (جزيرة سهيل)
Serabit el-Khadim	*Serabit* or *Serabit el-Khadim* (ancient turquoise mines site)	(No Greek name; mining site)	(No Roman name)	Serabit el-Khadim (سرابيط الخادم)
Tanis	*Djanet* (ṯꜥ-nīs)	Tanis (Τάνις)	Tanis	San el-Hagar (صان الحجر)

The Egyptian Gods An Illustrated Introduction

Name	Ancient Egyptian	Greek	Roman	Modern Arabic
Tebtunis	*Tebtynis* or *Tjebtunis* (lower Egypt site)	Tebtunis (Τεβτούνις)	Tebtunis	Tebtunis (تبوتنيس)
Thebes	*Waset* (wꜣs.t)	Thebes (Θῆβαι)	Thebae	Luxor / Al-Uqsur (الأقصر)
Toshka	(No specific ancient name known; Nubian region)	(No Greek name known)	(No known Roman name)	Toshka (توشكى)

Symbols and Objects

Ankh

The Ankh is a symbol that represents life, in the earthly and eternal sense. It is often seen in the hands of deities and pharaohs in Egyptian art, symbolising their power to give or sustain life. Its use in funerary iconography reflects a belief in the afterlife and the soul's journey beyond death. Worn as an amulet it also symbolises protection, and is associated with spiritual well-being and ancient wisdom.

Atef

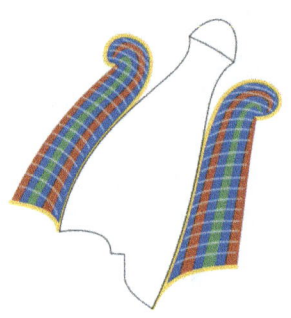

The Atef is the crown worn by Osiris. It consists of the white crown of Upper Egypt with two ostrich feathers on either side. The feathers symbolise *ma'at* (balance, cosmic order, justice, and truth). In religious art it symbolises Osiris's role as lord of the afterlife and judge of the dead. Its elaborate form sets it apart from other royal crowns, making Osiris unique among the gods.

The Benben Stone

The Benben Stone is the primeval mound that arises from the primordial waters of Nu, the first land to rise from chaos. In the Pyramid Texts it is said to have turned into a small pyramid, located in Heliopolis where Atum is said to dwell. In the Memphis tradition, the god Tatenen is the personification of the primeval mound. It is associated with the top stone of a pyramid, which is called a *benbenet* or pyramidion.

Cap Crown

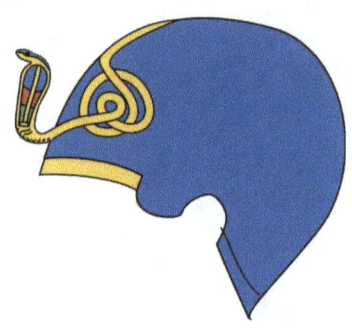

The Cap Crown is a royal headdress often worn by pharaohs during religious rituals and ceremonial occasions. Unlike other crowns it has a rounded close-fitting shape resembling a soft cap. It is typically coloured blue or white and is sometimes adorned with simple decorations. It is a symbol of divine authority and the pharaoh's connection to the gods.

Cartouche

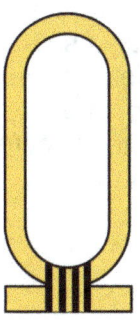

The cartouche is an oval or oblong symbol used in writing to enclose and highlight a royal name, often that of a pharaoh. It means that the name inside is sacred, divinely protected, and will endure for all time. It is often carved on monuments, tombs, and personal objects like amulets. It helps to identify and honour rulers in life and the afterlife. It is a powerful marker of status and legitimacy.

Crook and Flail

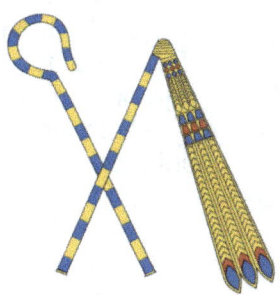

The Crook and Flail is a symbol of kingship and divine authority. It is traditionally associated with Osiris and is later adopted by the pharaohs. The crook, shaped like a shepherd's staff, symbolises the pharaoh's role as the protector and guide of his people, like a shepherd with his flock. The flail, often interpreted as a tool for threshing grain, represents the ruler's duty to provide for and discipline the nation. It is often shown crossed over the chest of gods and kings in tomb art and statues. It signifies authority and benevolence.

Deshret

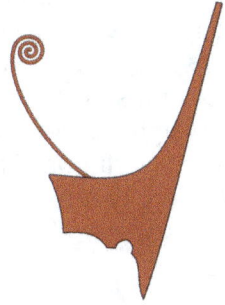

The Deshret is the Red Crown of Lower Egypt, the northern region of the country. It has a distinctive flat top with a tall, thin, spiral-like extension at the front.

Djed

The Djed is a symbol of stability, endurance, and strength. It is often associated with Osiris. It resembles a column with a broad base and a series of horizontal lines or bars near the top. It is believed to represent Osiris's spine, and by extension, his resurrection and the idea of eternal life. It is commonly used in amulets to offer protection and ensure the deceased's safe passage to the afterlife. In rituals, the 'Raising of the Djed' ceremony celebrates renewal and the triumph of order over chaos.

The Egyptian Gods An Illustrated Introduction

Eye of Horus

The Eye of Horus represents protection, health, and restoration. According to myth, Horus loses his eye in a battle with Set, but the eye is magically restored. It is a symbol of healing and wholeness. It is widely used as an amulet to ward off evil, ensure safety, and promote well-being, both in life and the afterlife. It also symbolises royal power and divine watchfulness.

Eye of Ra

The Eye of Ra represents protection, royal authority, and power. Unlike the Eye of Horus, which emphasises healing and restoration, the Eye of Ra is often seen as a fierce and aggressive force, embodying the sun's destructive energy used to defend Ra against his enemies. Sometimes it is personified as a goddess, sometimes Sekhmet, Hathor, or Wadjet, acting as Ra's protector and punisher.

Feather of Ma'at

The Feather of Ma'at represents balance, cosmic order, justice, and truth. It is associated with the goddess Ma'at, who personifies these principles. The feather plays a crucial role in the Weighing of the Heart ceremony, where the deceased's heart is weighed against the Feather of Ma'at to determine their worthiness for the afterlife. A heart lighter or equal in weight to the feather means the person has lived a virtuous life. The feather symbolises moral integrity and the ideal of living in harmony with the universe.

Hedjet

The Hedjet is the White Crown of Upper Egypt, the southern part of the country. It has a tall, conical shape with a pointed top.

Hemhem

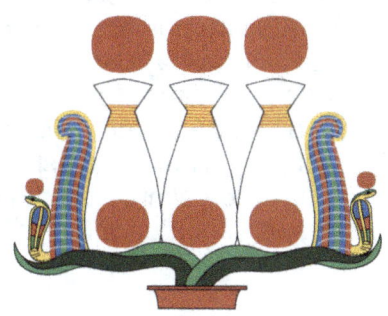

The Hemhem is an elaborate and ornate royal headdress. It is often described as a 'triple Atef'. It features ostrich feathers and uraei (rearing cobras) on either side, topped with sun disks. It is worn by pharaohs during ceremonies or in battle. Its dramatic design emphasises the king's strength and his connection to the gods in moments of significant religious or military importance.

Hennu

The Hennu is a sacred symbol representing the ceremonial barque or boat used to transport gods during religious festivals and funerary rites. It is often associated with the journey of the sun god Ra across the sky and through the underworld each night. The Hennu is believed to carry divine presence, allowing the gods to travel between worlds to ensure cosmic order. Models or depictions of the Hennu are placed in tombs to aid the deceased's journey in the afterlife.

Hypocephalus

The Hypocephalus is a small, circular amulet used in funerary practices, typically placed under the head of the deceased. It symbolises the sun, warmth, illumination, and protection in the afterlife. It is believed to radiate magical energy and connect the deceased to the regenerative power of the sun god Ra.

Khat

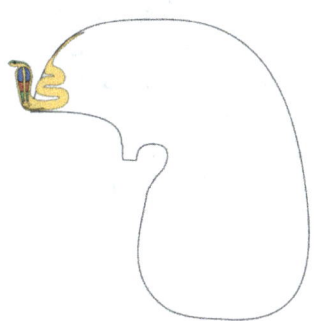

The Khat is a head covering worn by pharaohs and nobility. Unlike the more elaborate crowns, the Khat is a plain fitted cloth that drapes down the sides and back of the head, often tied at the back or held in place by a band. It is traditionally worn during daily activities or informal occasions, allowing the wearer practicality while maintaining a prestigious appearance.

Khepresh

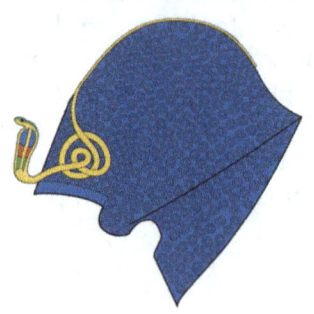

The Khepresh, also known as the Blue Crown or war crown, is a royal headdress often worn by pharaohs during ceremonial occasions and military campaigns. It has a rounded, close-fitting shape resembling a helmet, typically coloured deep blue and decorated with golden disks or uraei (rearing cobras). The Khepresh symbolises royal power, divine protection, and the pharaoh's role as a warrior and defender of Egypt.

Menat

The Menat is a ceremonial necklace and ritual object associated with the goddess Hathor. It typically consists of a string of beads with a counterweight at the back, allowing it to hang comfortably around the neck. The Menat is believed to have protective and magical properties, often used in religious ceremonies and worn by priests and priestesses. It symbolises fertility, rebirth, and divine favour, and its sound was thought to please the gods, especially Hathor, helping to invoke her blessings.

Nebu

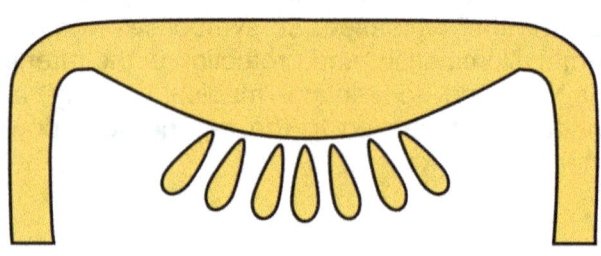

The Nebu is the hieroglyphic symbol for gold, a metal highly prized in ancient Egypt for its incorruptibility. It represents eternity, divine perfection, and the immortality of the gods. The symbol appears in hieroglyphs to denote gold and, by extension, wealth, power, and sacred qualities. Gold, and the Nebu symbol, is closely associated with the sun god Ra and used to emphasise the eternal nature of the pharaohs.

Nemes

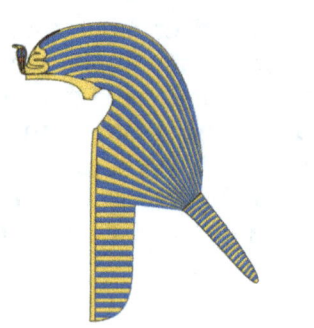

The Nemes (sometimes spelled *Nemss*) is the striped headcloth worn by pharaohs as a symbol of their royal authority. It covers the crown and the back of the head, often extending over the shoulders, and is typically depicted with horizontal or vertical stripes in art and sculpture. Unlike a crown, the Nemes is a cloth headdress rather than a rigid ornament, and it is famously seen on the golden mask of Tutankhamun.

Ouroboros

The Ouroboros is an ancient symbol depicting a serpent or dragon eating its own tail, forming a continuous circle. While not originally Egyptian, it appears in various cultures, the Ouroboros is adopted in later Egyptian symbolism to represent eternity and the endless cycle of life, death, and rebirth. It embodies the idea of something constantly recreating itself, the eternal nature of the universe, and the concept of infinity. In Egyptian contexts, it often appears in funerary art and mystical texts, emphasising timelessness, and regenerative powers.

Pschent

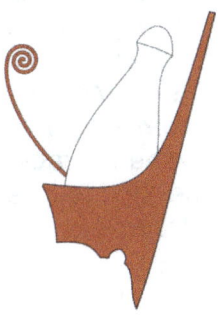

The Pschent is the Double Crown of Upper and Lower Egypt. It combines the Hedjet (the White Crown of Upper Egypt) and the Deshret (the Red Crown of Lower Egypt). The Pschent represents the pharaoh's sovereignty over the entire land of Egypt, and his role as a unifier and protector of the nation.

Serekh

The Serekh is a symbol used to represent a pharaoh's royal name, often appearing on monuments, pottery, and seals. It consists of a rectangular or trapezoid frame resembling a palace façade, topped with the image of a Horus falcon. Inside the frame, the pharaoh's name is written in hieroglyphs. The Serekh serves as a royal emblem before the widespread use of the cartouche and highlights the ruler's connection to the god Horus.

Shen Ring

The Shen Ring is a symbol shaped like a loop of rope tied in a continuous circle with no beginning or end, symbolising eternity, protection, and infinity. The word 'shen' itself means 'encircle' or 'protect'. Often held by gods or pharaohs in Egyptian art, the Shen Ring symbolises the eternal protection they receive and offer their people. It is commonly used in amulets and inscriptions to invoke lasting safety and unending power.

Shuti Crown

The Shuti Crown is a headdress with two tall ostrich feathers standing upright side by side. It is closely associated with the god Amun and is sometimes worn by pharaohs in religious and ceremonial contexts. The feathers symbolise balance, cosmic order, justice, and truth, echoing the principles of the goddess Ma'at.

Sistrum

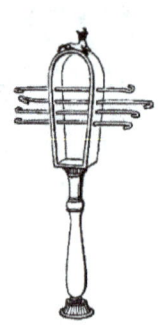

The Sistrum is a ritual ankh-shaped rattle instrument that represents cosmic order and divine sound. When shaken, the small rings or loops of thin metal on its movable crossbars produce a sound that can vary from a soft clank to a loud jangling. Its name in ancient Egyptian language was 'sekhem' or 'sesheshet' because of the sound it made when it rattled. The sistrum is associated with the goddesses Hathor, Bastet, Isis, Sekhmet, and Neith.

Situla

The Situla is a small bucket-shaped vessel used in ancient Egyptian rituals to pour libations or carry sacred liquids. It is closely linked to deities such as Isis and Hathor, symbolising fertility, rebirth, and divine nourishment, and is metaphorically imagined as being filled with the life-giving waters of the sacred Nile.

Solar Barque

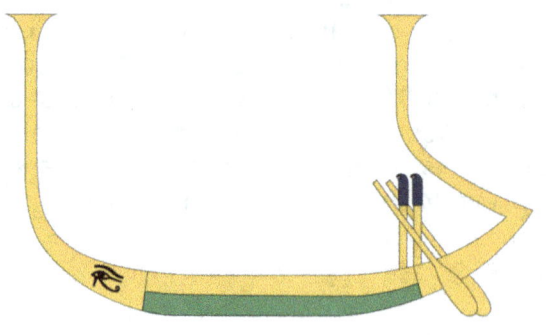

The Solar Barque is the sacred boat believed to carry the sun god Ra across the sky during the day and through the underworld at night. This journey symbolises the cycle of life, death, and rebirth, as Ra battles darkness and chaos to bring light and order to the world. The Solar Barque is often depicted in tombs and temples, representing the eternal passage of the sun and the promise of regeneration for the deceased in the afterlife.

Sun Disk

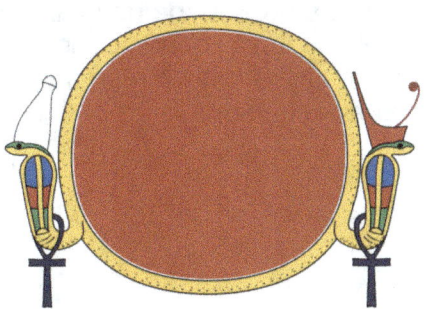

The Sun Disk is a prominent symbol of the sun god Ra and the life-giving power of the sun. Usually depicted as a bright circular disk, it often appears above the heads of gods such as Ra (later Amun-Ra), Hathor, Horus, Sekhmet, Bastet, Wadjet, and Khepri. In the case of Aten, the personification of the Sun Disk, it is shown with sun rays ending in hands, showing the sun's active nurturing force.

Tyet

The Tyet, also known as the Knot of Isis or the Isis Knot, is a looped knot similar in shape to the Ankh but with arms curved downwards. As the name suggests, it is associated with Isis and her magical powers. It is often used as a protective amulet. In funerary contexts it symbolises the protective and nurturing qualities of Isis, ensuring the deceased's safety and rebirth in the afterlife.

Uraeus

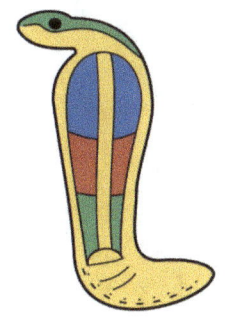

The Uraeus is a stylised cobra, depicted upright, rearing, and with its hood expanded. It is worn on the forehead of pharaohs and gods. It represents the goddess Wadjet, the protector of Lower Egypt, who is believed to spit fire at the pharaoh's enemies. The Uraeus guards the pharaoh from harm and protects their legitimate right to rule.

Vulture Crown

The Vulture Crown is a headdress traditionally worn by queens and goddesses. It features a stylised vulture with outstretched wings, often combined with the Uraeus (rearing cobra) on the forehead. The vulture represents the goddess Nekhbet, the protector of Upper Egypt, who watches over the pharaoh and the nation.

Was-Sceptre

The Was-Sceptre is a symbol of power, dominion, and authority. It is a long staff topped with a stylised animal head and a forked base. The Was-Sceptre is associated with the gods and pharaohs. It is often depicted in the hands of deities or rulers in art and hieroglyphs, and it represents strength, prosperity, and well-being.

Winged Sun

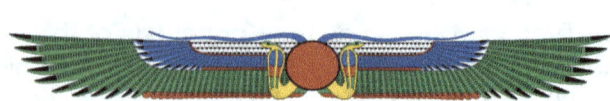

The Winged Sun is a sun disk flanked by outstretched wings, often accompanied by uraei (rearing cobras) on either side. It represents the life-giving energy of the sun god Ra and the idea of the sun's all-encompassing reach. The Winged Sun is commonly placed above temple entrances and on sacred objects to guard against evil and ensure the favour of the gods.

Images: Wikipedia Creative Commons, Public Domain

The Ogdoad: The Eight Gods of Hermopolis

The Primordial Waters
Nu   Naunet

Infinity and Endlessness
Heh   Hauhet

Darkness
Kek   Kauket

 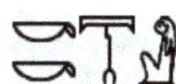

Hiddenness, Air, or Invisibility
Amun   Amunet

 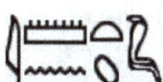

The Ogdoad

The Ogdoad are the eight primordial gods (four pairs or couples) representing the cosmic conditions before the world existed. The name 'Ogdoad' comes from the Ancient Greek *'ogdoás'* (*'ὀγδοάς'*) meaning 'the eight' or 'the eightfold'. In Ancient Egyptian the Ogdoad were called *'ḫmnyw'* / *'Khemenyu'* also meaning 'the eight'[1].

---

[1] Butler, E. P. (2009, March 19). Hermopolitan Ogdoad. Retrieved March 17, 2025, from https://henadology.wordpress.com/theology/netjeru/hermopolitan-ogdoad/

Hermopolis

The centre of worship of the Ogdoad is Hermopolis, near modern day el-Ashmunein in Middle Egypt[2]. Hermopolis was an important city on the boundary of Upper and Lower Egypt from as far back as the Old Kingdom until it was abandoned during the Muslim conquest of Egypt in the middle of the 7th Century CE. The name Hermopolis comes from the Ancient Greek 'Ermoúpolis' ('Ερμούπολις) meaning 'the city of Hermes'. In Ancient Egyptian the city of Hermopolis was called 'ḫmnw' / 'Khemenu', literally 'eight' after the eight gods who were worshipped there[3]. Texts of the Late Period describe the Ogdoad as having the heads of frogs (male), and the heads of snakes (female)[4]

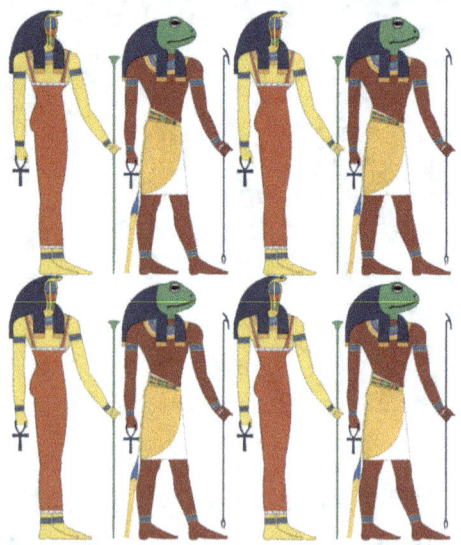

A depiction of the Ogdoad based on a Roman era relief at the Hathor temple in Dendera
Wikipedia Creative Commons, Public Domain

The Ogdoad, The dawn of civilization - Egypt and Chaldaea (1897)
Wikipedia Creative Commons, Public Domain

Ogdoad, The Place of Truth, Deir el Medina
Wikipedia Creative Commons, Public Domain

---

[2] G. Mussies in: Matthieu Sybrand Huibert, Gerard Heerma van Voss (eds.), Studies in Egyptian Religion: Dedicated to Professor Jan Zandee (1982), p. 92.
[3] G. Mussies in: Matthieu Sybrand Huibert, Gerard Heerma van Voss (eds.). (1982), p. 92.
[4] Smith, Mark (2002), On the Primaeval Ocean, p. 38

The Ennead: The Nine Gods of Heliopolis

The Ennead

The Ennead (The Great Ennead) are the nine gods representing the creation of the cosmos according to the traditions of Heliopolis. The name 'Ennead' comes from the ancient Greek 'enneás' ('έννεάς'), meaning 'the nine'. In Ancient Egyptian the Ennead were called 'psḏt' / 'Pesedjet' also meaning 'the nine' in it's feminine form.

The Ennead begins with Atum, the self-created god who emerged from the primordial waters of Nu. Atum then produced his children Shu (air) and Tefnut (moisture), who in turn gave birth to Geb (earth) and Nut (sky). From the union of Geb and Nut came four children: Osiris, Isis, Seth, and Nephthys.

Heliopolis

The centre of worship of the Ennead is Heliopolis, in modern day Cairo, Lower Egypt. Heliopolis was one of the most important spiritual and intellectual centres in Ancient Egypt, as it was the birthplace of Egyptian solar theology. It remained a historical and symbolic site through Greek and Roman rule. It finally fell into decline during the spread of Christianity when temples were closed, repurposed, or abandoned between the 4th and 6th centuries CE. The name Heliopolis comes from the Ancient Greek 'Hēlíoupólis' ('Ἡλίουπόλις') meaning 'the city of the sun'. In Ancient Egyptian the city of Heliopolis was called 'iwnw' / 'Iunu' / 'Jwnw' meaning 'The Pillars', perhaps referring to the tall pillars or obelisks that were prominent in the temple architecture of the city.

The Theban Triad

The Theban Triad

The Theban Triad are the three gods representing balance, continuity, and divine authority, uniting male, female, and child in a harmonious whole.
Amun is the father, the creator, king of the gods, representing hidden divine power and legitimacy of rule.
Mut is the mother, symbolising nurturing, maternal power, royal authority, and queenship.
Khonsu is the son, the moon god who governs time, healing, and the cyclical nature of life.

Thebes

The Theban Triad's centre of worship is Thebes, near modern day Luxor, Upper Egypt. Thebes was an important city which rose to prominence during Middle and New Kingdom, becoming the political and religious capital of Egypt, until 664 BCE when it was sacked by the Assyrians under Ashurbanipal, during Egypt's 26th Dynasty. The name Thebes comes from the Ancient Greek '*Thêbaí*' ('*Θῆβαι*'), from Egyptian '*tꜣ-jpy*' / '*Thebes*' > '*thejpt*', meaning 'the temple' or 'the inner sanctum'.

The Memphite Triad

The Memphite Triad

The Memphite Triad are the three gods representing creation, protection, healing, and rebirth.
Ptah is the father, representing creative power, thought and speech.
Sekhmet is the mother, symbolising divine wrath, protection, and the power to destroy or heal.
Nefertem is the son, representing beauty, renewal, and the life giving qualities of the lotus and the sun.

Memphis

The Memphite Triad's centre of worship is Memphis, near modern day Cairo. Memphis was one of the oldest and most important cities in Egypt. It was a centre of religion, culture, art, and architectural innovation. The name Memphis comes from the Ancient Greek *'Mémphis'* (*'Μέμφις'*), from the Egyptian *'mn-nfr'* / *'mn-nfr-ppy'*, meaning *'The Beauty of Pepy Endures'*. In Ancient Egyptian name for Memphis is *'Ineb-Hedj'*, meaning 'The White Walls', possibly referring to the walls of the royal residence.

29

The Elephantine Triad

The Elephantine Triad

The Elephantine Triad are the three gods representing the Nile River's life-giving power, fertility, and protection of Egypt's southern frontier.

Khnum is the father, god of the source of the Nile and creation, believed to fashion humans on a potter's wheel.

Satis is the mother, goddess of the Nile's annual flood and military protection.

Anuket is the daughter, goddess of the Nile's nourishment, fertility, flow and abundance.

Elephantine Island

The Elephantine Triad's centre of worship is Elephantine Island near modern day Aswan, Upper Egypt. Elephantine Island was a strategic and significant site at Egypt's southern border and it was believed to be the mythical source of the Nile. The name Elephantine comes from the Ancient Greek *'Elephantínē'* (*'Ἐλεφαντίνη'*), meaning 'elephant' or 'ivory'. The Ancient Egyptian name for Elephantine was *'Abu'* / *'Abw'*, also meaning 'elephant' or 'ivory', possibly in reference to the ivory trade or the shape of the island.

The Abydos Triad

The Abydos Triad

The Abydos Triad are the three gods representing death, resurrection, divine kingship, and protection.

Osiris, the father, is a god of the afterlife, resurrection, and the underworld.

Isis, the mother, is a goddess of magic, motherhood, and healing.

Horus, the son, is the sky god and symbol of living kingship and protection.

Abydos

The centre of worship for the Abydos Triad is Abydos near modern-day Al-Balyana, Upper Egypt. Abydos was considered the burial place of Osiris, making it one of the most spiritually significant cities in ancient Egypt. It remained a site of pilgrimage into the Greco-Roman period, but then lost its prominence under Christian and Islamic rule. The name Abydos comes from the Ancient Greek 'Ábudos' ('Άβυδος') from the Egyptian 'ꜣbḏw' / 'abedju', meaning 'elephant mountain' or 'elephant of the mountain'.

The Four Sons of Horus

From left to right: Imsety, Duamutef, Hapy, and Qebehsenuef
Wikipedia Creative Commons, Public Domain

The Four Sons of Horus collectively represent the protection of the internal organs of the deceased during mummification and burial. Each son is associated with a specific canopic jar, an internal organ, and a protective goddess. They serve to safeguard the body for the afterlife:

- Imsety protects the liver, protected by Isis (Greek '*Amesethis*' / '*Ἀμεσέθις*', from Egyptian '*Jmsty*', possibly meaning 'He of the Dill').
- Duamutef protects the stomach, protected by Neith (Greek '*Toumaúteph*' / '*Τουμαύτεφ*', from Egyptian '*Dwꜣ-mwt.f*' / '*dua-mut.ef*', meaning 'He Who Worships His Mother').
- Hapy protects the lungs, protected by Nephthys (Greek '*Hápys*' / '*Ἅπυς*', from Egyptian '*Ḥpy*', meaning 'He of Haste').
- Qebehsenuef protects the intestines, protected by Serket (Greek '*Kebesenōph*' / '*Κεβεσενώφ*', from Egyptian '*Qbḥ-sn.w.f*' / '*Qebehsenuef*', meaning 'He Who Refreshes His Brothers').

The 42 Judges of Ma'at

Wikipedia Creative Commons, Public Domain

The 42 Judges of Ma'at are minor gods whose function is to judge the souls of the dead in the afterlife, along with Osiris, in the Weighing of the Heart ceremony.

Each of the gods is assigned to one of the 42 nomes (provinces) of ancient Egypt, and presides over a specific moral principle that the deceased must claim innocence of during the confession. Egyptologist R. H. Wilkinson[5] and the Papyrus of Ani[6] give slightly different details:

No.	Name of Judge	Nome	Sin (Wilkinson)	Sin (Papyrus of Ani)
1	Usekh-nemmt ('Far-Strider')	Heliopolis	Spoke falsehood	Committed sin
2	Hept-khet ('Fire-Embracer')	Kheraha	Committed robbery	Committed robbery with violence
3	Fenti ('Nosey One')	Hermopolis	Acted with rapaciousness	Stole
4	Am-khaibit ('Swallower of Shades')	"The Cavern"	Committed murder	Slew others
5	Neha-her ('Dangerous One')	Rosetau	Stole	Stole grain
6	Ruruti ('Double Lion')	"The sky"	Destroyed food	Purloined offerings
7	Arfi-em-khet ('Fiery Eyes')	Letopolis	Acted with crookedness	Stole the property of a god
8	Neba ('Flame')	"Came forth backwards"	Stole offerings	Uttered lies
9	Set-qesu ('Bone Breaker')	Heracleopolis	Lied	Carried away food unlawfully
10	Utu-nesert ('Green of Flame')	Memphis	Took food unlawfully	Uttered curses
11	Qerrti ('You of the Cavern')	"The West"	Was sullen	Committed adultery

---

[5] Wilkinson, Richard H., The Complete Gods and Goddesses of Ancient Egypt, Thames & Hudson, 2003, ISBN 0-500-05120-8. pp. 84–5.
[6] Mark, Joshua J. "The Forty-Two Judges". World History Encyclopedia. Retrieved 18 June 2025.

No.	Name of Judge	Nome	Sin (Wilkinson)	Sin (Papyrus of Ani)
12	Kenemti ('White of Teeth')	Faiyum	Transgressed moral or divine law	Blasphemed
13	Hetch-abhu / Shezmu ('House of Nature')	"The shambles"	Killed a sacred bull	Consumed the heart (i.e., acted with cruelty or hatred)
14	Ta-retiu ('Eater of Entrails')	"House of Thirty"	Committed perjury	Attacked another
15	Unem-snef ('Lord of Truth')	Maaty	Stole bread	Was deceitful
16	Unem-besek ('Wanderer')	Bubastis	Eavesdropped	Stole cultivated land
17	Neb-Maat ('Pale One')	Heliopolis	Babbled needlessly	Eavesdropped
18	Tenemiu ('Doubly Evil')	Andjet	Disputed unjustly	Slandered another
19	Sertiu ('Wememty-Snake')	"Place of execution"	Committed adultery	Was angry without just cause
20	Tutu ('See Whom You Bring')	"House of Min"	Behaved improperly	Committed sexual misconduct
21	Uamenti ('Over the Old One')	Imau	Terrorized others	Seduced another's partner
22	Maa-antuf ('Demolisher')	Xois	Transgressed	Defiled oneself
23	Her-uru ('Disturber')	Weryt	Was hot-tempered	Terrorized others
24	Khemiu ('Youth')	Heliopolitan nome	Ignored the truth	Transgressed the law
25	Shet-kheru ('Foreteller')	Wenes	Caused disturbance	Was unjustly angry
26	Nebheru ('You of the Altar')	"the secret place"	Deceived or hoodwinked	Ignored the words of truth
27	Hraf-haf ('Face Behind Him')	"Cavern of wrong"	Committed illicit acts	Caused others to weep
28	An-hetep-f ('Hot-Foot')	"The dusk"	Neglected one's duties	Committed acts of violence
29	Sera-kheru ('You of the Darkness')	"The darkness"	Quarrelled	Stirred up strife
30	Neb-heru ('Bringer of Your Offerings')	Sais	Acted with undue restlessness	Acted with undue haste
31	Sekhriu ('Owner of Faces')	Nedjefet (13th / 14th Upper Egyptian nome)	Was impatient	Pried into the affairs of others

The Egyptian Gods   An Illustrated Introduction

No.	Name of Judge	Nome	Sin (Wilkinson)	Sin (Papyrus of Ani)
32	Neb-abui ('Accuser')	Wetjenet	Damaged the image of a god	Spoke excessively or without restraint
33	Owner of Horns	Asyut	Spoke excessively or idly	Carried away sacred offerings of the dead
34	Nefertem	Memphis	Did wrong or beheld evil willingly	Wronged others
35	Temsep/Tem-Sepu	Busiris	Performed conjuration against the king	Performed witchcraft against the king
36	Ari-em-ab-f ('You Who Acted Willfully')	Tjebu	Obstructed or diverted the flow of water	Stopped the flow of a neighbour's water
37	Ahi ('Water-Smiter')	"The abyss"	Was loud-voiced in arrogance or anger	Raised one's voice arrogantly
38	Uatch-rekhit ('Commander of Mankind')	"Your house"	Reviled or cursed a god	Cursed a god
39	Nehebkau	The Harpoon Nome	Acted with arrogance	Acted with arrogance
40	Neheb-nefert ('Bestower of Powers')	"The city"	Showed favouritism or self-preference	Stole the bread of the gods
41	Hetch-abhu ('Serpent With Raised Head')	"The cavern"	Acquired dishonest wealth	Slew cattle belonging to a god
42	Neb-abui ('Serpent Who Brings and Gives')	"The silent land"	Committed blasphemy	Snatched away the bread of a child or showed contempt for the god of one's city

The Weighing of the Heart ceremony from the Temple of Hathor at Deir el-Medina
Wikipedia Creative Commons, Public Domain

Aker: Guardian of the Horizons

Left: Two variations of 'Aker' in hieroglyphs

Left: The hieroglyphic symbol for 'horizon'

Aker is an earth god, an underworld god, and the guardian and personification of the horizons: the boundaries between the earth and the land of the living above, and the underworld below.

For the Ancient Egyptians, the eastern and western horizons are marked by mountain peaks, both sides of which are part of the universal cosmic mountain, which rises up on either side of the Nile valley to hold up the heavens, literally cradling civilisation.

Each evening the sun god descends into the western horizon, into the land of *Manu*, which represents death and the journey into the underworld and the afterlife. Each morning, the sun god rises again in the eastern horizon, from the land of *Bakhu*, which represents life, birth, and rebirth into the land of the living. His name means 'one who bends', and he is also referred to as 'He who is looking forward and behind'[7].

Aker prevents the forces of chaos (harmful spirits or serpents) from entering the world, and protects the sun god on his journey, either by bearing him on his back, or as a ferryman on his barque[8]. While Aker doesn't appear to have any extended narrative myths like Osiris or Isis, he holds a cosmic and protective role, as a symbolic gateway and guardian.

Aker is depicted in a variety of forms, a lion-headed figure, a figure with two lion heads facing left and right, a single reclining lion with his mouth wide open, two reclining lions with their torsos merged together as one, with the two heads at either end looking away from eachother, or two merged torsos of reclining sphinxes with human heads.

Depictions of Aker also contain a hieroglyphic symbol for 'horizon', consisting of a large sun disk in the centre, and the east and west mountain tops on either side[9]. Other inscriptions, wall paintings, and reliefs focus on Aker's role in protecting those travelling through the underworld, suggesting that Aker is more of a god of the underworld, in some cases a personification of the underworld[10].

Aker does not have major dedicated temple complexes dedicated to him, but statues of Aker are positioned outside the entrances to important temples and other buildings, a practice continued by the Greeks and Romans.

---

[7] Pat Remler: Egyptian Mythology, A to Z. Infobase Publishing, 2010, ISBN 1438131801, pp. 4 & 5.
[8] A type of sailing vessel
[9] Remler, 2010.
[10] Geraldine Pinch: Egyptian Mythology: A Guide to the Gods, Goddesses, and Traditions of Ancient Egypt. Oxford University Press, Oxford (UK) 2004, ISBN 0195170245, page 99.

The Early Dynastic Period: Aker first appears in the tombs of the pharaohs Hor Aha and Djer who ruled from around c3050 to c3000 BCE. In Djer's tomb at Abydos, Aker is shown devouring three hearts, perhaps symbolising the purification of souls[11].

The Old Kingdom: The Pyramid Texts mention Aker in several spells as a protector of the deceased, particularly in his role as a guardian of the horizon, ensuring the safe passage of the pharaoh into the afterlife. His role is perhaps most fully described in the Pyramid Texts of the pharaoh Teti, who died around c2333 BCE[12].

- Spell 275 describes the deceased wearing a special garment, opening the double doors of heaven, going to the boundary of the horizon (Aker), laying the special garment down on the ground, and then becoming like the Great One who is in Crocodilopolis (The solar deity Sobek or Sobek-Ra)[13].
- Spell 581 describes the deceased arriving in the 'broad-hall of Osiris' where 'Aker stands up for thee', along with other protective guardians, helping the deceased in their passage through the underworld[14].

The Middle Kingdom: The Coffin Texts expand on the Pyramid Texts, emphasising the role of Aker as a protector, alongside other gods who protect the deceased on their journey through the underworld and into the afterlife.

The New Kingdom: The Book of the Dead further describes Aker as a guardian of the horizon, invoking him to provide protection as the soul makes its journey.

The Late Period: The two lions of Aker (*Akeru*), also known as *Ruti* ('two lions'), are given their own names: *Sef* or *Sefe* ('yesterday'), and *Tuau* or *Duaj* ('tomorrow').

Sef or *Sefe*

- Yesterday
- Left-facing
- West-facing
- Guarding the Western Horizon
- The Land of *Manu*
- The Underworld
- Death, the journey to the underworld, and the afterlife

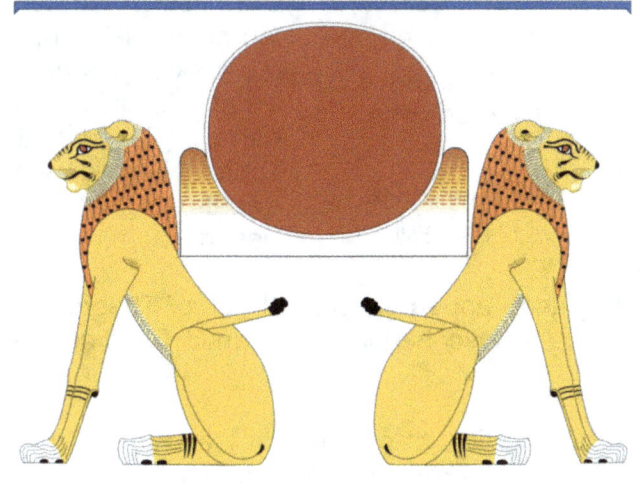

Tuau or *Duaj*

- Tomorrow
- Right-facing
- East-facing
- Guarding the Eastern Horizon
- The Land of *Bakhu*
- The Land of the Living
- Life, birth, rebirth

Aker, Wikipedia Creative Commons, Public Domain

Perhaps the closest parallel Greco-Roman god to Aker is the Roman god Janus, a god of thresholds, gates, beginnings, and endings, depicted with two faces, one looking forward and one backward. Aker could be prayed to for protection during journeys (especially during the afterlife), safety from chaos or danger, or for stability during transitions.

---

[11] Peter Kaplony: Die Inschriften der ägyptischen Frühzeit, 3rd edition. Harrassowitz, Wiesbaden 1963, pp. 65.
[12] Leitz, 2002.
[13] Sacred Texts (2004, June 2). The Pyramid Texts, Translation by Samuel A. B. Mercer (1952). Retrieved March 20, 2025, from https://www.sacred-texts.com/egy/pyt/pyt14.htm
[14] Sacred Texts (2004, June 2).

Amun: The Hidden One and Supreme Creator

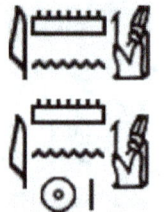

Left: 'Amun' in hieroglyphs

Left: 'Amun-Ra' in hieroglyphs

Amun is the primordial god of that which is hidden, air, wind, creation, kingship and divine authority. He is the supreme creator, and the king of the gods. He is everywhere at once, and his presence can be felt, but never seen[15]. His name means 'the hidden one', 'invisible', or 'the secret one'[16]. He first created himself, then the other gods, and then brought the world into being. Amun, together with his wife and female counterpart Amunet are members of the Ogdoad. Amun later became fused with the sun god Ra to become Amun-Ra (*Amon-Ra, Amon-Re, Amun-Re*)[17], worshipped as the supreme creator, a champion of the poor and the troubled, the upholder of *ma'at*, and a figure central to personal piety[18]. As Amun-Ra rose in prominence in the Theban tradition, his female counterpart or consort Amunet was gradually replaced by the mother goddess Mut (*Maut, Mout*). Amun-Ra and Mut had a son, the moon god Khonsu, and the three of them became known as the Theban Triad[19]. Amun is depicted as a man wearing a tall crown plumed with two large ostrich feathers. He was first depicted with red-brown skin, then with blue skin, later with a sun disk on his head, and then with the head of a ram. Amun's main centres of worship are at Karnak (Thebes), the Luxor Temple (Thebes), Tanis (Northeastern Delta), Gebel Barkal and Napata (Nubia), and the Siwa Oasis (Western Desert).

The Old Kingdom: Amun begins to appear as a local god of Thebes, possibly evolving from a more ancient hidden god of the air. He is described in the Pyramid Texts as a primordial deity and a symbol of creative force[20].

The First Intermediate Period: Political fragmentation leads to the rise of local Theban rulers. The Theban 11th Dynasty promotes Amun, likely identifying him as a local god of wind or air.

The Middle Kingdom: Amun becomes the protective patron of the city of Thebes (replacing the god Montu or Montju[21]). Thebes gains political power and becomes an important religious centre whose name means 'the temple', or 'the inner sanctum'[22]. The Ancient Egyptians call the city Waset ('$w^3s.t$')

---

[15] Armour, Robert A. Gods and Myths of Ancient Egypt. Cairo: The American University in Cairo Press, 2001.
[16] Hart, George (2005). The Routledge Dictionary of Egyptian Gods and Goddesses. Abingdon, England: Routledge. p. 21. ISBN 978-0-415-36116-3. Archived from the original on 30 July 2024. Retrieved 7 January 2016.
[17] Stark, 2007.
[18] Arieh Tobin, Vincent (2003). Redford, Donald B. (ed.). The Essential Guide to Egyptian Mythology. Oxford Guides. Berkley Books. p. 20. ISBN 0-425-19096-X.
[19] Wilkinson, John Gardner (2013). Modern Egypt and Thebes. Cambridge University Press. p. 282. ISBN 978-1-108-06510-8. Retrieved 10 December 2019.
[20] Hill, J. (2017, August 23). Amun. Retrieved March 19, 2025, from https://ancientegyptonline.co.uk/amun/
[21] Warburton, David (2012). Architecture, Power, and Religion: Hatshepsut, Amun and Karnak in Context. Lit. ISBN 978-3-643-90235-1.

meaning 'the city of the sceptre', or 'the sceptre of the pharaohs'[23]. Amun is merged with the sun god Ra to become Amun-Ra (*Amon-Ra, Amon-Re, Amun-Re*). As Amun-Ra, he is additionally depicted with a sun disk above his head.

Amun, Wikipedia Creative Commons, Public Domain

The Second Intermediate Period: The Theban royal line continues Amun worship despite Hyksos rule in the north. Amun becomes a symbol of Theban resistance.

The New Kingdom: Amun-Ra is promoted to the status of a national god by Ahmose I, the first pharaoh of the New Kingdom, because he believes that Amun has helped him against the rival Hyksos Dynasty, driving them out of Lower and Middle Egypt.

The Amarna Period (c1353 to c1336 BCE): Amun is temporarily abandoned when the pharaoh Amenhotep IV changes his name to Akhenaten ('Effective for the Aten') and moves from Thebes to Akhetaten ('Horizon of the Aten', now known as Amarna). Akhenaten then imposes the worship of the sun god Aten (Atenism) above all others.

Restoration and Late New Kingdom: After the death of Akhenaten, his son Tutankhaten ('living image of Aten') changes his name to Tutankhamun ('living image of Amun') and restores religious traditions, returning Amun-Ra to prominence. From this point on Amun-Ra is depicted with blue skin, symbolising his association with air and primeval creation. As Egypt expands further south into the Kingdom of Kush in Lower and Upper Nubia (Southern Egypt and Northern Sudan), the chief solar deity of the Kushites is depicted with the head of a ram. As the Kushites are brought under Egyptian rule, Amun-Ra takes on this ram-headed aspect, first with ram horns, and then the head of a ram with curved green horns. Amun-Ra also absorbs the identity of the fertility god Min and is also called Amun-Min or Amun-Ra-Min.

The Third Intermediate Period: Amun's cult remains strong, particularly in Upper Egypt. Egypt is divided, pharaohs rule from Tanis in the north, Amun's priests rule Thebes in the south.

The Late Period: Nubian, and Persian rulers adopt Amun to legitimize power. The Kushite kings (25th Dynasty) of Nubia deeply venerate Amun, making Napata and Jebel Barkal new centres of his worship.

The Ptolemaic Period: Amun is syncretised with Zeus (Zeus-Ammon). Greek rulers respect Egyptian religion, and the oracle of Amun at Siwa Oasis gains fame (visited by Alexander the Great).

The Roman and Byzantine Periods: The worship of Amun declines and is eventually suppressed with the spread of Christianity. Amun's imagery and theology influence later concepts of hidden divinity and the power of oracles. The Romans identify him with Jupiter and called him Jupiter Ammon.

As Amun-Ra, a combination of rulership and solar power, he could be equated with a Greek Zeus-Helios, or a Roman Jupiter-Sol. Amun or Amun-Ra could be prayed to for protection, fertility, success, divine guidance, and mercy.

---

[22] Wiktionary (2025, January 28). Thebes. Retrieved March 17, 2025, from https://en.wiktionary.org/wiki/Thebes
[23] Global Egyptian Museum (n.d.). Was-sceptre. Retrieved March 17, 2025, from https://www.globalegyptianmuseum.org/glossary.aspx?id=397

Amunet: The Invisible One and Primordial Mother

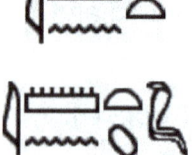

Left: Two variations of 'Amunet' in hieroglyphs

Amunet is the primordial goddess of the air, of all that is unseen, breath, the force that existed before the creation of the world, the cosmic elements, hidden power, and protective wisdom[24][25][26][27][28].

As her name suggests, she is the female counterpart of the god Amun. Her name is the feminine form of 'the hidden one', 'invisible', or 'the secret one'[29]. Amunet and her male counterpart Amun are members of the Ogdoad.

Amunet is also syncretised with the goddess Neith in some late texts at Karnak (Thebes). She is commonly depicted holding a staff and wearing the Deshret (a red crown) associated with the rule of Lower Egypt[30], even though she was worshipped mainly in Upper Egypt (Thebes and Hermopolis). She is often depicted in coronation scenes and temple reliefs as a divine protector of the pharaoh.

Amunet is venerated alongside Amun at Karnak (Thebes) where she has her own chapels and is honoured in rituals connected to kingship and creation. She is also venerated in Hermopolis where statues and reliefs show her standing behind the pharaohs, offering divine protection, guidance, and support as a protective maternal goddess[31], sometimes with the Aknh symbol meaning 'life', 'live', 'cause to live', or 'nourish'.

The Old Kingdom: Amunet does not appear in Old Kingdom texts or temple inscriptions. The Theban region, later her cult centre, is not yet politically prominent. Her later association as the female counterpart of Amun likely has its roots in pre-existing local dualistic theology (male-female divine pairs).

The First Intermediate Period: With political decentralisation, local Theban cults begin to rise in importance. Early forms of Amun begin to appear in Theban contexts, possibly alongside a female consort who may be an early version of Amunet.

---

[24] Pinch, G. (2002). *Handbook of Egyptian Mythology*. ABC-CLIO
[25] Daniel, Robert W. (2013). Two Greek Magical Papyri in the National Museum of Antiquities in Leiden: A Photographic Edition of J 384 and 395 (=PGM XII and XIII). Springer-Verlag. p. 64. ISBN 978-3-663-05377-4.
[26] Henrichs, Albert (2013). Papyri Graecae magicae / Die griechischen Zauberpapyri. Walter de Gruyter. p. 123. ISBN 978-3-11-095126-4.
[27] Wilkinson, Richard H. (2003). The Complete Gods and Goddesses of Ancient Egypt. Thames & Hudson. ISBN 0-500-05120-8.
[28] Hart, George (1986). A Dictionary of Egyptian Gods and Goddesses. Routledge. ISBN 0-415-05909-7.
[29] Hart, George (2005). The Routledge Dictionary of Egyptian Gods and Goddesses. Abingdon, England: Routledge. p. 21. ISBN 978-0-415-36116-3. Archived from the original on 30 July 2024. Retrieved 7 January 2016.
[30] Wilkinson, R. H. (2003). *The Complete Gods and Goddesses of Ancient Egypt*. Thames & Hudson.
[31] Teeter, E. (2011). *Religion and Ritual in Ancient Egypt*. Cambridge University Press.

The Middle Kingdom: The city of Thebes rises to political dominance as Theban rulers unify Egypt. Their local gods Amunet and Amun become more prominent and take on a national significance. This significance is reinforced by the Ogdoad tradition at Hermopolis, and from this point on, the centre of worship of Amunet and Amun shifts from Hermopolis to Thebes. As Amun is increasingly merged with Ra to become Amun-Ra, the king of the gods, Amunet's relationship with Amun evolves. Amunet is adapted to fit into Thebes' theological and political system, where she plays a prominent role in coronation rituals and royal ceremonies as a divine legitimiser of rule and authority[32].

Amunet, Wikipedia Creative Commons, Public Domain

The Second Intermediate Period: Amunet appears to begin a gradual decline in visibility. At around the same time, the goddess Mut ('Mother') begins to appear in the Theban tradition.

The New Kingdom: Worship of Amunet and Amun continues, particularly in the major temple at Karnak (Thebes), but the cult is regionally more fragmented. In some cases Amunet and Mut coexist in some rituals. Gradually however, Amunet is reduced in prominence as the goddess Mut becomes chief consort of Amun. One of the most famous representations of Amunet is a life-size statue from the Luxor Temple at Thebes, showing Amunet embracing Tutankhamun.

The Third Intermediate Period: Amunet retains her presence in rituals and ceremonies at Karnak (Thebes). Local priesthoods maintain the cult of Amunet, especially those loyal to the traditional Theban religion.

The Late Period: Amunet is still mentioned in priestly cosmological texts and is still present in the temple reliefs. The Ogdoad remains important in Hermopolitan religion.

The Ptolemaic Period: Amunet retains a minor ceremonial role, sometimes syncretised or paralleled with Greek goddesses like Rhea or Hestia, and her role becomes more symbolic in theology rather than being widely practised.

The Roman Period: Amunet's syncretism or parallel with the Greek goddesses Rhea and Hestia translate across to the Roman equivalent goddesses Ops and Vesta. However, traditional Egyptian religion gradually declines under Roman rule, particularly with the emergence of Christianity.

The Byzantine Period: With the Christianisation of Egypt, the temples of Amun and associated deities are closed. Amunet's worship ceases as pagan cults are suppressed under imperial edicts. Her memory persists only in magical and Hermetic texts, where she is sometimes listed among archaic divine names representing hidden feminine forces.

The closest possible parallel to Amunet is the Greco-Roman goddess Nyx / Nox, the personification of night and the unseen beginnings of existence.

People could pray to Amunet for protection and guidance, spiritual insight or wisdom, fertility and creation, renewal and life-force, ritual purification, or divine favour.

---

[32] Bleeker, C. J. (1973). *The Egyptian God Amun*. Brill.

Anput: Goddess of the Embalming and the Dead

Left: 'Anput' in hieroglyphs

Anput is a goddess of embalming and of the dead, and is sometimes described as a goddess of mourning. Mourning rituals include offerings and prayers invoking Anput to guide the soul of the deceased safely through the afterlife and to comfort the grieving. Anput is the feminine counterpart of the god Anubis[33].

Anput is associated with funerals and the mummification process. She is also a guardian of tombs and one of the deities who safeguard the deceased during their journey through the underworld.

Anput is sometimes associated with the protection of the deceased during the 'Weighing of the Heart' ceremony. She assists in the protection of the deceased during the judgement process.

Anput is also associated with protection in the desert, which ancient Egyptians view as a realm of the dead. Ancient Egyptians bury their dead in the western desert and necropolises beyond the fertile Nile valley. The West, associated with the setting sun, becomes a metaphor for death, and the 'Land of the West' a euphemism for the afterlife. The chaos and danger of such a dry, lifeless, hostile, and inhospitable environment, is a stark contrast to the fertile Nile valley.

Anput appears in the Pyramid Texts and is named as the mother of the goddess Kebechet, the serpent who "refreshes and purifies" the pharaoh, bringing cooling and purifying water to the spirits of the dead as they wait for the completion of their mummification.

Anput is depicted as a woman with a headdress showing a reclining jackal, and in some cases with the head of a jackal (similar to her counterpart Anubis who also has the head of a jackal), but this depiction is very rare[34]. Jackals are strong symbols of the dead and the afterlife for ancient Egyptians as they are commonly seen around cemeteries, scavenging shallow graves[35], which leads to their association with tombs, death, and burial practices. Sometimes the reclining jackal on Anput's headdress is depicted perched on a feather, representing the Feather of Ma'at, against which the heart of the deceased is weighed and judged. Located in Upper Egypt, Anput's main centre of worship is Cynopolis (Greek: 'City of the Dog / Jackal'), known to the Egyptians as Hardai or Ta-senet.

The First Intermediate Period: Funerary religion becomes increasingly localised. The nome of Cynopolis ('City of the Dog / Jackal') in Middle Egypt may have early local traditions that later contribute to Anput's formation.

---

[33] Wilkinson, Richard H. (2003). The Complete Gods and Goddesses of Ancient Egypt. Thames & Hudson. p. 190
[34] Hill, J (2010). "Gods of ancient Egypt: Anput". Ancient Egypt Online. Retrieved 5 June 2017.
[35] Wilkinson 1999, p. 262 (burials in shallow graves in Pre-Dynastic Egypt); Freeman 1997, p. 91 (rest of the information).

The Middle Kingdom: The earliest references to Anput begin to appear. She is mentioned in funerary texts and stelae (inscribed stone or wooden slabs), primarily as the female counterpart or wife of Anubis. Her cult is most likely centred in the 17th Upper Egyptian nome, whose capital is Hardai (Greek: Cynopolis, 'the City of the Dog / Jackal'). In this period, she symbolises protection of the deceased and guardianship of the necropolis, sometimes associated with mummy wrappings and embalming rituals.

Anput, Wikipedia Creative Commons, Public Domain

The Second Intermediate Period: Limited evidence survives, but local Theban and Cynopolitan traditions of funerary deities remain active. Anput is probably venerated in local necropolis rituals as Anubis's consort and assistant.

The New Kingdom: The first major depictions of Anput begin to appear, particularly in Theban tombs and temple texts, during what is the peak of the Theban religious tradition. Anput is typically shown as a woman wearing a headdress with a jackal standard, signifying her link to Anubis and funerary rites. Anput is listed among the divine protectors of the dead, and is present in rituals concerning embalming and burial. Her protective presence is invoked to watch over the mummified body and guide the soul safely through the underworld.

The Third Intermediate Period: Anput continues to appear in funerary texts and tomb art, often in a symbolic or supportive role, rather than as the direct focus of independent worship. Her iconography remains linked to the mortuary cult of Anubis, and her worship becomes more fragmented as local priesthoods take over religious leadership.

The Late Period: Revivals of older religious traditions and increasing attention to local deities helps to maintain Anput's symbolic role in some regional cults in this period.

The Ptolemaic Period: Anput's role becomes increasingly ritualistic and theological rather than widespread in popular worship. She appears in temple scenes, occasionally alongside Anubis in depictions of embalming and mummification. Anput is not syncretised with any Greek deities in the same way as other more prominent gods like Isis or Anubis are during this period.

The Roman Period: Traditional Egyptian funerary religion continues under Roman rule, especially in Upper Egypt. Anput's name still appears in magical papyri and funerary texts, where she functions as a protective guardian of mummification and tombs. Artistic depictions persist in temple scenes involving Anubis.

The Byzantine Period: With the spread of Christianity and the imperial bans on traditional Egyptian religion, Anput's worship ceases. In late Coptic magical texts and Hermetic writings, faint echoes of her protective and funerary aspects may persist, reinterpreted through Christian or Gnostic symbolism (as with many old Egyptian deities).

A possible parallel of Anput in Greek / Roman religion is Hekate / Trivia. They are both associated with protection, guiding souls, and funerary magic. People could pray to Anput for protection of the deceased, guidance for souls, assistance with funerary rituals, safety for tombs and sacred places, support for the living.

Anubis: God of the Afterlife

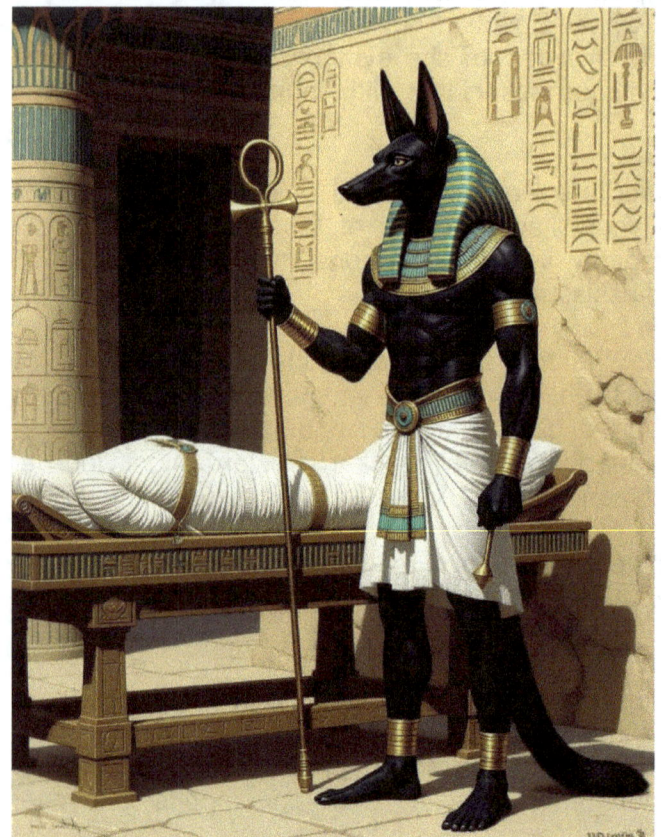

Left: Two variations of 'Anubis' in hieroglyphs

Anubis is a god of funerals, funerary rituals, the protector of graves, and a guide to the underworld. The name 'Anubis' is from Greek ('Άνουβις'). Before the Greeks arrived in Egypt in around the 7th century BCE, he was known as 'Apnu' or 'Inpu', meaning 'a royal child'. The root 'inp' means 'to decay'.

Anubis attends the 'Weighing of the Heart' ceremony, in which the deceased's heart is weighed against the Feather of Ma'at and judged to determine whether the soul is allowed to enter the realm of the dead. He is mentioned in the story of Osiris. After Osiris is murdered and dismembered by his brother Set, the goddess Isis (Osiris's wife) searches for and reassembles his body. Anubis helps to embalm Osiris, wrapping him and performing the first mummification ritual, allowing Osiris to become lord of the underworld.

Anubis is variously portrayed as the son of Ra and Nephthys, the cow goddess Hesat, cat-headed Bastet, or Osiris (later Serapis) and Isis[36]. His female counterpart is Anput, with whom he fathered the goddess Kebechet, the serpent who "refreshes and purifies" the pharaoh, bringing cooling and purifying water to the spirits of the dead as they wait for the completion of their mummification.

Anubis is associated with, and almost identical to, the god Wepwawet, also a god of funerary rituals and war, but with grey or white fur on his head instead of black. It is assumed that these two figures were eventually combined[37]. Anubis is depicted as a jackal or a man with a jackal's head[38]. Jackals are strong symbols of the dead and the afterlife for ancient Egyptians as they were commonly seen around cemeteries, likely scavenging shallow graves[39], which led to their association with tombs, death, and burial practices. Located in Upper Egypt, Anubis's main centre of worship is Cynopolis (Ancient Greek: 'City of the Dog'), known to the ancient Egyptians as *Hardai* or *Ta-senet*.

The Early Dynastic Period: The earliest mentions of Anubis appear in funerary texts and artefacts. He is invoked as a protector of graves, and is closely associated with royal burials. He appears in full animal form with the head and body of a jackal[40].

---

[36] Hart, George (1986), A Dictionary of Egyptian Gods and Goddesses, London: Routledge & Kegan Paul, ISBN 978-0-415-34495-1.
[37] Gryglewski 2002, p. 145.
[38] Turner, Alice K. (1993). The History of Hell (1st ed.). United States: Harcourt Brace. p. 13. ISBN 978-0-15-140934-1.
[39] Wilkinson 1999, p. 262 (burials in shallow graves in Pre-Dynastic Egypt); Freeman 1997, p. 91 (rest of the information).
[40] Wilkinson, Toby A. H. (1999), Early Dynastic Egypt, London: Routledge

The Old Kingdom: Anubis becomes a central deity in funerary religion. He appears in the Pyramid Texts where he embalms the deceased, guides the soul through the underworld, and oversees the ritual of 'opening the mouth' ('*wepet-er*'). This ceremony was an important ritual designed to restore the deceased's sensory and vital functions, such as breathing, seeing, hearing, speaking, and eating, thereby enabling them to partake in the afterlife. This ritual was integral to the transformation of the deceased into 'akh', a blessed and effective spirit capable of interacting with the divine realm[41].

Anubis, Wikipedia Creative Commons, Public Domain

The First Intermediate Period: Worship of Anubis becomes more widespread, including among non-royals. As burials become more democratised, Anubis becomes accessible to commoners as a guide in the afterlife.

The Middle Kingdom: Anubis is gradually replaced by Osiris[42], but continues as a major funerary deity. He appears frequently in the Coffin Texts and in tomb decorations. As the cult of Osiris rises, Anubis's role shifts to that of a guardian and embalmer of Osiris. He begins to function as an assistant rather than a primary judge of the dead.

The New Kingdom: Anubis is featured prominently in scenes from the Book of the Dead. He presides over the 'Weighing of the Heart' ceremony alongside Thoth and Osiris. His cult centres at Cynopolis ('City of the Dog') in Upper Egypt. Popular amulets and statues of Anubis are used in burials.

The Third Intermediate and Late Periods: Anubis remains an important god in tomb art and funerary practices. He blends more closely with the Greek god Hermes (Roman: Mercury) during the Latte Period.

The Ptolemaic Period: Anubis is syncretised with Hermes in Hellenistic (Greek) beliefs where he evolves into Hermanubis, a hybrid deity combining Anubis and Hermes. He acts as a psychopomp (a guide of souls).

The Roman Period: Worship of Anubis (or Hermanubis) continues alongside other Egyptian gods under Roman influence, spreading to Rome. He appears in temples and shrines across the Roman world such as Pompeii. Tomb paintings depict Anubis as holding the hand of the deceased to guide them to Osiris[43]. Eventually the worship of Egyptian gods declines with the spread of Christianity and with the Roman banning of pagan worship.

The closest equivalent to Anubis in Greco-Roman mythology is Hermes Psychopompos (Hermes in his role as the soul-guide). The Romans carried this identification forward, referring to him as Mercurius Psychopompos, and later Hermanubis (Hermes + Anubis), especially in Roman Egypt.

People could pray to Anubis for protection of the deceased, safe passage through the underworld, proper performance of funerary rites, purification and preservation, protection against evil spirits or desecration of graves, guidance and comfort for grieving families.

---

[41] Hill, J. (n.d.). The Opening of the Mouth. Retrieved June 3, 2025, from https://ancientegyptonline.co.uk/openingofthemouth/
[42] Freeman, Charles (1997), The Legacy of Ancient Egypt, New York: Facts on File, ISBN 978-0-816-03656-1.
[43] Riggs, Christina (2005), The Beautiful Burial in Roman Egypt: Art, Identity, and Funerary Religion, Oxford and New York: Oxford University Press

Anuket: Fertility Goddess of the Nile

Left: 'Anuket' in hieroglyphs

Anuket is a goddess of fertility, nourishment, fresh water, and the Nile, particularly its cycle of flooding, which is vital to agriculture and survival in ancient Egypt. As a goddess of the Nile, she personifies the life-giving waters that flow from Nubia into Egypt, making her especially significant around the cataracts of the Nile[44], the shallow stretches and whitewater rapids around Aswan.

Her name is thought to mean 'the clasper' or 'the embracer'[45], referring to the way the life-giving waters of the Nile embrace the land, wrapping around it and blessing it with fertility and life. Some depictions of Anuket poetically show her with outstretched arms in an embracing posture, believed to visually echo the shape of the Nile with its two tributaries.

The various traditions agree that Anuket is the granddaughter of Ra. In the Elephantine / Nubian tradition, Anuket is the daughter of Khnum and Satis, the sister of Sobek, the wife or consort of Khnum, and the mother of Heka (a god of magic). In the Heliopolitan tradition, Anuket is the daughter of Khnum only, with less emphasis on Satis, who is either her mother or sister. In other traditions Anuket is the daughter of Satis only, with less emphasis on Khnum.

In the Elephantine tradition, Anuket, Khnum, and Satis together form the Elephantine Triad, and like her mother Satis, Anuket also serves as a protector of Egypt's southern border and its expansion into Nubia, from which she is sometimes referred to as 'the Nubian'[46]. Anuket and Satis have both been referred to as the Eye of Ra, along with Bastet, Hathor, and Sekhmet[47].

Anuket is depicted wearing a crown of reeds or ostrich feathers. The reeds represent the vegetation of the Nile. Anuket's sacred animal and spiritual emblem is the gazelle, known for its speed and elegance. In certain ancient rituals to Anuket, gazelles are set free as offerings, a symbolic act of releasing life or abundance. The gazelle's speed and grace mirror the swift, graceful flow of the Nile, linking Anuket to qualities of speed, movement, grace, and agility.

The Pre-Dynastic and Early Dynastic Periods: Anuket does not yet appear in the archaeological or written record. However, the First Cataract region near Aswan holds sacred significance, and local Nubian and Upper Egyptian peoples venerate the Nile and its life-giving powers. These southern traditions lay the foundation for the later worship of Anuket.

---

[44] Hart, George (2005), The Routledge Dictionary of Egyptian Gods and Goddesses, Revised Edition, p. 28
[45] "Anoukis" , Encyclopædia Britannica, vol. II (9th ed.), New York: Charles Scribner's Sons, 1878, p. 90
[46] Abdelhakim, Walaa Mohamed; Zein, Mohamed; Mosallam, Amr (1999-12-01). "The Sexual Symbolism of the Votive Beds' Decorations and Its Relation to Their Function". The International Journal of Tourism and Hospitality Studies. 4 (1): 162–143. doi:10.21608/ijthsx.2023.180510.1040. ISSN 2785-9843.
[47] Hill, J. (2010). "Anuket". ancientegyptonline.co.uk. Ancient Egypt Online. Retrieved 2016-10-26.

The Old Kingdom: The earliest references to Anuket appear at Elephantine Island and Lower Nubia, where she is worshipped as a local river goddess. She is linked to the Nile cataracts, crucial for controlling water flow and irrigation.

The First Intermediate Period and Middle Kingdom: During periods of political change, Anuket's cult remains local but continuous. Priests at Elephantine maintain her worship, and she becomes increasingly defined as the daughter of Khnum and Satis, forming the Elephantine Triad. In the Middle Kingdom, her role as a fertility goddess and nurturer of crops and life becomes more prominent, and worship begins to expand as Egyptian influence grows deeper into Nubia.

Anuket, Wikipedia Creative Commons, Public Domain

The Second Intermediate Period and New Kingdom: Even amid political fragmentation, worship continues at Elephantine. In the New Kingdom, the cult reaches its height, with temples and shrines established at Sehel, Philae, and Elephantine. Festivals such as the Festival of Anuket celebrate the Nile inundation, during which offerings are thrown into the river to give thanks for life and fertility. Artistic depictions show her as a woman with a tall feathered headdress, sometimes nursing the pharaoh, symbolising divine nourishment and legitimacy.

The Third Intermediate and Late Periods: Anuket maintains a strong regional following in Upper Egypt and near Nubia. Artistic representations grow more elaborate, occasionally merging aspects with Hathor. Local devotion remains strong at Elephantine, appearing on temple reliefs and votive offerings, even as national devotion to Isis and Osiris rises.

The Ptolemaic Period: Under Ptolemaic rule, the cult remains active in southern sanctuaries. Anuket is identified with the Greek goddess Hestia (Vesta)[48]. Temples at Philae and Elephantine depict her alongside Isis and other Nile deities, maintaining her traditional symbols of reeds, the Nile, and the gazelle, though Greek artistic influences appear.

The Roman and Byzantine Periods: Worship continues under Roman rule, particularly in southern Egypt, but gradually declines with the spread of Christianity. By the early Byzantine era, her cult persists at Philae, appearing in the last pagan reliefs. In AD 535, Emperor Justinian orders the closure of Philae's temples, formally ending Anuket's worship, though local folk practices celebrating the Nile's life-giving flood survive.

There isn't a direct one-to-one Greek or Roman equivalent to Anuket, but there are some thematic parallels. The Naiads (Greek) / Nymphae (Roman) are river and freshwater spirits. The Potamoi (Greek) are river gods, guardians of streams and rivers. Tiberinus (Roman) is a river god associated with the river Tiber, in much the same way that Anuket is associated with the Nile. In the discourse known as Interpretatio Graeca ('Greek Interpretation'), Anuket is compared to Hestia (Roman: Vesta). She has also been compared to Artemis (Roman: Diana) due to shared associations with fertility, water, and nature, however this is not documented in Greek sources. Anuket could be prayed to for a good flooding of the Nile, fertility, abundance, prosperity, protection of travellers and fishermen, safe travel on the Nile, or protection from the dangers of the river.

---

[48] "Anoukis" , Encyclopædia Britannica, vol. II (9th ed.), New York: Charles Scribner's Sons, 1878, p. 90

Apis: The Sacred Bull of Memphis

Left: Four variations of 'Apis' in hieroglyphs

Apis is a sacred bull originally worshipped in Memphis (his primary cult centre), Saqqara, and Alexandria. He is referred to as 'Herald of Ptah', 'Messenger of Ptah', 'Living Soul of Ptah' ('*Ba-en-Ptah*'), and 'The Great God' ('*Neter Aa*').

Apis manifests divine power on earth, symbolises death and rebirth, and acts as an oracle or divine intermediary, his movements are interpreted as prophecies, his breath is believed to cure disease, and his presence blesses those around him with strength.

Apis does appear in religious texts and ritual traditions. Details of the mummification ritual of the sacred bull are written within the Apis Papyrus[49] [50]. Sometimes the body of the bull is mummified and fixed in a standing position on a foundation made of wooden planks.

Apis is the son of the goddess Hathor and assigned a significant role in her worship, being sacrificed and reborn. He is depicted as a black and white bull with a sun disk above his head, a symbol shared with his mother Hathor. Later Apis also serves as an intermediary between humans and other powerful deities such as Ptah[51], Osiris, and Atum.

The Early Dynastic Period: The origins of Apis worship begin in Memphis[52]. Early pharaohs associate themselves with Apis as a symbol of divine strength and earthly authority.

The Old Kingdom: Apis becomes firmly associated with the god Ptah, the creator god of Memphis. Apis is seen as Ptah's living manifestation, an embodiment of the deity on earth. Each Apis bull is chosen based on specific markings, housed in Memphis, and treated with great honour during its life. A special window is created in the temple through which he can be viewed, and on certain holidays, he is led through the streets of the city, decorated with jewellery and flowers. It is believed that the cow who gives birth to

---

[49] Vos R.L. (1993). The Apis Embalming Ritual - P. Vindob. 3873. Peeters publishers 1992. ISBN 978-90-6831-438-0. Archived from the original on 2015-07-02. Retrieved 2015-07-02.
[50] Christina Riggs (5 June 2014). Unwrapping Ancient Egypt: The Shroud, the Secret and the Sacred (p.81). Bloomsbury Publishing 5 Jun 2014, 336 pages. ISBN 978-0857855077. Retrieved 2015-07-02.
[51] Ceram, C. W. (1967). Gods, Graves, and Scholars: The Story of Archaeology. Translated by Garside, E. B.; Wilkins, Sophie (2nd ed.). New York: Alfred A. Knopf. pp. 130–131.
[52] Kahl, Jochem (2007). "Ra is My Lord": Searching for the Rise of the Sun God at the Dawn of Egyptian History. Otto Harrassowitz Verlag. p. 59. ISBN 978-3-447-05540-6.

the selected bull conceives him by a flash of lightning from the heavens, or from moonbeams. She is also treated specially and given a special burial.

Apis, Wikipedia Creative Commons, Public Domain

The First Intermediate Period: Despite political instability, Apis worship continues locally in Memphis, though less sponsored by the state.

The Middle Kingdom: Apis's prominence grows along with Memphis's political recovery. The bull is increasingly linked to Hathor and Osiris, foreshadowing later associations with the afterlife and resurrection.

The New Kingdom: Worship of Apis reaches national significance. Apis becomes closely tied to Osiris, seen as Osiris-Apis after death. Elaborate burial rituals are conducted for deceased Apis bulls, reflecting the belief in the bull's continued divine existence in the afterlife. A burial site is established at the Serapeum of Saqqara, a vast underground necropolis for Apis bulls. From the reign of Ramesses II onwards, bulls are buried in interconnected underground galleries[53] [54].

The Third Intermediate Period: Despite Egypt's political fragmentation, Apis worship remains strong. A priestly class at Memphis maintains the cult of Apis, with continued burials at the Serapeum.

The Late Period: Apis continues to be revered as a divine oracle; people consult the bull for guidance. The popularity of Apis strengthens as national identity solidifies under foreign threat. Apis bulls are embalmed with royal style rituals.

The Ptolemaic Period: The Apis cult is synthesised with Greek religious ideas. Serapis is created, a Graeco-Egyptian deity combining Apis, Osiris, Hades, and Zeus. Serapis becomes the official god of the Ptolemaic dynasty. His cult centre is moved to Alexandria, where it attracts both Egyptian and Greek followers. The Serapeum of Alexandria becomes one of the greatest temples in the Greek world.

The Roman Period: Worship of Apis and Serapis continues under Roman rule. Serapis becomes widely worshipped across the Roman Empire, especially in Greece, Italy, and North Africa. Apis bulls are still honoured in Egypt, and their burials continue at Saqqara into the early Roman period. With the rise of Christianity, pagan cults like that of Serapis and Apis are gradually suppressed. The destruction of the Serapeum at Alexandria in 392 CE marks a symbolic end to the public worship of Serapis and Apis.

In the same way that Apis is seen as Ptah's living manifestation, the Greco-Roman god Zeus (Jupiter) also appears in bull form in some myths. Apis could be prayed to for fertile livestock, agricultural abundance, strength and vitality, protection of Memphis and Egypt, blessings of kinship and stability, and divine favour in the afterlife.

---

[53] Griffith, Francis Llewellyn (1911). "Apis". In Chisholm, Hugh (ed.). Encyclopædia Britannica. Vol. 2 (11th ed.). Cambridge University Press. p. 168.
[54] "Serapeum of Saqqara- Madain Project (en)". madainproject.com. Retrieved 2022-11-22.

Aten: The Sun Disk

Left: Aten' in hieroglyphs

Aten is a god of the sun disk, representing the visible disk of the sun in the sky, and the life-giving energy of the sun. The word Aten appears in the Old Kingdom as a noun meaning 'disk', referring to anything flat and circular; the sun was referred to as the 'disk of the day' where the sun god Ra was thought to reside[55]. In this sense, the 'silver Aten' was sometimes used to refer to the moon[56]. It has also been suggested that a more correct translation of Aten would be 'orb' or 'sphere' rather than disk[57]. In earlier religious texts before the reign of Akhenaten, Aten is referred to as 'the Aten of Ra' ('the disk of Ra'). He is depicted as a sun disk with sun rays ending in hands, often shown reaching out to bless the pharaoh and his family. Aten is briefly elevated to the status of sole deity and worshipped at the temporary capital city Akhetaten (modern day Amarna) during what is known as the Amarna Period (c1353 to c1336 BCE). This period is also called the Amarna Episode, the Amarna Revolution, and the Amarna Heresy.

The Pre-Dynastic and Early Dynastic Periods: Sun worship exists in a general form, but Aten is not yet personified or central. Solar deities such as Ra begin to emerge, and solar symbolism becomes more prominent in royal iconography.

From The Old Kingdom to the Second Intermediate Period: Aten appears as a minor aspect of the sun god, often depicted simply as the solar disk. He remains a minor sun deity. Worship of the sun focuses mainly on Ra and other established deities. Worship of Aten is primarily through royal inscriptions acknowledging the sun's life-giving power.

The New Kingdom: Aten gains prominence under Amenhotep III, Akhenaten's father. Amenhotep III refers to Aten as "the Dazzling Sun Disk" and builds a sun temple to Aten in Karnak (Thebes). However, this is still within a polytheistic framework, Aten is one of many gods. Around year 4 of his reign, Amenhotep IV changes his name to Akhenaten ('Effective for the Aten') and begins promoting Aten as the supreme, sole god. Akhenaten launches a dramatic religious revolution. He suppresses worship of traditional gods, especially Amun, closes temples, seizes priestly wealth, and erases images of other deities. He builds a new capital city, Akhetaten (modern day Amarna), dedicated to Aten. He composes the 'Great Hymn to the Aten', emphasising Aten as the creator of life, universal god, and source of light and order. Aten is portrayed as a universal, invisible, abstract deity, with no anthropomorphic form. Only Akhenaten and his family are shown directly interacting with Aten, acting

---

[55] Redford, Donald B. (1984). Akhenaten, the heretic king. Princeton: Princeton University Press. pp. 170–172. ISBN 0-691-03567-9. OCLC 10099207

[56] Fleming, Fergus; Lothian, Alan (2003). The way to eternity: Egyptian myth. Duncan Baird Publishers. p. 52. ISBN 0-7607-3930-7. OCLC 52728250

[57] Khamneipur, Abolghassem (2015). Zarathustra: myth, message, history (1st ed.). Victoria, BC, Canada: Friesen Press. p. 81. ISBN 978-1-4602-6881-0. OCLC 945369209

as intermediaries between god and people. Aten is symbolised as a sun disk with days ending in hands, sometimes holding ankhs (symbols of life). After Akhenaten's death, short-lived successors continue Aten worship in a weakened form. Smenkhkare or the female pharaoh Neferneferuaten (possibly Nefertiti) rule briefly. Signs emerge of a partial religious rollback, but Atenism remains dominant. Tutankhaten ('living image of Aten') changes his name to Tutankhamun ('living image of Amun'), signalling a return go Amun worship. He restores the old gods and reopens their temples. The capital is moved back to Thebes. Aten temples are abandoned, and the Aten cult is officially dismantled. Horemheb, a general who becomes a pharaoh, leads a total purge of Atenism. Akhenaten is declared a heretic. His monuments are dismantled, names and images erased or defaced. The Amarna period is officially suppressed in Egyptian history. Aten is reduced to a minor solar symbol again. The name and figure of Akhenaten are omitted from pharaoh lists and historical records. Egypt reverts to traditional polytheism, centred again around Amun-Ra, Osiris, Isis, and others. Worship of Aten, also known as 'Atenism', is one of the earliest known experiments in monotheism, the idea that there is only one true god, or henotheism, the worship of one god without denying the existence of other gods.

From The Third Intermediate to the Ptolemaic Period: Aten worship declines sharply after Akhenaten's death, and he remembered mostly in historical texts. Temples are abandoned, and traditional polytheistic practices resume. Greek rulers and priests focus on syncretic deities like Serapis and Hellenised forms of Egyptian gods. Aten becomes a historical curiosity rather than a living cult, and receives little or no active worship.

The Roman Period: Aten remains an obscure figure. Egyptian religion survives in rural areas, but Aten is not central. Roman administration prioritises Isis, Serapis, and other cults.

The Byzantine Period: Aten worship ceases completely. Christianity spreads throughout Egypt, ending the practice of ancient Egyptian religion, including all solar cults associated with Aten.

Aten, Wikipedia Creative Commons, Public Domain

Aten is perhaps less of a deity and more of an abstract divine principle, so comparisons with Greek and Roman gods are more conceptual. There is of course Helios / Sol, the personification of the sun, the sun's daily journey across the sky, and also power and authority. Apollo, a god of sun, light, healing, and life-giving energy is later syncretised with Helios / Sol. Aten could be prayed to for life and vitality, agricultural abundance, health and protection, blessings from the pharaoh, spiritual enlightenment, and cosmic harmony.

Atum: The Primordial Creator

Left: 'Atum' in hieroglyphs

Atum is a god of creation, the setting sun, completion, eternity, kingship, the primeval mound, the universe, and order. His name is thought to be derived from the ancient Egyptian verb '*tm*' which means 'to complete' or 'to finish', and so he is interpreted as being 'the complete one', and 'the finisher of the world', which he returns to watery chaos at the end of the creative cycle. As creator he gives everyone their soul from his vital force, essence, or '*ka*'[58]. Atum creates himself from the chaotic primordial waters of Nu as one of the first gods to exist. He brings order from chaos by emerging on the Benben Stone[59]. According to the Temple Texts from Heliopolis, and the Pyramid Texts, Atum creates the first gods: Shu (air), and Tefnut (moisture). Shu and Tefnet then give rise to Geb (Earth) and Nut (Sky), whose children become the rest of the Ennead: Osiris, Isis, Set, and Nephthys.

He represents the sun in its evening form, travelling into the underworld at night. He is often merged with Ra as Ra-Atum, symbolising the sun's full cycle, from creation (morning) to death (evening). As a god of completion, Atum embodies the end of things, just as he begins them. He is linked to royal authority, and the pharaohs are considered to be the earthly embodiment of Atum in their divine role. By creating the world and the gods, Atum upholds *ma'at*. His continued existence ensures the world does not fall back into chaos (Nu). He is depicted as a man wearing the Pschent (the double crown of Upper and Lower Egypt). This shows Atum's connection to kingship, and his role as the father of the gods. He is often depicted with red or dark skin, linking him to the setting sun (Ra-Atum) and creation from clay or matter. In some creation myths, Atum is shown or described as a snake, representing his role as a primordial being who will return to his serpent form at the end of time when the world dissolves back into chaos (Nu)[60]. He carries the was-sceptre (a symbol of power) and an Ankh (a symbol of life), emphasising his divine authority and life-giving powers. When he is fused with the sun god Ra to become Atum-Ra, he appears with a sun disk above his head, especially in solar temples or texts.

Atum was worshipped at Heliopolis, his primary and most important centre, the spiritual heart of the Ennead[61]. He was also worshipped to a lesser extent at Memphis, his secondary centre of worship, which although primarily focused on the god Ptah, acknowledges Atum as part of their creation theology. At Thebes, Atum is honoured in texts and rituals, especially when merged with Ra as Ra-Atum, although Amun-Ra is mostly dominant there. At Abydos and Saqqara Atum is mentioned in funerary texts as the god who welcomes the deceased pharaohs into the afterlife.

---

[58] Wilkinson, Richard H. (2003). The Complete Gods and Goddesses of Ancient Egypt. Thames and Hudson. ISBN 0-500-05120-8.
[59] The British Museum. "Picture List" (PDF). Archived (PDF) from the original on 2013-09-22. Retrieved 2012-04-04.
[60] Wilkinson, Richard H. (2003).
[61] Wilkinson, Richard H. (2003).

Atum, Wikipedia Creative Commons, Public Domain

The Early Dynastic Period: Atum appears as one of the earliest creator gods in Egyptian cosmology. In Heliopolis, he is revered as the self-created deity who brings forth the first gods. Atum is closely associated with the Benben Stone and the solar cult of Heliopolis.

The Old Kingdom: Atum is fully integrated into royal ideology and theology. The Pyramid Texts describe Atum as the creator god who gives birth to Shu and Tefnut by spitting. Atum is often identified with the setting sun, completing the solar triad with Khepri (rising sun) and Ra (midday sun). Atum becomes associated with the pharaoh, helping them ascend into the heavens.

The Middle Kingdom: The worship of Atum continues, now more often merged with Ra, forming the composite deity Ra-Atum or Atum-Ra. The Ennead is fully developed with Atum at the top as the first god in the creation myth, followed by Shu, Tefnut, Geb, Nut, Osiris, Isis, Set, and Nephthys[62].

The New Kingdom: Atum's role as creator and solar deity is preserved in religious texts like the Book of the Dead and the Coffin Texts. Atum is invoked in royal tombs and funerary texts, reaffirming his role in rebirth and the afterlife. He becomes more symbolic of the setting sun and completion, as Ra (in his Atum aspect) travels into the underworld.

The Third Intermediate Period: Reverence of Atum continues, often in the context of solar religion, and the syncretisation of solar gods and creator gods. His role becomes more theological and philosophical, symbolising the end of the day, old age, and the return to the primordial chaos before rebirth.

The Late Period: Atum retains significance but is often overshadowed by other deities like Amun and Osiris. Heliopolis remains a centre of theological learning, preserving Atum's role in the creation myth.

The Ptolemaic and Roman Periods: Atum continues to be venerated in a more abstract, theological form. Temples and priesthoods still acknowledge him as a primeval creator. The Greeks equate him with the universal principles or the Greek god of the sun Helios (Roman: Sol).

The Byzantine Period: Atum's active worship has largely ceased. Christianity dominates Egypt, and ancient temples close. However, Atum's image endures in philosophical writings and in the cultural memory of Egypt as a self-created god who embodies the origins of all existence.

Greek and Roman gods have some similarities with Atum. Helios / Sol represents aspects of the setting sun and solar symbolism. Chaos / Phanes (from the Orphic tradition) is similar to Atum as a self-created being emerging from primordial chaos. Cronus / Saturn is a primordial father figure who like Atum exists before other gods. Zeus / Jupiter in his creative aspect, like Atum, is a supreme being, father of gods and men. People could pray to Atum for creation and renewal, light and life, order and stability, protection in death and the afterlife, and completion and fulfilment.

---

[62] Dunand, Françoise; Zivie-Coche, Christiane (2004). Gods and men in Egypt : 3000 BCE to 395 CE. Ithaca, NY: Cornell University Press. ISBN 0801488532. OCLC 937102309

Bastet: Leonine Warrior and Feline Protector

Left: 'Bastet' in hieroglyphs

Bastet is a goddess whose role evolves over time. She is initially a warrior goddess of war and battle, a fierce defender of the pharaoh and the sun god Ra, a guardian of the home, and a protector against disease and evil spirits[63]. As her warrior aspect softens, she also becomes a goddess of cats, childbirth, dance, domesticity[64], fertility, grace, healing, joy, motherhood, music, perfume, the moon, the sun, and women's secrets. The domesticated cat becomes sacred to Bastet and cats are mummified and buried in her honour. The name Bastet is translated as 'She of the ointment jar'[65] or 'She of the perfume jar', the hieroglyph for an ointment jar '*bas*' being part of her name. She is the daughter of Ra and Isis, and the sister or twin aspect of Sekhmet. Her consort is Ptah, and their sons are Nefertem and Maahes[66]. Bastet is also related to Wadjet, one of the oldest Egyptian goddesses from the Southern Delta, who was known as the 'Eye of the Moon'[67].

Bastet is sometimes referred to as the 'Eye of Ra'[68] when the sun god Ra sends out his daughter to punish humanity for their rebellion. The Eye of Ra is also sometimes personified as Sekhmet, but in other versions, Bastet takes on this role. Once pacified, Bastet becomes a protector and a nurturer, but retains the power to destroy when provoked. Bastet is first depicted as a lioness or a woman with a lioness head, carrying or wearing a sistrum, with a solar disk encircled by a uraeus (cobra) on her head, linking her to Ra. She is sometimes shown with a protective knife, especially when slaying the serpent Apep[69]. She is later depicted as a cat or a woman with a cat's head, often elegant and serene. Sometimes she is depicted holding kittens, representing fertility and motherhood. She wears a red or white dress and a menat necklace, a symbol of femininity and celebration.

Bastet was mainly worshipped at Bubastis (*Per-Bastet*, 'House of Bastet') in the eastern Nile Delta (modern day Tell-Basta, near Zagazig) with large temples dedicated to her, and numerous cat cemeteries indicating the sacred role of cats in her cult. She was also worshipped in Memphis alongside her consort Ptah, and thereby linked to the Memphite Triad (Ptah, Sekhmet, and Nefertem). Her connection to Sekhmet is especially important here, with the two seen as dual aspects of the

---

[63] Mark, Joshua J. (July 24, 2016). "Bastet". World History Encyclopedia. Archived from the original on April 17, 2021. Retrieved December 5, 2018.
[64] Pinch, Geraldine (2002). Egyptian Mythology: A Guide to the Gods, Goddesses, and Traditions of Ancient Egypt. New York, New York: Oxford University Press. p. 115.
[65] Quirke, Stephen (1992-08-01). Ancient Egyptian Religion. London: British Museum Press. ASIN B01K2D7BYM.
[66] Pinch, Geraldine (2002). Egyptian Mythology: A Guide to the Gods, Goddesses, and Traditions of Ancient Egypt. New York, New York: Oxford University Press. p. 115.
[67] Wilkinson, Richard H. (2003). The Complete Gods and Goddesses of Ancient Egypt. Thames & Hudson. p. 176
[68] Darnell, John Coleman (1997). "The Apotropaic Goddess in the Eye". Studien zur Altägyptischen Kultur. 24: 35–48. JSTOR 25152728.
[69] Pinch, Geraldine (2002). Egyptian Mythology: A Guide to the Gods, Goddesses, and Traditions of Ancient Egypt. New York: Oxford University Press. p. 130.

same divine force. Leontopolis ('City of Lions', modern day Tell el-Muqdam) is known for its lion and lioness cults. It is possible that in her earlier lioness form, Bastet was worshipped here alongside or in place of Sekhmet or other lioness deities.

Bastet in her later feline form, Wikipedia Creative Commons, Public Domain

The Pre-Dynastic and Early Dynastic Periods: Bastet begins as a local lioness or cat deity in the Nile Delta, particularly associated with the region that later becomes Bubastis (Per-Bastet). Bastet first appears as a lioness-headed goddess in early religious texts and imagery. She is originally a fierce warrior and solar deity associated with protection, much like the lioness goddess Sekhmet.

The Old Kingdom and First Intermediate Periods: Bastet is mentioned in the Pyramid Texts, one of the oldest religious texts in the world. Her role is protective, especially of the pharaoh and the sun god Ra. As central authority weakens, local cults flourish, and Bastet's worship strengthens in her home city, Bubastis. She becomes increasingly seen as a guardian of households and fertility to ordinary Egyptians as well as kings.

The Middle Kingdom and Second Intermediate Periods: Bastet begins to be depicted with both lioness and domestic cat features. The cult centre in Bubastis (Tell Basta) begins to grow. Despite political disruption, Bastet remains beloved among the populace. Her role as a nurturing yet vigilant goddess of the home resonates strongly. She often appears as a woman with a cat's head or as a seated cat, symbolising grace, fertility, and divine protection.

The New Kingdom and Third Intermediate Periods: Bastet's dual nature is emphasised, fierce protector and nurturing mother. She becomes associated with fertility, childbirth, and music. She is often depicted holding a sistrum and sometimes with kittens. She is linked more closely to domestic cats, which were revered in Egyptian homes. Worship of Bastet spreads throughout Egypt. Cat burials and Bastet figurines increase as people seek her protection and blessings.

The Late Period: Her cult centre at Bubastis becomes one of the most significant pilgrimage sites. Large festivals (like the famous Feast of Bastet) draw tens of thousands. Thousands of cat mummies are buried as offerings. Her role as a household protector and guardian of women is emphasised.

The Ptolemaic Period: Bastet is syncretised with the Greek goddess Artemis (Roman: Diana), goddess of the hunt and protector of women. Worship continues under Greek rule with adjustments to fit Hellenistic sensibilities. The Greeks call her Ailuros (Koine Greek: αἴλουρος, 'cat').

The Roman and Byzantine Periods: Bastet worship fades with the spread of Christianity and the decline of traditional Egyptian religion. Bubastis and other temples are eventually abandoned or destroyed. Yet her image lives on in Egyptian art and legend, and the reverence for cats in Egyptian culture persists, echoing her ancient role as the gentle, watchful guardian of home and life.

In Bastet's later gentler form, she resembles Artemis (Diana), a goddess of the hunt, protector of women and children, and guardian of animals. Both also have connections to the moon in later traditions. In her domestic and household-protective aspects, Bastet also shares traits with Hestia / Vesta, a goddess of the hearth and home. People could pray to Baste for protection of the home and family, fertility and childbirth, health and healing, joy, music, and protection from evil spirits and snakes.

Bat: Goddess of the Cosmos and Fertility

Left: 'Bat' in hieroglyphs

Bat is a goddess of cattle, fertility, music, dance, joy, celebration, protection, the cosmos, the sky, and femininity. She is one of the oldest goddesses dating back to the Pre-Dynastic Period and late Palaeolithic cattle herding cultures. Her name is believed to be linked to the ancient Egyptian word '*ba*' with the feminine '*-t*' ending[70]. In ancient Egyptian religion, a person's '*ba*' roughly equates to one's personality or emanation, which is often translated as 'soul'. Bat is believed to protect individuals and offer spiritual safety and divine favour.

She is associated with the cosmos and the celestial sphere, particularly through her connection with the sistrum[71], one of the most frequently used sacred instruments in ancient Egyptian temples. She is believed to help maintain harmony in the universe. As an early goddess of music and dance, Bat is invoked during celebrations and festivals, bringing joy, ecstasy, and emotional uplift. She has a nurturing aspect, connected with cattle and fertility, representing plenty, nourishment, and maternal care, especially in farming and pastoral contexts. In later periods she becomes merged with the goddess Hathor[72].

Bat is depicted with a human face, but with cow ears, and long inward-curving horns (sometimes described as lyre-shaped or resembling a sistrum frame). In some rare cases, she has been depicted in full cow form, like Hathor. One difference between Bat and Hathor is that Hathor's cow horns curve outward, whereas Bat's horns curve inward, sometimes described as lyre-shaped. The differences in these horns may have some visual meaning, or it might just be because of different breeds of cattle herded in different territories. When depicted on the head or handle of the sistrum, Bat is depicted with her face in mirror symmetry (two faces back to back), symbolising her omnipresence and cosmic balance, as mentioned in the Pyramid Texts:

> "*I am Praise; I am Majesty; I am Bat with Her Two Faces; I am the One Who Is Saved, and I have saved myself from all things evil*"[73].

Bat was mainly worshipped in Sheshesh (also known as Hu or Diospolis Parva) in Upper Egypt, in modern day Hu near Abydos. The centre of her cult was known as the 'Mansion of the Sistrum'[74]. She was venerated as a local deity long before Egypt was unified. She was sometimes referred to as 'The Lady of Sheshesh'.

---

[70] Barbara Lesko Great Goddesses, 100, p. 81
[71] Wilkinson, Richard. H. Reading Egyptian Artp. 213 Thames and Hudson 1992. ISBN 0-500-27751-6
[72] Wilkinson, Richard H. The Complete Gods and Goddesses of Ancient Egypt, p.172 Thames & Hudson. 2003. ISBN 0-500-05120-8
[73] R. O. Faulkner, The Ancient Egyptian Pyramid Texts, Oxford 1969, p. 181, Utterance 506
[74] Hart, George. The Routledge Dictionary of Egyptian Gods and Goddesses, p. 47 2nd Edition Routledge. 2005. ISBN 0-415-34495-6

The Pre-Dynastic Period: Bat originates as a local cow goddess, associated with fertility, the cosmos, and the pharaoh's power. Her imagery often includes cow horns and a human face.

Bat, Wikipedia Creative Commons, Public Domain

The Early Dynastic Period: Bat's worship is well established by the time of Narmer (possibly the first unifying pharaoh of Egypt). She is depicted on ceremonial artefacts like the Narmer Palette[75], where a bovine face with curved horns appears on both sides of the top.

The Old Kingdom: Bat is considered a protective deity of the pharaoh, invoked during ceremonies involving the pharaoh's divine authority. Her imagery appears on sistra, especially the arch-shaped sistrum that becomes associated with her, and the goddess Hathor.

The First Intermediate Period: As central authority weakens, local deities regain importance, and Bat's cult continues regionally in Hu. However, Hathor's worship spreads more widely, and her attributes increasingly overlap with Bat's. Even so, Bat retains her identity as a symbol of unity, bridging human and divine realms through her association with music and the afterlife.

The Middle Kingdom: Worship of Bat begins to decline in favour of the increasingly popular Hathor, who shares many of Bat's characteristics. Hathor absorbs much of Bat's iconography, especially the cow horns and sistrum.

The Second Intermediate Period: Bat's independent cult diminishes significantly, though her imagery continues in religious iconography.

The New Kingdom and Third Intermediate Periods: Bat is no longer actively worshipped as a separate deity; her attributes are fully assimilated into Hathor's cult. Her imagery continues as a symbolic motif in temple art and ritual objects.

The Late Period: A revival of archaic deities includes Bat. Theological texts and temple reliefs celebrate Egypt's ancient heritage. Her name occasionally appears alongside Hathor's.

The Ptolemaic Period: Under Greek rule, Bat's identity remains merged within Hathor's cult. However, her name continues to appear in inscriptions at Dendera, where Hathor's temple preserves imagery derived from Bat's iconography.

The Roman Period: Bat is no longer an object of independent worship, but her symbolic features remain in use.

The Byzantine Period: By this period, Bat's worship has long ceased. However, her iconography and theological role live on in the Egyptian imagination, transmitted through Hathor's legacy and preserved in the religious art of the late temples.

Hathor, who absorbs Bat, becomes associated with love, beauty, music, and joy. These traits link her (and by extension Bat) to Aphrodite / Venus. People could pray to Bat for fertility and motherhood, protection and harmony, divine favour and joy, and spiritual or cosmic balance.

---

[75] Wilkinson, Richard H. (2003). The Complete Gods and Goddesses of Ancient Egypt. New York: Thames & Hudson. ISBN 978-0-500-05120-7. OCLC 1085905646.

Bennu: God of Creation and Resurrection

Bennu is a god of creation, cyclical rebirth, renewal, the sun and sunrise, and by extension life, resurrection, and eternity. His name means 'to rise' or 'to shine', derived from the verb '*weben*' / '*wbn*' which means 'to rise in brilliance'[76] or 'to rise radiantly', often used to describe the rising of the sun.

In the Heliopolitan tradition, Bennu emerges from the primordial waters of Nu and lands on the Benben Stone. He then cries out, the sound of which initiates and determines the nature of creation itself, including the first sunrise, with which he is associated. He is sometimes referred to as 'He who came into being by himself'[77]. Bennu can even be seen as an aspect or manifestation of Atum at the moment of creation. Different texts suggest that Bennu either emerges with Atum or symbolises the moment of creation alongside him[78]. In this sense he is regarded as the creator's spark. When Atum becomes merged with the sun god Ra as Atum-Ra or Ra-Atum, Bennu then also becomes associated with Ra as well. He is then also regarded as the '*ba*' ('soul') of Ra, or the living symbol of the sun's daily rebirth, and the ever renewing solar soul.

Left: Two versions of 'Bennu' in hieroglyphs

As a symbol of rebirth and renewed life after death, he is also associated with Osiris[79], the god who dies, is resurrected, and becomes ruler of the afterlife, guaranteeing renewal for all beings. Because of this overlapping function, Bennu comes to be regarded as the 'ba' ('soul') of Osiris in some traditions. In the Book of the Dead, spell 83 describes the deceased transforming into a Bennu bird: "I am the Bennu, the soul of Ra, the guide of the gods to the Underworld". In the Papyrus of Ani, Bennu is linked to Ra (solar rebirth) and Osiris (resurrection in the Duat). In Coffin Texts and later temple hymns, Osiris's resurrection is paralleled to the daily rebirth of the sun, and Bennu embodies the same cyclical rebirth.

These different ideas and beliefs are fused together so that Ra is reborn each morning, Osiris is renewed through Ra's life force and reborn each year (and eternally in the afterlife), and Bennu symbolises the mechanism of renewal itself, the living spark that ensures the eternal cycle continues. Bennu also serves as a spiritual manifestation or divine messenger, and he appears on funerary scarab amulets as a symbol of rebirth[80]. He is commonly depicted as a mythical heron-like bird, grey

---

[76] Hart, George (2005). The Routledge Dictionary of Egyptian Gods and Goddesses (Second ed.). New York: Routledge. pp. 48–49. ISBN 0-415-34495-6.
[77] Hart, George (2005)
[78] Hart, George (2005).
[79] Wilkinson, Richard H. (2003). The Complete Gods and Goddesses of Ancient Egypt. London: Thames & Hudson. p. 212. ISBN 0-500-05120-8.
[80] Hart, George (2005).

or purple, with a long beak, streamlined body, and two long crest feathers on its head, modelled on the yellow-billed or grey heron, a bird native to the Nile and seen as sacred. The heron's behaviour, living alone, nesting in high places, may have contributed to its symbolic link with divinity, uniqueness, and elevation.

Bennu did not have widespread independent cult or large temples dedicated to him, but he was venerated within the religious centres of other major deities with whom he was closely associated, especially Ra, Atum, and Osiris. He was worshipped at Heliopolis[81], the primary centre of the sun god Ra, and the focus of the Heliopolitan creation myth, along with the Benben Stone.

Bennu, Wikipedia Creative Commons, Public Domain

The Pre-Dynastic Period: There is no direct evidence of Bennu worship during this time, but solar bird imagery and ideas relating to the sun rising from the primeval waters may be precursors to the later Bennu myths.

The Old Kingdom: The earliest textual references to Bennu appear in the Pyramid Texts in the context of the afterlife and solar rebirth. Bennu is associated with the sun god Ra and Atum, as a divine being that emerges from the Benben Stone. Bennu symbolises self-creation and cyclic renewal.

The Middle Kingdom: Theological ideas about creation become more structured, and Bennu appears more frequently in cosmological texts. He is seen as an aspect of Atum-Ra, acting as the '*ba*' ('soul') of the sun god.

The New Kingdom: Bennu's identity is well developed and integrated into Heliopolitan theology. He is also described as the lord of jubilees[82], and the herald of the gods. Artistic depictions show Bennu as a heron-like bird (possibly a grey heron or sacred bird), often wearing a crown (Atef[83] or solar disk). He is mentioned in the Book of the Dead and other funerary texts as a symbol of resurrection and eternal life.

The Third Intermediate and Late Periods: Bennu continues to appear in religious texts and temple iconography, especially in association with Ra, Osiris, and the sun's rebirth. Worship is limited to priestly and theological circles, rather than mass public worship. Bennu is particularly associated with Heliopolis, the city of the sun god.

The Greco-Roman Period: Bennu becomes increasingly associated with the Greek phoenix. The idea of a self-reborn bird that rises from ashes may stem from earlier Egyptian Bennu traditions. Writers like Herodotus[84] and Pliny the Elder mention an Egyptian bird resembling the phoenix, likely inspired by Bennu. Bennu's symbolism lives on in Roman and Hellenistic art and thought, though often in syncretised form.

Bennu's self-renewing nature, emerging from flames or from itself is thought to be the original inspiration for the phoenix legends that developed in Greek mythology. Bennu could be prayed to for rebirth and resurrection, new beginnings and creation, and longevity and continuity.

---

[81] Wilkinson, Richard H. (2003). The Complete Gods and Goddesses of Ancient Egypt. London: Thames & Hudson. p. 212. ISBN 0-500-05120-8.
[82] Wilkinson, Richard H. (2003)
[83] Wilkinson, Richard H. (2003)
[84] Lecocq, Françoise (2009). "L'œuf du phénix. Myrrhe, encens et cannelle dans le mythe du phénix" (PDF). Schedae. 6 (1: L'animal et le savoir, de l'Antiquité à la Renaissance): 73–106. Archived from the original (PDF) on 2016-03-03. Retrieved 2016-09-13.

Bes: The Household Protector

Left: 'Bes' in hieroglyphs

Bes is a god and protector of households, mothers, children, and childbirth. He later comes to be regarded as the defender of everything good and the enemy of all that is bad[85]. His female counterpart is the goddess Beset[86]. He is not typically worshipped in temples but is venerated in homes, especially through wall paintings, amulets, furniture carvings, and cosmetic jars and mirrors (he is also a protector of personal beauty and health). The word '*bes*' means 'cat' in Nubian, which suggests a possible Nubian or southern origin of Bes[87]. It is also possible that the name Bes originates from either '*bs*' meaning 'flame', or '*bz*' meaning 'to be initiated' or 'to introduce'[88].

Bes protects mothers and children and guards women during childbirth. He also protects newborns and infants from evil spirits, illness, and misfortune. Amulets and household objects with Bes's image are common in homes. He specialises in driving away demons, bad dreams, and evil influences. He is invoked for protection during sleep, especially for children. Images of Bes are carved on beds and headrests to guard against nightmares. People believe that he watches over them during sleep and prevents nocturnal attacks from spirits. His fierce appearance (lion-like features, tongue out, with weapons raised) is meant to scare off harmful forces. He is associated with celebration, music, and dance, often shown playing a tambourine or harp, or dancing. He appears in festivals and joyful occasions, especially those related to fertility, love, or home life. He has no major myths, but he appears across all periods of Egyptian history as a beloved and personal protector.

He is associated with Taweret[89], a goddess of childbirth and fertility[90]. Bes and Taweret are often depicted together on household items, amulets, and furniture[91]. They are invoked together during pregnancy and childbirth. Bes also shares some aspects of music and joy with the goddess Hathor. Both are connected to festivals, dancing, and beauty. In some celebrations, images of Bes appear alongside Hathor's cult objects. The goddess Bastet is also a protector of households and women, like Bes. Both deities can have ferocious and joyful aspects, defending against evil while also bringing

---

[85] El-Kilany, Engy (2017). "The Protective Role of Bes- image for Women and Children in Ancient Egypt" (PDF). Journal of Association of Arab Universities for Tourism and Hospitality. 14 (2): 19–28. doi:10.21608/jaauth.2017.48140 – via Google Scholar.
[86] Weingarten, Judith (2015). "The Arrival of Bes[et] on Middle-Minoan Crete". In Jana Mynárová; Pavel Onderka; and Peter Pavúk (eds.). There and Back Again – the Crossroads II. Proceedings of an International Conference Held in Prague, September 15-18, 2014. Prague: Czech Institute of Egyptology, Faculty of Arts of the Charles University. pp. 181–196. ISBN 978-80-7308-575-9.
[87] Mackenzie, Donald A. (1907). Egyptian myth and legend. With historical narrative, notes on race problems, comparative, etc. London: The Gresham Publishing. p. 312
[88] El-Kilany, Engy (2017).
[89] "Statue of the Goddess Taweret". The Fitzwilliam Museum. Retrieved 2024-03-02.
[90] Kelley, Erika (2022). "Coping with Trauma: Evidence that Suggests the Ancient Egyptians used Transpersonal Psychology to Cope with Birth-Related Trauma". History in the Making. 15 – via Google Scholar.
[91] van Oppen de Ruiter, Branko (17 April 2020). "Lovely Ugly Bes! Animalistic Aspects in Ancient Egyptian Popular Religion". Arts. 9 (2): 51. doi:10.3390/arts9020051. ISSN 2076-0752.

peace and happiness to the home. Bes is sometimes linked to Ra or Horus in magical texts where he serves as a guardian against enemies of these solar gods. In these roles, Bes takes on a warrior-like aspect, standing against chaos or demonic threats (like the serpent Apep). Unlike most Egyptian gods who are shown in profile, Bes is shown full face, confronting danger head on. He is often depicted as a dwarf[92] with leonine features, symbolising strength and ferocity despite his small size.

Bes, Wikipedia Creative Commons, Public Domain

The Pre-Dynastic Period: There is no direct evidence of Bes worship yet. Some scholars suggest that figures with protective or grotesque features in early art may hint at proto-Bes deities or apotropaic (evil-warding) spirits.

The Old Kingdom: Bes does not appear yet as a fully formed deity in this period. Protective household spirits, especially those guarding women and children, may be precursors to Bes. Some dwarfish servants and entertainers are depicted in tomb art, possibly forming the mythological base for Bes.

The Middle Kingdom: The first clear appearances of Bes-like figures begin to emerge, possibly as part of apotropaic magic (e.g. magical knives, protective amulets, etc.). These early representations are not yet standardised, and Bes may be a class of sprits (like 'Bes-entities') rather than a singular god.

The New Kingdom: Bes becomes a popular and fully recognised deity in Egyptian religion. He appears widely in domestic art and household objects, cosmetics containers, headrests, mirrors, childbirth scenes (alongside the goddess Taweret). Bes is invoked in magical spells, charms, and rituals for protection, fertility, and joyful celebrations. He is frequently portrayed with lion-like features, a protruding tongue, a feathered headdress, and musical instruments (like tambourines and harps, etc.).

The Third Intermediate and Late Periods: Worship of Bes continues to flourish across all levels of society. Bes becomes syncretised with foreign protective spirits, reflecting increasing cultural exchange (e.g. Nubian or Levantine deities). Worship of Bes spreads as far north as the area of Syria, as far west as the Balearic Islands of Spain, and later into the Roman and Achaemenid Empires[93]. Bes is especially popular among commoners, and his worship spreads beyond temples into everyday life. Some temples and chapels dedicated to Bes appear, though he is still primarily a household deity.

The Ptolemaic and Roman Periods: Bes remains immensely popular during the Greco-Roman era. His imagery spreads to Mediterranean and Near Eastern culture, where he is adopted or blended with local protective spirits and deities. In Roman Egypt, Bes often appears on coins, amulets, mosaics, and even military standards. His cult reaches beyond Egypt into parts of the Levant, Cyprus, and Rome. Sometimes referred to as 'Besas', his iconography becomes increasingly stylised and widespread.

Bes is perhaps similar to the satyrs of Greek mythology, with their jovial, musical, and fertility related aspects, also depicted as bearded with animal features. People could pray to Bes for protection from evil, childbirth and family health, joy, music, celebration, love, and fertility.

---

[92] Carr, Karen (2017-06-18). "Who was the African god Bes?". Quatr.us Study Guides. Retrieved 2023-07-05.
[93] Abdi, Kamyar (2002). "Notes on the Iranianization of Bes in the Achaemenid Empire". Ars Orientalis. 32: 133–162. JSTOR 4629595.

Geb: God of the Earth, and Father of Snakes

Left: 'Geb' in hieroglyphs

Geb is a god of the earth[94] and vegetation, earthquakes, and snakes. His name is believed to derive from a word related to 'earth' or 'earthly realm'. He is the personification of the earth itself; his body is literally the land, mountains, valleys, and soil. He lies beneath the sky goddess Nut, forming the physical foundation of the world. Together with Nut, Geb is the father of Osiris, Isis, Set, and Nephthys.

Geb is a member of the Ennead. The priests of Heliopolis consider Geb to be the father of the sun, believing that he and Nut lay the cosmic egg from which the sun emerges.

As the personification of the earth, Geb allows crops to grow. The earth is also referred to as 'The House of Geb'. It is believed that his laughter creates earthquakes. He is also loosely associated with the god Aker, as both of them represent different aspects of the earth[95], Geb as the living, fertile land, and Aker as the underworld and the boundary between them. Because snakes live in the earth, Geb is also seen as having dominion over them, both dangerous serpents and protective forces.

Geb sometimes intervenes in disputes, like the conflict between Osiris and Set, by assigning rulership or judgement. He is associated with judgement in the afterlife[96], occasionally mentioned in texts like the Pyramid Texts as playing a role in legitimising kingship and justice.

In the beginning, Geb (Earth) and Nut (Sky) are locked in a tight embrace[97]. Their father, Shu (Air), is ordered by Ra (Atum) to separate them, creating the space where the world would exist[98]. Geb becomes the Earth, lying below, while Nut becomes the sky, arching above. This separation allows life to begin on Earth. Geb inherits the throne of the gods from his father Shu and later passes it on to his son Osiris. Geb is considered a divine king, and after ruling, he divides the world among his children. He gives Osiris rule over the living, which leads to the conflict with Set, Osiris's brother. In some versions, Geb acts as judge, choosing Osiris over Set as rightful ruler. When Set kills Osiris, Geb mourns and becomes involved in resolving the dispute between Horus and Set over kingship. In some versions, Geb grants Horus the throne after judgement.

Geb is depicted in various symbolic ways that highlight his connection to the earth, fertility, and kingship. He is often shown with green or black skin, green representing vegetation and the living earth, and black symbolising the fertile soil of the Nile. His attire includes significant royal regalia, such

---

[94] Pinch, Geraldine (2002). Handbook of Egyptian Mythology. Handbooks of World Mythology. ABC-CLIO. p. 135. ISBN 1-57607-763-2.
[95] Dunand, Francoise (2004). Gods and Men in Egypt 3000 BCE to 395 CE. Armand Colin. p. 345. ISBN 9780801488535.
[96] Pinch, Geraldine (2002). Handbook of Egyptian Mythology. Santa Barbara: ABC-CLIO. pp. 76, 77, 78. ISBN 9781576072424.
[97] Meskell, Lynn Archaeologies of social life: age, class et cetera in ancient Egypt Wiley Blackwell (20 Oct 1999) ISBN 978-0-631-21299-7 p.103
[98] Van Dijk, Jacobus (1995). "Myth and Mythmaking in Ancient Egypt" (PDF). Jacobusvandijk. Retrieved 26 May 2017.

as the Atef crown, Hedjet crown of Upper Egypt, and the Deshret crown of Lower Egypt. In some depictions, he is shown lying flat to represent the earth itself, with the sky goddess Nut arched above him, held apart by their father Shu. Geb is sometimes covered in plants and shown touching animals and humans, emphasising his role as the source of all life. A goose, his sacred animal, is often seen on his head or nearby. Additionally, he may hold a crook and flail, traditional emblems of kingship and authority.

Geb, Wikipedia Creative Commons, Public Domain

The Early Dynastic Period: Geb begins to appear in early religious texts and is included in emerging creation myths. His role as the earth god and ancestor of divine rulers is being solidified.

The Old Kingdom: Geb is formally part of the Ennead, one of the most influential divine families. He appears frequently in the Pyramid Texts, where he grants the pharaoh dominion over the Earth and acts as a judge and divine father. The pharaoh is referred to as the 'Heir of Geb'.

The First Intermediate Period: In a time of political instability, worship of Geb continues but is less visible due to general decline in centralised religious activity.

The Middle Kingdom: Geb has a renewed prominence in religious texts and art. He appears in Coffin Texts, taking on more roles in the afterlife and maintaining his status as earth god and creator.

The New Kingdom: There is widespread depiction of Geb in temple walls and tombs, especially in creation myths and cosmology. He appears in the Book of the Dead and in temple complexes like Karnak and Luxor (Thebes). He is often depicted lying beneath the goddess Nut in cosmological scenes. He occasionally appears in judgement scenes reinforcing his association with order and legitimacy.

The Third Intermediate and Late Periods: Worship centres such as Heliopolis, Memphis, and Edfu continue to include Geb in broader religious rituals. Local variants and cults reinterpret Geb's role alongside other chthonic (underworld) deities like Aker.

The Ptolemaic Period: Under Greek rule, Geb is syncretised with Cronus[99], the Greek god later linked to fertility and the harvest (Roman: Saturn). Priests in cities like Tebtunis identify Geb with Soknebtunis-Geb, blending Greek and Egyptian traditions. He is still seen as a cosmic ancestor, but less frequently the focus of direct worship.

The Roman and Byzantine Periods: Geb continues to be venerated in funerary texts and temple inscriptions, but worship becomes increasingly symbolic. Egyptian religion gradually declines as Christianity spreads, and the worship of Geb ends with the suppression of pagan religions in Egypt.

As an embodiment of the earth, the Greek / Roman counterpart to Geb (male) is Gaia / Terra Mater (female). In Egyptian tradition the earth is masculine and the sky is feminine, but in the Greek tradition it is the opposite. People could pray to Geb for fertility and abundance, stability and prosperity, peace and safety, and continuity and inheritance.

---

[99] Rondot, Vincent (2013). Derniers visages des dieux d'Égypte. Iconographies, panthéons et cultes dans le Fayoum hellénisé des IIe–IIIe siècles de notre ère [Last faces of the gods of Egypt. Iconographies, pantheons and cults in the Hellenized Fayoum of the 2nd–3rd centuries AD] (in French). Paris: Presses de l'université Paris-Sorbonne; Éditions du Louvre. pp. 75–80, 122–127, 241–246.

Hapi: The Flooder of the Nile

Left: 'Hapi' in hieroglyphs

Hapi is a god of the annual flooding of the Nile (the 'Arrival of Hapi')[100]. He is referred to as lord of the fish and birds, the marshes, the river bringing vegetation, and 'Lord of Neper' (a god of grain)[101]. He personifies the annual flooding of the Nile, which is critical for agriculture, bringing nutrient rich silt that makes the land fertile for crops[102]. Without Hapi's blessing, people believe they would face famine.

Hapi is a bringer of prosperity, abundance, and nourishment. He is often described as making the land green and fruitful. He is sometimes depicted tying together the lotus (a symbol of Upper Egypt) and the papyrus (a symbol of Lower Egypt), symbolising the unification of Upper and Lower Egypt through the Nile[103].

Hapi doesn't appear in any major mythological narratives or stories like other gods. There are no surviving myths that tell us about Hapi's adventures, conflicts, or origins in a narrative sense. Instead, Hapi functions more like a cosmic force or natural principle than a character in mythological stories. Hapi is closely associated with Khnum, who is believed to control the sources of the Nile, especially at Elephantine Island, where the Nile's floodwaters are thought to originate. While Khnum controls the flow, Hapi personifies the flooding itself and the life-giving water. In some texts, Khnum and Hapi work together to bring the flood. Hapi is also symbolically associated with Osiris in terms of fertility, vegetation, and the cycles of nature, all of which are embodied by the Nile. In some symbolic readings, the annual inundation is like the resurrection of Osiris. In a cosmological context, Hapi is associated with Geb (Earth)[104] and Nut (Sky) as a part of the natural forces sustaining balance. Geb and Nut form the physical universe, and Hapi's flood is what activates the fertility of Geb. Hapi is part of the *ma'at* that these deities help maintain.

Hapi is depicted as a man with large breasts and a round belly, symbolising fertility and abundance, often painted blue or green to represent water and vegetation. He is often depicted carrying offerings, plants, or water jugs. Sometimes he's shown as twin figures representing the Nile's two sources (from Upper and Lower Egypt). He can be considered gender-fluid or gender-ambiguous by modern standards[105]. He is depicted wearing a beard[106] and a traditional male kilt or loincloth, and he is addressed in texts using male pronouns and titles, but at the same time he has distinctly feminine physical traits. He has prominent breasts, symbolising nourishment, fertility, and abundance, and like

---

[100] Wilkinson, Richard H. (2003). The Complete Gods and Goddesses of Ancient Egypt. Thames & Hudson. ISBN 978-0-500-05120-7., p.106
[101] Wilkinson (2003), p.117
[102] Wilkinson (2003), p.106
[103] Wilkinson (2003), p.107
[104] Wilkinson (2003), p.105
[105] "15 LGBT Egyptian Gods". www.advocate.com. 2016-09-20. Retrieved 2022-12-25
[106] Wilkinson, Richard H. (2003). The Complete Gods and Goddesses of Ancient Egypt. Thames & Hudson. ISBN 978-0-500-05120-7., p.107

the Nile itself is seen as the 'mother of all' even though personified by a male god. He was mainly worshipped at Elephantine Island in Upper Egypt, in the Temple of Khnum. This island near the first cataract is believed to be the mythical source of the Nile's inundation[107]. Local belief was that Hapi's floodwaters rose from beneath Elephantine Island in underground caverns or sacred caves. He was also worshipped at Thebes (Luxor) in temples such as Karnak (Thebes), and Memphis (Lower Egypt).

Hapi bearing offerings, Wikipedia Creative Commons, Public Domain

The Pre-Dynastic Period: The Flooding of the Nile is already seen as sacred and life-giving. There is no direct evidence of Hapi yet, but early religious practices honour natural forces like the river.

The Early Dynastic Period: The foundations of state religion take shape. Hapi may begin to be personified, but references are still limited.

The Old Kingdom: The first clear references to Hapi as a deified personification of the Nile flood are found. He appears in Pyramid Texts, offering provision and sustenance to the deceased pharaoh. He is linked to the pharaoh's role as a maintainer of *ma'at*.

The Middle Kingdom: Worship of Hapi becomes visible and widespread. The Hymn to the Nile is written during this period, praising Hapi directly: "Hail to you, Hapi, who comes forth from the Earth... to give life to Egypt". Hapi is seen as a benevolent, essential force, not part of mythological dramas, but present in daily life.

The New Kingdom: Hapi is featured in temple reliefs, especially at Karnak (Thebes). He appears in scenes of royal ritual, blessing the pharaoh with prosperity. He is sometimes shown in dual form (Hapi of Upper Egypt and Lower Egypt) tying the two lands together. He is associated with gods like Khnum (controller of the source of the Nile), Osiris (fertility), and Amun-Ra (state religion).

The Third Intermediate and Late Periods: Hapi continues to appear in temples and tombs. The Nile's role remains central, especially as political unity weakens, the emphasis on *ma'at* increases. Hapi's worship persists in both state religion and popular belief. There are more regional depictions of Hapi in dual form, particularly in temples at Philae Island and Esna.

The Ptolemaic and Roman Periods: Hapi continues to appear in temple scenes, especially in Upper Egypt (Philae Island and Dendera). The Ptolemies co-opt Nile symbolism to legitimise rule, Hapi is shown blessing the foreign rulers. Depictions of Hapi become more elaborate, but still rooted in older forms.

The Byzantine Period: With the rise of Christianity and the decline of traditional Egyptian religion, Hapi's worship fades. The Nile continues to be venerated symbolically, but Hapi as a deity disappears from religious practice.

Parallels with Hapi in Greco-Roman mythology include the Potamoi (river gods), especially Nilus, who becomes the Romanised god and divine spirit of the river Nile. People could pray to Hapi for a fertile, well balanced inundation of the Nile, abundance, nourishment, and prosperity, harmony, balance, and unity in the land, and sustenance for both the living and the dead.

---

[107] Wilkinson, Richard H. (2003). The Complete Gods and Goddesses of Ancient Egypt. Thames & Hudson. ISBN 978-0-500-05120-7., p.108

Hathor: Goddess of the Sky, and the Afterlife

Left: 'Hathor' in hieroglyphs

Hathor is one of the most multi-faceted[108] deities of ancient Egypt. She is a goddess of love, beauty, music, dance, joy, motherhood, fertility, the sky, the sun, the afterlife, foreign lands, mining, and trade. She presides over love, femininity[109], feminine beauty, and attraction. Ancient Egyptians look to her for guidance in personal relationships[110].

As a goddess of joy, music, and celebration, she inspires happiness and emotional ecstasy[111]. She is often shown with a sistrum and a menat necklace[112]. Her name means 'House of Horus' or 'My House is the Sky'[113], representing her as the mother or consort of Horus[114], providing a symbolic dwelling place for him. As a goddess of motherhood and fertility, she assists in childbirth and nurtures infants. She is also the divine mother of the pharaohs[115], often shown embracing or breastfeeding them, legitimising their rule[116].

Hathor is one of the Egyptian deities people turn to in times of personal distress or illness. Commonly depicted as a cow, cow-headed woman, or woman with cow horns, Hathor symbolises fertility and nourishment. She is associated with life-giving milk, the earth's bounty, and feminine generative power.

Hathor is also a sky goddess, linked with the sun god Ra, either as his daughter, his eye, or his consort. In the Book of the Heavenly Cow, humanity rebels against Ra, who sends his eye (the Eye of Ra) to punish them. The eye takes the form of Hathor, but in a wrathful and destructive aspect, often identified as Sekhmet. Hathor / Sekhmet goes on a killing spree, almost destroying humanity with terrifying ferocity. Ra regrets the destruction and tries to stop her, but she is too bloodthirsty. Ra tricks her by pouring beer, dyed red to look like blood, across the land. Hathor drinks it, gets drunk, and falls asleep, ending the massacre. She wakes as her gentle, loving self again[117]. Ra then decides to retreat from the earth. Hathor, as the Celestial Cow, lifts Ra into the sky on her back. She becomes the sky itself, with stars decorating her body. Hathor is also a protector of travellers, miners, and traders[118]. She was worshipped in Serabit el-Khadim in the Sinai Peninsula, a site of turquoise mines in the Sinai

---

[108] Wilkinson, Richard H. (2003). The Complete Gods and Goddesses of Ancient Egypt. Thames & Hudson. ISBN 978-0500051207.
[109] Troy, Lana (1986). Patterns of Queenship in Ancient Egyptian Myth and History. Acta Universitatis Upsaliensis. ISBN 978-9155419196.
[110] Bleeker, C. J. (1973). Hathor and Thoth: Two Key Figures of the Ancient Egyptian Religion. Brill. ISBN 978-9004037342.
[111] Graves-Brown, Carolyn (2010). Dancing for Hathor: Women in Ancient Egypt. Continuum. ISBN 978-1847250544.
[112] Meeks, Dimitri; Favard-Meeks, Christine (1996) [French edition 1993]. Daily Life of the Egyptian Gods. Translated by G. M. Goshgarian. Cornell University Press. ISBN 978-0801431159.
[113] Bleeker, C. J. (1973).
[114] Lesko, Barbara S. (1999). The Great Goddesses of Egypt. University of Oklahoma Press. ISBN 978-0806132020.
[115] Lesko, Barbara S. (1999).
[116] Pinch, Geraldine (1993). Votive Offerings to Hathor. Griffith Institute. ISBN 978-0900416545.
[117] Graves-Brown, Carolyn (2010).
[118] Yellin, Janice W. (2012). "Nubian Religion". In Fisher, Marjorie M.; Lacovara, Peter; Ikram, Salima; D'Auria, Sue (eds.). Ancient Nubia: African Kingdoms on the Nile. The American University in Cairo Press. pp. 125–144. ISBN 978-9774164781.

Desert. She was revered there as 'Lady of Turquoise'. In the Book of the Dead, Hathor emerges from a sycamore tree[119], greets and welcomes the dead, offers them food, drink, and guides them through the dangerous underworld and the afterlife[120]. Hathor's most well-known depiction is that of a beautiful woman, wearing a sun disk on her head encircled by a cobra and cow horns. She is also depicted as a giant cow, holding up the sky, or with her body representing the sky, with the sun and the stars decorating her. Her main centre of worship is Dendera in Upper Egypt, her most important and best preserved temple[121].

Hathor, Wikipedia Creative Commons, Public Domain

The Early Dynastic Period: Hathor begins to appear in royal iconography. She is associated with the pharaoh as his divine mother or nurturer[122].

The Old Kingdom: Hathor is fully established as a major goddess. She is known as 'Mistress of the West' (goddess of the dead), closely tied to the afterlife and royal tombs in the Pyramid Texts. She is worshipped at Dendera, and Serabit el-Khadim from this time onwards.

The Middle Kingdom: Hathor's worship expands significantly. She becomes more closely linked with music, love, and beauty. Her titles include 'Mistress of Music', and 'Lady of Jubilation'. She is important in funerary literature like the Coffin Texts.

The New Kingdom: Hathor is widely venerated and incorporated into royal temples, such as Deir el-Bahri and Luxor (Thebes). She has a major role in the afterlife as the mother of Horus and the pharaoh. She is associated with the Eye of Ra and myths of destruction and renewal.

The Third Intermediate and Late Periods: Hathor's cult persists, especially in local temples like Dendera. Increasing syncretism with Isis begins, blending their identities.

The Ptolemaic Period: The Temple of Hathor at Dendera is rebuilt and expanded. Greek rulers associate Hathor with Aphrodite (Roman: Venus). Her iconography and cult rituals are preserved and even flourish under Greek rule and influence.

The Roman and Byzantine Periods: Worship of Hathor continues, often alongside Isis, who by now has absorbed many of her attributes. Hathor is still honoured at Dendera and other temple sites. With the rise of Christianity and imperial bans on pagan worship, Hathor's temples are closed. Her cult ceases as an organised religion, but elements of her imagery and function persist in folk traditions and later goddess figures.

Hathor is most commonly equated with the Greek / Roman goddess Aphrodite / Venus. Hathor could be prayed to for love, fertility, joy, music, beauty, emotional fulfilment, maternal care, protection, happiness in life, and peace in death.

---

[119] Roberts, Alison (2000). My Heart My Mother: Death and Rebirth in Ancient Egypt. NorthGate Publishers. ISBN 978-0952423317.
[120] Assmann, Jan (2005) [German edition 2001]. Death and Salvation in Ancient Egypt. Translated by David Lorton. Cornell University Press. ISBN 978-0801442414.
[121] Gillam, Robyn A. (1995). "Priestesses of Hathor: Their Function, Decline and Disappearance". Journal of the American Research Center in Egypt. 32: 211–237. doi:10.2307/40000840. JSTOR 40000840.
[122] Gillam, Robyn A. (1995).

Hauhet: Primordial Goddess of Infinity

Left: 'Hauhet' in hieroglyphs

Hauhet is a primordial goddess of infinity, eternity[123], boundlessness, primordial chaos, the infinite expanse, pre-creation, the unknown, and cosmic potential.

Her name means 'infinity' or 'limitless'. Her name is the feminine form of her male counterpart Heh[124]. She is referred to as 'Lady of Infinity', 'She Who Is Boundless', 'Mistress of the Primordial Expanse', 'The Infinite One', 'She Who Embraces Eternity', and 'Goddess of the Limitless Waters'.

She personifies the female aspect of infinity, representing the boundless, formless, expanse that existed before the world began. She helps sustain the chaotic, watery abyss (Nu) from which the first act of creation arose[125]. She exists outside of time, yet she is necessary for time, space, and life to begin.

Her male counterpart is Heh (*Huh*), and together they are one of the four pairs of gods of the Ogdoad.

Hauhet is most commonly depicted as a woman the head of a cobra, possibly wearing a simple headdress, sometimes with the hieroglyph for 'infinity' or similar symbols.

The main centre of worship for Hauhet was at Hermopolis (*Khemenu*), near modern day el-Ashmunein in Middle Egypt[126]. Other sites of theological significance such as Thebes, Heliopolis, and Abydos also mention Hauhet in funerary texts such as the Coffin Texts and the Pyramid texts..

The Pre-Dynastic Period: There is no direct evidence of Hauhet by name, but early concepts of primordial chaos and cosmic duality begin to form in proto-religious beliefs.

The Early Dynastic Period: Conceptual foundations of creation myths emerge, but Hauhet is not yet mentioned in surviving sources.

The Old Kingdom: The earliest references to the Ogdoad begin to appear in pyramid texts from this period, though not all members are explicitly named. Among them, Hauhet, whose name means 'endlessness' or 'infinity', embodies one of the feminine aspects of chaos or boundlessness, and was likely conceptualised during this time, even if not independently worshipped. Her male counterpart,

---

[123] Wilkinson, Richard H. (2003). The Complete Gods and Goddesses of Ancient Egypt. Thames & Hudson. p. 109
[124] Wilkinson, Richard H. (2003).
[125] Allen, James P. Genesis in Egypt: The Philosophy of Ancient Egyptian Creation Accounts. Yale Egyptological Seminar, 1988
[126] G. Mussies in: Matthieu Sybrand Huibert, Gerard Heerma van Voss (eds.), Studies in Egyptian Religion: Dedicated to Professor Jan Zandee (1982), p. 92.

Heh (also known as Huh), features more prominently in later iconography, suggesting a gradual development in the theological prominence of these deities.

Hauhet, Wikipedia Creative Commons, Public Domain

The Middle Kingdom: The Hermopolitan cosmology, cantered in the city of Hermopolis, becomes increasingly defined and gains prominence in religious thought. Within this framework, the Ogdoad is more clearly articulated, with Hauhet paired with her male counterpart Heh, both embodying the concept of infinite space or eternity[127]. Although Hauhet gains theological significance as a feminine personification of infinity and features in religious writings and temple theology, she does not emerge as a goddess of individual cult worship, remaining a conceptual figure who appears mainly alongside her consort.

The New Kingdom: During this time, theological syncretism continues as the Theban Triad and solar cults dominate, yet some cosmological texts, including versions of the Book of the Dead and Coffin Texts, reference the Ogdoad. Hauhet remains present in funerary and cosmological literature as part of creation mythology, but there is no evidence of temples or independent worship dedicated to her.

The Late Period: A revival of older theological traditions takes place alongside the rise of temple building and the reassertion of local cults, with Hermopolis Magna remaining a key theological centre. Temple inscriptions and cosmological representations continue to reference the Ogdoad, including Hauhet, who maintains her role as a mythological figure rather than a goddess of daily worship. Egyptian priests preserve and teach the Ogdoad cosmology, ensuring Hauhet's ongoing relevance within priestly and temple theology, particularly in Hermopolis.

The Ptolemaic and Roman Periods: Under Greek and later Roman rule, Egyptian religion becomes highly syncretic[128], with the Ogdoad, including Hauhet, appearing in esoteric religious texts and later Hermetic writings[129]. While Hauhet's theological role is preserved in temple inscriptions and religious literature, worship remains symbolic, and no direct cult develops. The priesthoods maintain interest in cosmological systems, integrating Ogdoad myths into Greco-Egyptian religious thought, but public religious life increasingly centres on more popular deities such as Isis, Horus, and Serapis.

The Byzantine Period: The Byzantine period marks the end of pagan worship in Egypt, as the rise of Christianity[130] leads to the closure of temples and the decline of traditional religious practices[131]. Consequently, Hauhet's theological role fades, surviving only in historical and textual records of ancient Egyptian religion.

As the personification of primordial infinity and endlessness, Hauhet could be compared to the Greek Aion or the Roman Aeternitas. As a primordial feminine principle, she could be equated with Chaos, a feminine void at the beginning of time. Hauhet has a cosmological role, but not a devotional one as such, and there is no evidence of direct popular worship or any prayers addressed to her.

---

[127] Wilkinson, Richard H. (2003). The Complete Gods and Goddesses of Ancient Egypt. Thames & Hudson. p. 109
[128] Peacock, David (2000), The Roman Period, pp. 437–38.
[129] Mahé 1978–1982. Mahé also demonstrated numerous other Egyptian influences on the Hermetica (cf. Bull 2018, pp. 9–10).
[130] "The History of Religion in Egypt" (PDF). Center for Middle Eastern Studies, University of Arizona. Retrieved 2025-03-26.
[131] Procopius Bell. Pers. 1.19.37

Heh: Primordial God of Infinity

Left: Two variations of 'Heh' in hieroglyphs

Heh is a god of eternity, infinite time, boundlessness, the immeasurable, the endless, and the concept of millions (as a symbol of countless years or infinity). The main meaning of the Egyptian word *ḥeḥ* is 'million' or 'millions', and so he is a personification of this concept. His name is also believed to mean 'flood', referring to the watery chaos of Nu that existed before the creation of the world[132]. Heh personifies the infinite aspect of the primordial waters[133]. He is referred to as 'Lord of Eternity', 'He of Millions of Years', 'Bearer of Infinity', and 'Personification of Infinity'.

Heh represents infinite time or eternity, maintains the eternal cycle of creation, and supports royal and cosmic longevity. Heh sometimes supports Shu, a god associated with the air, in supporting the sky goddess Nut[134]. His female counterpart is Hauhet[135], which is the feminine form of his name, and together Heh and Hauhet are one of the four pairs of gods of the Ogdoad[136].

Heh is depicted as a male human figure, often seated or kneeling. He is almost always holding notched palm ribs in one or both hands[137]. These represent the passing of time, especially 'millions of years'[138], referring to the ancient Egyptian practice of carving notches on palm ribs to count years. Along with the palm ribs, shen rings are often shown below them, above them, or above or around his head.

In some depictions Heh is shown standing, offering the palm fronds and the shen rings to the pharaoh, and in others he is depicted in multiple forms, up to eight figures, emphasising boundlessness. In the Book of the Heavenly Cow, eight Heh gods are depicted together with Shu supporting Nut, who has taken the form of a cow[139]. In the Ogdoad he is depicted as a frog, or a man with the head of a frog. Depictions of Heh are also used in hieroglyphics to represent one million, which is considered equivalent to infinity in Ancient Egyptian mathematics, thus he is known as the 'god of millions of years'. As a member of the Ogdoad his main centre of worship is Hermopolis, where he is venerated as part of cosmological doctrine, not as an independent deity with a personal myth or cult.

---

[132] Allen, James P. Genesis in Egypt: The Philosophy of Ancient Egyptian Creation Accounts. Yale Egyptological Seminar, 1988
[133] Allen, James P. Middle Egyptian: An Introduction to the Language and Culture of Hieroglyphs. Cambridge University Press, 2000
[134] Pinch, Geraldine (2002). Handbook of Egyptian Mythology. p. 139.
[135] Wilkinson, Richard H. (2003). The Complete Gods and Goddesses of Ancient Egypt. Thames & Hudson. p. 109
[136] Wilkinson, Richard H. (2003).
[137] Owusu, Heike (2008). Egyptian Symbols. New York, NY: Sterling. p. 73.
[138] Remler, Pat (2010). Egyptian Mythology, A to Z. New York: Chelsea House.
[139] Pinch, Geraldine (2004). A Guide to the Gods, Goddesses, and Traditions of Ancient Egypt. Oxford University Press. pp. 75, 77. ISBN 0-19-517024-5.

The Old Kingdom: The earliest references to Heh appear in the Pyramid Texts, especially in cosmological contexts. Heh is not worshipped as a personal deity, but appears as a concept in the background of royal funerary theology, linked to the eternal afterlife of the pharaoh. No temples or shrines dedicated to Heh exist at this time.

Heh, Wikipedia Creative Commons, Public Domain

The Middle Kingdom: Heh's role becomes more defined in Coffin Texts, where he appears in the Ogdoad. Heh and his female counterpart Hauhet represent eternity and boundlessness, part of the cosmic conditions before creation. Heh is still not worshipped independently, but acknowledged as part of Egypt's cosmological system.

The New Kingdom: This is the peak of Heh's symbolic visibility, especially in royal tombs and temples. He is depicted frequently offering 'millions of years' to pharaohs[140], especially in mortuary temples and tomb art (e.g. the Valley of the Kings and Queens, Thebes). Heh appears in the Book of the Dead and other funerary texts as a symbol of infinite time. There is still no temple or independent worship, Heh functions within state theology.

The Late Period: There is continued use of Heh in temple reliefs, especially in temples like those at Karnak (Thebes) and Esna, where cosmological themes are emphasised. The Ogdoad's theological role is reaffirmed in revived priestly cosmologies. Heh remains a theological figure, not a personal or civic god.

The Ptolemaic Period: Hellenistic rulers of Egypt adopt and preserve Egyptian religious symbolism. Heh still appears in temple iconography and is occasionally blended or harmonised with Greek philosophical concepts of time and infinity. His image is still used in royal contexts, affirming eternal rulership and cosmic order under Greco-Egyptian rule.

The Roman Period: Heh continues to appear occasionally in temple art, but by the end of the Roman period, Egyptian temple religion fades, and so does Heh's active use. He survives only in art and texts as a symbol, not worshipped as a figure.

As the personification of eternity and boundless time, Heh is comparable to the Greek Aion and the Roman Aeternitas, both personifications of eternity. He is also philosophically comparable to Chronos / Saturn, the personification of time. Heh could be prayed to for eternal life, both for gods and humans, longevity or 'millions of years' of prosperity or rule, cosmic stability, the assurance that time and existence continue forever, and immortality in the afterlife, where the soul endures endlessly.

---

[140] Remler, Pat (2010). Egyptian Mythology, A to Z. New York: Chelsea House.

Heqet: Goddess of Fertility and Regeneration

Left: 'Heqet' in hieroglyphs

Heqet is a goddess of fertility, childbirth, rebirth, midwifery, creation, life, and renewal. Her name comes from the root '*ḥq*', meaning 'to rule', or 'sceptre'. She is referred to as 'She Who Hastens Birth'[141], 'Goddess of Childbirth', 'Lady of the Birth House', 'Bringer of Life', 'She of the Frog Form'.

Heqet speeds and assists childbirth, animates the body with life ('*ka*'), presides over fertility and conception, protects infants and mothers, and she is a symbol of resurrection and rebirth. She is mentioned in creation mythology alongside Khnum, the ram-headed god and divine potter who forms human beings on his potter's wheel using Nile clay[142].

Heqet is associated with the goddess Taweret, as they are both protectors of childbirth. Heqet speeds up labour, whereas Taweret (depicted as a pregnant hippopotamus) wards off evil during labour. Heqet is also associated with Bes, who is a protector of mothers, children, and the household. He protects mothers and infants from evil spirits and misfortune. In childbirth rituals, Bes, Tawaret, and Heqet often form a protective triad. In the Temple of Kom Ombo, Heqet was worshipped alongside Ra as the parents of Heru-ur[143].

Heqet is depicted as a frog[144], sitting upright or squatting. Frogs are sacred to Heqet because after the annual Nile flood, frogs appear in huge numbers, an ancient symbol of fertility and abundance. The frog's life cycle (from tadpole to adult) also symbolises transformation and rebirth. Heqet is also depicted as a woman with a frog's head, particularly in temple art and magical amulets, sometimes holding an ankh or a knife (to cut the umbilical cord), and with a headdress or a hieroglyphic symbol of her name.

Heqet's primary cult centre is Qus in Upper Egypt. This location is known for temples dedicated to Heqet and Khnum, where they were worshipped as partners in creation. Another early centre where Heqet was venerated is Herwer (near Asyut) in Middle Egypt, often associated with local fertility rites. Evidence of frog amulets and inscriptions suggests popular devotion, particularly among women. Heqet also appears in birth related rituals, mortuary texts, temple reliefs, and resurrection symbolism at Abydos, which was a major religious centre for the cult of Osiris. At the Dendera Temple Complex and at Philae Island (Temple of Isis), Heqet appears in temple reliefs at a birthing house (*Mammisi*).

---

[141] Lichtheim, M. (1973). Ancient Egyptian Literature. Vol. 1. p. 220.
[142] Wilkinson, Richard H. (2003). The Complete Gods and Goddesses of Ancient Egypt. Thames & Hudson. p. 229
[143] Minas-Nerpel, Martina (2017). Offering the ij.t-knife to in the Temple of Isis at Shanhur. In: Illuminating Osiris. Egyptological Studies in Honor of Mark Smith (Material and Visual Culture of Ancient Egypt 2). Lockwood Press, Atlanta, 2017, p.264
[144] Armour, Robert A. (2001). Gods and Myths of Ancient Egypt. American University in Cairo Press. p. 116.

Heqet is shown taking part in the divine birth of Horus as one of the goddesses assisting Isis in the delivery.

Heqet, Wikipedia Creative Commons, Public Domain

The Early Dynastic Period: The earliest evidence of Heqet appears in this period. She is associated with fertility and regeneration, possibly already connected with frogs and childbirth, and likely worshipped in local cults in Upper Egypt. Early frog statuettes are often thought to be depictions of her[145].

The Old Kingdom: Heqet is named in Pyramid Texts, especially in the context of rebirth and resurrection. She begins to be linked to creation mythology, and possibly paired with Khnum. She is revered as a helper goddess who grants life and assists birth.

The Middle Kingdom: Worship of Heqet increases in prominence, especially at Qus and other Upper Egyptian sites. She has a strong connection to the god Khnum as she animates the bodies that he forms on the potter's wheel. Amulets and frog iconography become widespread, especially among women. Heqet often appears in magical spells and birth-related texts.

The New Kingdom: Heqet appears in temple art, particularly in birth houses (*Mammisi*) attached to temples like Dendera and Philae Island. Her role as a divine midwife is solidified; she assists in the mythical birth of Horus. She is popular in household religion, appearing on amulets, and in prayers and childbirth invocations[146] [147]. Her worship spreads more broadly across Egypt.

The Third Intermediate Period: Heqet has a continued presence in domestic and magical contexts, although she is overshadowed by major deities like Isis and Amun, she remains popular in folk religion.

The Late Period: Heqet continues to appear in ritual and magical texts, including Demotic and Greek-influenced spells. Temples such as those at Philae Island and Esna include depictions of Heqet in birth related reliefs.

The Ptolemaic Period: Worship of Heqet continues under Greek rule, especially in temple birth houses where Heqet still plays a role in divine births. Amulets and spells invoking Heqet remain in use. She is integrated into Hellenistic religious practices, though in a diminished role compared to earlier periods. A temple is dedicated to Horus and Heqet at Qus[148] [149].

The Roman and Byzantine Periods: The last phase of formal temple of worship of Heqet, she is still represented in Philae Island temple reliefs. Her cult declines along with traditional Egyptian religion as Christianity spreads. Her symbolism (e.g. a frog as a life symbol) occasionally survives in folk traditions.

Heqet is comparable to the Greek / Roman goddess Eileithyia / Lucina, a goddess of childbirth. She could be prayed to for protection during labour, ease of delivery, and strength for mother and child.

---

[145] Wilkinson, Toby A. H. (1999). Early Dynastic Egypt. Routledge. p. 286.
[146] "Frog Amulet". The Cleveland Museum of Art. 30 October 2018. Retrieved 4 November 2021.
[147] Capel, A. K.; Markoe, G. E., eds. (1996). Mistress of the House, Mistress of Heaven. Hudson Hills Press. p. 72. ISBN 1-55595-129-5.
[148] Porter, Bertha and Moss, Rosalind. Topographical Bibliography of Ancient Egyptian Hieroglyphic Texts, Reliefs and Paintings, V Upper Egypt: Sites (Volume 5). Griffith Institute. 2004.
[149] Wilkinson, Richard H., The Complete Temples of Ancient Egypt, Thames and Hudson, 2000, pp 152, ISBN 0-500-05100-3

Heru-ur: God of the Sky, Sun and Moon

Left: 'Heru-ur' in hieroglyphs

Heru-ur is a god of the sky, war, kingship, protection, hunting, the sun, and the moon. 'Heru' (or 'Horus') means 'falcon' or 'the distant one', and 'Ur' means 'great' or 'elder'. He is a guardian deity, especially of the pharaoh[150] who is considered his earthly embodiment. He protects *ma'at* and defends Egypt from chaos and foreign enemies. He battles the forces of chaos, often represented by Set. He embodies the ideal ruler, just, strong, and victorious. His association with the falcon and the sky represents him 'watching from above'. His right eye (The Eye of Ra) represents the sun, and his left eye (The Eye of Horus) represents moon[151].

In earlier traditions, before the myth became centred on Horus the Younger, Heru-ur was the god who fought Set for the right to rule Egypt after the death of Osiris, or simply in a cosmic struggle between order and chaos. Heru-ur and Set are seen as opposing cosmic forces who must share rulership of Egypt, Heru-ur ruling Lower Egypt, and Set ruling Upper Egypt.

Heru-ur is sometimes merged with Ra to form Ra-Horakhty ('Ra-Horus of the Horizons'), a sky god and falcon with Ra's solar power, representing the rising sun and the daily rebirth of light. Montu is a Theban falcon-headed war god, and like Heru-ur, he represents military strength and royal valour. Khonsu, the moon god of Thebes, is sometimes linked with Heru-ur through their celestial roles, both of them being associated with lunar and solar elements. In some Theban traditions Khonsu is depicted as a falcon-headed youth, blurring the lines with Horus imagery. Heru-ur is often confused with or merged with Horus the Younger, the son of Isis and Osiris. In many later myths, the roles of Heru-ur and Horus are combined, with Horus the Younger inheriting many of Heru-ur's traits, such as being a sky god, battling with Set, and being the protector of kingship. Sopdu is an eastern desert and sky god, sometimes portrayed as a falcon and associated with protection of the eastern border. Heru-ur is depicted as a falcon either soaring or perched, as a falcon-headed man he is shown wearing a crown or double-crown (Pschent) representing unifying rule of Upper and Lower Egypt, and sometimes with a sun disk above his head or a uraeus on his crown. He is also sometimes depicted as a Hieracosphinx (a falcon headed lion).

Heru-ur was worshipped at Hierakonpolis. He was also worshipped at Edfu in Upper Egypt. Edfu is best known for Horus the Younger, but early traditions merged with Heru-ur. The great Temple of Horus, built in the Ptolemaic period, honours Horus Behdetite, a falcon who retains many of Heru-ur's older attributes, especially as a sky god and warrior. Letopolis near modern day Ausim in the Nile Delta of Lower Egypt is a centre for Horus in his form as a celestial falcon, sharing many attributes of Heru-ur. Alongside Sobek the crocodile god, Heru-ur was also worshipped as a solar and protective

---

[150] Pearson, Patricia O'Connell; Holdren, John (May 2021). World History: Our Human Story. Versailles, Kentucky: Sheridan Kentucky. p. 29. ISBN 978-1-60153-123-0.
[151] Darnell, John Coleman (1997). "The Apotropaic Goddess in the Eye". Studien zur Altägyptischen Kultur. 24: 35–48. JSTOR 25152728.

deity, the son of Ra and Heqet[152], the husband of his sister-wife Tasenetnofret, and the father of the child god Panebtawy[153], at the dual temple at Kom Ombo, south of Edfu in Upper Egypt.

Heru-ur, Wikipedia Creative Commons, Public Domain

The Pre-Dynastic Period: Heru-ur emerges as a local falcon deity in Hierakonpolis, one of the earliest religious and political centres in Upper Egypt. He is likely to have been a totemic sky and kingship god representing the ruling elite. His association with falcons, the sky, and divine rule begins here.

The Early Dynastic Period: Heru-ur becomes closely tied to the pharaoh, who is regarded as the living embodiment of Horus. Royal iconography, such as the Narmer Palette, shows kings as falcons or accompanied by falcons.

The Old Kingdom: In the Pyramid Texts, Heru-ur appears as a sky god and protector of the pharaoh in the afterlife. He is invoked alongside Ra and other major deities in royal funerary spells. His eye symbolism (sun and moon) becomes important in solar theology.

The Middle Kingdom: Theological developments begin to merge Heru-ur with other Horus forms, especially Horus son of Isis (Harsiesis). He remains an important god of kingship, but narrative myths now shift toward Horus the Younger as the son who avenges Osiris. Heru-ur retains a more cosmic and timeless role in temple inscriptions and hymns.

The New Kingdom: Heru-ur is often syncretised with Ra as Ra-Horakhty, a powerful solar god. He is still invoked in temples and tombs as a warrior and protector, especially in his role as a falcon god who defeats chaos. Edfu and Kom Ombo temples begin to elevate Horus in forms that include Heru-ur elements.

The Late Period: At Kom Ombo, Heru-ur is worshipped alongside Sobek in a major dual temple. His healing, solar, and protective aspects are emphasised. He is often indistinct from Horus the Younger, though he is still regarded as an ancient, powerful deity.

The Ptolemaic Period: In temples like Edfu, Heru-ur's legacy survives in the form of Horus Behdetite, a god of the sky, war, and protection. Mythical scenes (e.g. battling with Set) blend elements of Heru-ur and Horus son of Isis, showing the fusion of traditions. The Ptolemaic dynasty promotes him as a model of kingship, tying their rule to ancient legitimacy.

The Roman Period: Worship of Heru-ur continues under Roman rule, mostly in temples built or maintained by earlier dynasties. Heru-ur survives in syncretic Greco-Egyptian religion, often equated with the Greco-Roman god Apollo[154], but gradually loses distinct identity as temples close and Christianity spreads.

In Greco-Roman tradition Heru-ur could be equated with Apollo / Sol as a sky god or the sun. As a protector of kingship and order, he could be compared to Zeus / Jupiter. His falcon symbolism as 'all seeing' could be compared to Apollo or Hermes / Mercury. Heru-ur could be prayed to for royal authority and divine legitimacy, protection of the kingdom, victory over enemies, cosmic balance and order, clear vision, guidance, and protection.

---

[152] Minas-Nerpel, Martina (2017). Offering the ij.t-knife to in the Temple of Isis at Shanhur. In: Illuminating Osiris. Egyptological Studies in Honor of Mark Smith (Material and Visual Culture of Ancient Egypt 2). Lockwood Press, Atlanta, 2017, p.264
[153] Abdelhalim, Ali. (2019). Notes on the Bandeau-Texts of Columns of Kom Ombo Temple. Bulletin of the Center Papyrological Studies, p.298
[154] Strudwick, Helen (2006). The Encyclopedia of Ancient Egypt. New York: Sterling Publishing Co., Inc. pp. 158–159. ISBN 978-1-4351-4654-9.

Hesat: The Milk Goddess

Hesat is a goddess of milk, nourishment, motherhood, fertility, birth, cows, maternal care, kingship, divine sustenance, and the nurturing of the pharaoh. Her name comes from the word 'hesa' / 'ḥsꜣ' which relates to milk or nourishment. Hesat provides divine or sacred milk, nourishes gods, pharaohs, and purifies the dead with her milk. Milk from Hesat is sometimes described as the 'milk of life'[155] and used ritually in offerings and purification rites. She is often considered a form or aspect of Hathor. In some texts, Hesat is said to emanate from Hathor.

Hesat is associated with other cow goddesses such as Mehet-Weret, Bat, Nut (in cosmic cow form), Isis (occasionally in cow form), Neith (in some early cow associated roles), Sekhat-Hor, Ihet, Seret, Tayet, and Wenut. They all have overlapping roles, symbolising motherhood, nourishment, and fertility. Hesat is also associated with other bull deities such as Apis, Mnevis, Buchis, Khnum (sometimes depicted with bull horns), Montu (as the Buchis bull), Sema-wer, and Ageb-wer[156].

Left: Two variations of 'Hesat' in hieroglyphs

Hesat is depicted as a white cow[157]. She is sometimes depicted nursing the infant pharaoh or a young god. Like Hathor, Hesat is sometimes depicted with a sun disk above her head or between her horns, or a uraeus (rearing cobra), symbolising royalty and divine authority. Worship of Hesat was often integrated into the cults of related deities, particularly Hathor and Ra. Heliopolis is one of the oldest religious centres in Egypt, dedicated primarily to Ra and the Ennead. Hesat was worshipped there as a nourishing aspect of Hathor. Memphis is an early political and religious centre, in which Hesat was a maternal cow goddess associated with the sacred Apis bull cult. In some texts Hesat is the mother of Apis. Dendera is a major cult centre of Hathor where Hesat was worshipped as an aspect or emanation of Hathor.

The Pre-Dynastic Period: Cow deities appear in art and symbolism in association with fertility, nourishment, and motherhood. Early reverence for sacred cows is likely to have laid the foundation for later worship of Hesat, particularly in regions like Heliopolis and Memphis.

The Early Dynastic Period: In the development of divine kingship ideology, cows become important symbols of the mother of the pharaoh. Hesat's role begins to crystallise as a divine cow figure tied to royal legitimacy and nourishment.

---

[155] Mark, Joshua J.. "Hathor". World History Encyclopedia. World History Encyclopedia, 02 Sep 2009, https://www.worldhistory.org/Hathor/. Web. 23 Jun 2025.
[156] Von Lieven, Alexandra [in German] (2012). "Book of the Dead, Book of the Living: BD Spells as Sample Texts". The Journal of Egyptian Archaeology. 98: 249–67. doi:10.1177/030751331209800114.
[157] Metropolitan Museum of Art staff member. "Scarab with the Representation of Hathor as Cow". www.metmuseum.org. Retrieved 2018-12-03.

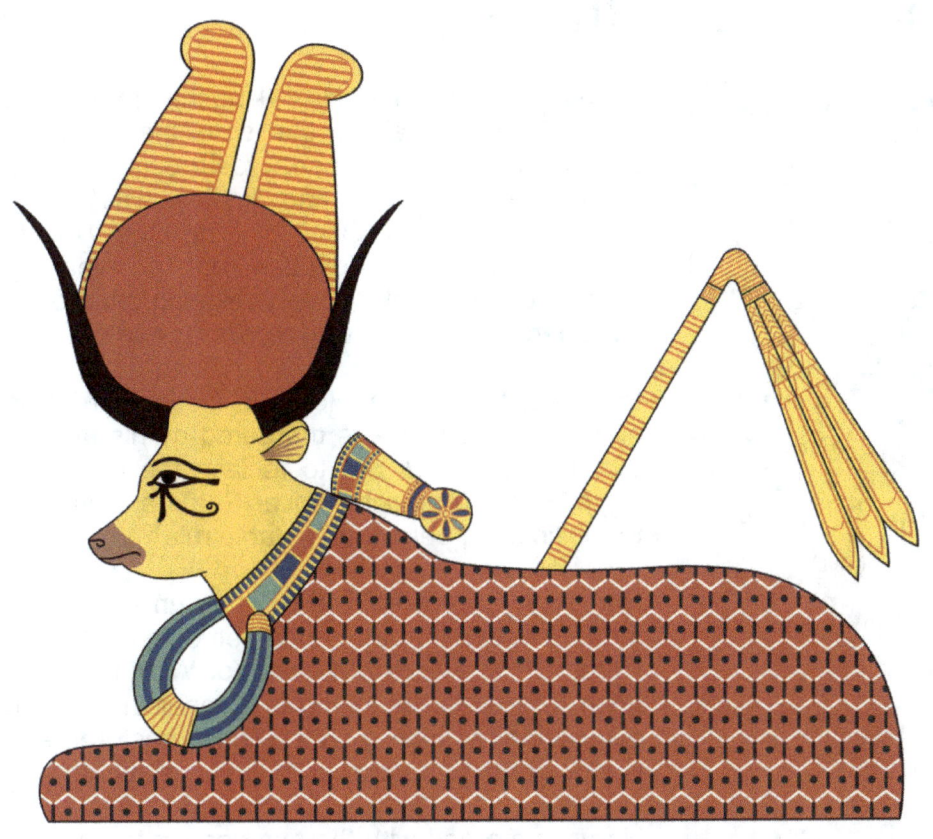
Hesat, Wikipedia Creative Commons, Public Domain

The Old Kingdom: The first clear references to Hesat appear in Pyramid Texts and early funerary literature. She is described as a nurse of the pharaoh and a source of divine milk. She is connected to the Apis bull cult in Memphis, and the Apis bull is said to be her offspring, solidifying her role in divine cattle theology.

The Middle Kingdom: There is increased integration of Hesat into funerary religion. She is invoked as a provider of sustenance to the dead, linking her to the afterlife and rebirth. Worship of Hesat continues as a sub-aspect of Hathor, who rises in prominence during this period.

The New Kingdom: Hesat is clearly associated with Hathor, especially in temples at Dendera and Heliopolis. She continues to appear in offering texts, healing spells, and royal rituals. Her milk is seen as divine sustenance for gods, pharaohs, and the deceased. She is possibly linked to the birth of Anubis in some local traditions.

The Third Intermediate and Late Periods: Hesat's worship becomes more symbolic and theological, rarely involving standalone temples. She is referred to in funerary texts, milk offerings, and cosmological hymns. Her association with Hathor and the Apis cult remains strong, especially in Memphis.

The Ptolemaic Period: Egyptian religion is reorganised and expanded under Greek rule, and temple theology is formalised. Hesat is closely linked with the goddess Isis[158]. She appears in elaborate temple texts, especially in Dendera, as part of Hathor's maternal and cosmic forms. Her imagery continues in rituals of birth, purification, and nourishment of the pharaoh.

The Roman Period: Traditional temples decline as Christianity rises and pagan cults are suppressed. Hesat's worship, like many traditional deities, fades out, surviving mainly in religious texts and symbolic motifs. Final echoes of her role persist in funerary magic, and syncretic Greco-Egyptian art.

As a nourishing mother and giver of milk, Hesat could be compared to the Greek / Roman goddess Hera / Juno. As a goddess of fertility, abundance, and life-giving, she could be equated with Demeter / Ceres. As a protector of kings and giver of divine milk, she could be compared to Amalthea, who nurtured the infant Zeus, a parallel of Hesat feeding divine kings.

---

[158] Wilkinson, Richard H. (2003). The Complete Gods and Goddesses of Ancient Egypt. Thames & Hudson. pp. 173–174

Horus: God of the Sun and the Sky

Left: 'Horus' in hieroglyphs

Horus is a god of the sky[159], kingship, protection, war, hunting, healing, the sun, the moon[160], divine order, vengeance, resurrection, royal power, guardianship, and justice. His name means 'The Distant One', or 'The One Who Is Above'[161], from the Egyptian root '$ḥr$' meaning 'face', 'height', or 'sky'. Every reigning pharaoh is considered to be the living Horus on earth[162].

In the myth of Osiris, Horus is the son of Osiris and Isis. After Osiris is murdered by his brother Set, Horus battles Set to reclaim the throne of Egypt[163]. Horus's victory over Set is a metaphor for unification, peace, and stable rule[164].

Horus's eyes are said to be the sun (right eye, the Eye of Ra) and the moon (left eye, the Eye of Horus)[165]. The 'Eye of Horus' (or Wedjat eye[166]) myth tells of Horus losing and regaining his left eye during his battles with Set. His restored eye is a powerful protective and healing symbol.

Horus is merged with the sun god Ra to become *Ra-Horakhty* ('Ra-Horus of the Horizons'). In Edfu on the west bank of the Nile in Upper Egypt, Horus becomes *Horus Behdety* ('Horus of Edfu'), a local warrior form of Horus. In the Theban tradition, Horus is the king of the living, and Osiris is the king of the dead, and the two become merged into one divine cycle. In various local cults, Horus is merged with Min, Sobek, and Khonsu. Horus is depicted as a falcon[167] or a falcon-headed man[168] wearing the Pschent double crown, and sometimes with the uraeus (rearing cobra).

In Upper Egypt Horus was worshipped at Hierakonpolis, one of the oldest religious centres in Egypt, also at Edfu, the site of the great Ptolemaic Temple of Horus, one of the best preserved temples in Egypt, and at Kom Ombo as Heru-ur ('Horus the Elder'). In Lower Egypt he was worshipped at

---

[159] Pearson, Patricia O'Connell; Holdren, John (May 2021). World History: Our Human Story. Versailles, Kentucky: Sheridan Kentucky. p. 29. ISBN 978-1-60153-123-0.
[160] "Horus". World History Encyclopedia. Archived from the original on 2021-04-14. Retrieved 2019-02-22.
[161] Meltzer, Edmund S. (2002). Horus. In D. B. Redford (Ed.), The ancient gods speak: A guide to Egyptian religion (pp. 164). New York: Oxford University Press, USA.
[162] Pearson, Patricia O'Connell; Holdren, John (May 2021). World History: Our Human Story. Versailles, Kentucky: Sheridan Kentucky. p. 29. ISBN 978-1-60153-123-0.
[163] "The Oxford Guide: Essential Guide to Egyptian Mythology", Edited by Donald B. Redford, Horus: by Edmund S. Meltzer, pp. 164–168, Berkley, 2003, ISBN 0-425-19096-X.
[164] te Velde, Herman (1967). Seth, God of Confusion: A Study of His Role in Egyptian Mythology and Religion. Probleme der Ägyptologie 6. Translated by van Baaren-Pape, G. E. (2nd ed.). Leiden: E. J. Brill. ISBN 978-90-04-05402-8.
[165] Wilkinson, Richard H. (1992). Reading Egyptian Art: A Hieroglyphic Guide to Ancient Egyptian Painting and Sculpture. Thames & Hudson. p. 186.
[166] Pommerening, Tanja, Die altägyptischen Hohlmaße (Studien zur Altägyptischen Kultur, Beiheft 10), Hamburg, Helmut Buske Verlag, 2005
[167] Wilkinson, Richard H. (2003). The Complete Gods and Goddesses of Ancient Egypt. Thames & Hudson. p. 202.
[168] Harvard. "Horus Falcon Wearing Crown of Upper and Lower Egypt with Uraeus | Harvard Art Museums". harvardartmuseums.org. Retrieved 2025-05-09.

Letopolis, where inscriptions mention him as a guardian of divine secrets and hidden power, and also at Heliopolis, the centre of solar religion in ancient Egypt, and at Memphis as the son of Osiris and Isis, where pharaohs are 'Horus in life' and 'Osiris in death'[169].

Horus, Wikipedia Creative Commons, Public Domain

The Pre-Dynastic Period: The earliest roots of the worship of Horus begin here. Horus appears as a falcon sky god in early iconography. Hierakonopolis becomes an early cult centre for Horus, associated with emerging royal authority.

The Early Dynastic Period: Horus becomes firmly linked to kingship. Horus is seen as the divine embodiment of the pharaoh, the protector of *ma'at*. Temple structures and falcon iconography support Horus's role in the state cult.

The Old Kingdom: Horus continues as the chief deity of kingship. Texts such as the Pyramid Texts mention Horus as the son of Osiris and the living king. The conflict between Horus and Set starts to appear in religious narratives. Kings identify themselves as Horus in life, and Osiris in death.

The Middle Kingdom: Horus regains prominence as the ideal ruler, especially through literature and temple inscriptions. Horus son of Isis becomes a more dominant form, emphasising the myth of Osiris and Horus. The Eye of Horus continues to be developed as a powerful symbol of protection and healing.

The New Kingdom: Horus is heavily emphasised in royal theology. He is worshipped in multiple forms: Ra-Horakhty (a syncretic sun god), Horus Behdety (a warrior god at Edfu), and Harpocrates[170] (a healing child god). His story with Isis and Osiris is widely depicted in tombs and temples. The Battle of Horus and Set becomes a standard mythological theme.

The Late Period: The revival of older religious traditions strengthens Horus's cult again. The Temple of Edfu is started late in this period. Horus is invoked in temple texts as a protector and a just ruler.

The Ptolemaic Period: The Temple of Horus at Edfu is completed between 237 and 57 BCE, becoming the major centre of worship for Horus. He is deeply incorporated into Greco-Egyptian religion. Greek forms like Harpocrates (Horus the Child) become popular across Egypt and the Mediterranean. Horus, Apis, and Osiris together become Serapis, a Greco-Egyptian deity.

The Roman and Byzantine Periods: Horus continues to be worshipped, often in syncretic forms. Temples like Philae Island still honour Horus and the Osirian triad. There is a gradual decline in Horus worship with the rise of Christianity, suppression of traditional cults, and closure of temples.

As a god of the sky and celestial vision, Horus is comparable with the Greek / Roman god Apollo or Helios / Sol. As a god of kingship and justice, he is comparable with Zeus / Jupiter. People could pray to Horus for divine kingship and authority, protection from enemies, victory and justice, cosmic balance, and divine insight.

---

[169] "The Oxford Guide: Essential Guide to Egyptian Mythology", Edited by Donald B. Redford, Horus: by Edmund S. Meltzer, pp. 164–168, Berkley, 2003, ISBN 0-425-19096-X.
[170] "- Moralia, De Iside et Osiride (Isis and Osiris), 12. (356A)". Archived from the original on 2023-04-03. Retrieved 2022-08-16.

Imentet: Goddess of the Afterlife

Left: 'Imentet' in hieroglyphs

Imentet is a goddess of the west, the afterlife, the necropolis, welcoming the dead, tombs, and the underworld. Her name comes from the word *imnt* ('west') with the feminine *–et* ending, together meaning 'She of the West'[171]. The West is the direction where the sun sets, a symbolic region associated with death and the afterlife, especially the necropolises where the dead were buried to the west of the Nile. In ancient Egyptian, *Amenti* or *Amentet* is the name of the location where the sun sets, and where the entrance to the underworld is located, although later the term began to be associated with graveyards and tombs as well[172].

Imentet welcomes and receives the souls of the deceased as they arrive at the entrance to Duat (the underworld)[173]. She offers them nourishment in the form of bread and water before they continue on their long journey to the Field of Reeds (*Aaru*), which is equated with the idea of paradise. She is the symbol of the afterlife's promise, the personification of the western necropolises, and she represents the hope of resurrection and eternal life. She appears in pyramid texts, coffin texts, iconography, tomb inscriptions, and the Book of the Dead.

Imentet is closely associated with the goddess Hathor who is also known as 'Lady of the West'. Both of them appear in tombs welcoming the dead. In many depictions, it's hard to distinguish between the two, leading some scholars to believe that Imentet may have originated as a local or funerary aspect of Hathor, Isis, or Nephthys[174] [175].

Imentet is depicted as a woman in a red sheath dress, wearing the hieroglyph for 'west' (*imnt*) on or above her head, holding an ankh (a symbol of life) and a sceptre or staff, and in welcoming poses greeting the dead[176]. She is sometimes depicted in winged form, like Isis and Nephthys[177], but this is rare. She is also sometimes depicted beneath or near the sacred tree of life, from which she looks out over the entrance to the Duat (underworld). Imentet was primarily worshipped and venerated in the Theban Necropolis on the west bank of Luxor (Thebes), and at Abydos as a supporting deity for Osiris who was the central figure there.

---

[171] Hill, Jenny (2010). "Amentet". Ancient Egypt Online. Retrieved 2016-10-25.
[172] Hill, Jenny (2010).
[173] Hill, Jenny (2010).
[174] Wilkinson, Richard H. (2003). The Complete Gods and Goddesses of Ancient Egypt. Thames & Hudson. pp. 145–146
[175] Wilkinson, Richard H. (2003).
[176] Hill, Jenny (2010).
[177] Hill, Jenny (2010).

The Early Dynastic Period: There is no confirmed evidence of Imentet during this time. Funerary beliefs were developing, but most known deities were focused on kingship and sky gods (e.g. Horus). If Imentet existed at all here, she had not yet emerged as a named figure.

The Old Kingdom: The earliest possible references to the concept of 'the West' (*Imentet, Amenti*) as a funerary realm appear in this period. Imentet may not yet have been personified as a goddess at this stage, but the idea of the west as the land of the dead was well established by this time. Deities like Hathor and Nephthys already appear in funerary roles.

Imentet, Wikipedia Creative Commons, Public Domain

The First Intermediate Period: There is less centralised religious control, but local beliefs flourish. There are some signs of increased personalisation in funerary beliefs, setting the stage for goddesses like Imentet to become more visible in the next era.

The Middle Kingdom: Imentet begins to appear as a personified figure in funerary texts and tomb decorations. She is mentioned in Coffin Texts as one of the deities who welcomes and sustains the dead. She is depicted in tomb scenes offering food and drink to the deceased. Her role overlap heavily with Hathor of the West.

The Second Intermediate Period: Amid fragmentation and instability. Funerary traditions persist, especially in Theban regions, where Imentet's associations are strongest.

The New Kingdom: This is the peak of her visual representation, especially in the Valley of the Kings and Queens (Thebes). Imentet appears regularly in tomb paintings and funerary papyri as a welcome of the dead and guardian of the western necropolis. She is sometimes shown emerging from the Tree of Life, offering sustenance. She may be syncretised with Hathor or Isis in Theban traditions at this time.

The Third Intermediate and Late Periods: Imentet continues to appear in funerary art, though less prominent than during the New Kingdom. There is decreasing religious innovation and more standardised religious practices. Imentet's role is largely subsumed under Hathor and Isis in funerary religion.

The Ptolemaic and Roman Periods: Imentet still appears sporadically in funerary contexts, especially in tombs that retain traditional Egyptian beliefs. Greek and Roman influence leads to the Hellenisation of Egyptian deities, and Imentet fades further as a distinct identity. Her image or role is occasionally preserved in conservative priestly traditions or local necropolis rituals.

The Byzantine Period: Worship of all traditional Egyptian deities declines rapidly with the rise of Christianity in Egypt. Imentet, as a minor and primarily symbolic goddess, disappears entirely from religious practice. She remains only in archaeological, artistic, and textual records.

As a goddess welcoming the dead, Imentet is comparable to the Greek / Roman goddess Hekate / Trivia or Persephone / Proserpina, who guides or receives souls into the afterlife, connected with transition and the underworld. As a personification of the western horizon, sunset, and death, she is comparable with Nyx / Nox and Thanatos / Mors. As a symbol of life after death and regeneration, she is comparable with Demeter / Ceres as part of the Persephone / Proserpina cycle. People could pray to Imentet for a safe and guided passage into the afterlife, spiritual sustenance, renewal, and eternal life.

Imhotep: God of Wisdom and Medicine

Imhotep is a god of architecture, construction, craftsmanship, healing, knowledge, magic, mediation, medicine, prophecy, rational thought, revelation, sacred geometry, scholarly learning, science, scribes, temple building, wisdom, and writing. He was originally a mortal human being who served as chancellor to the pharaoh Djoser in the 3rd Dynasty during the Old Kingdom. He designed the first known pyramid, the Step Pyramid of Saqqara (also known as the Pyramid of Djoser[178]). In the following 3,000 years after his death, he was gradually glorified and deified.

His name means 'He who Comes in Peace'[179], or 'The One who Comes with Peace'. He is also referred to as 'Son of Ptah'[180], 'Great of Magic', 'Lord of Healing', 'Prince of Peace', 'He Who Has Come with Peace', and 'Healer of Every Disease'. He heals the sick, inspires wisdom and knowledge, protects and guides builders and architects, acts as a divine mediator between humans and other gods, channels and controls magic, and guides righteous leadership and ethics.

Left: Three variations of 'Imhotep' in hieroglyphs

He is often invoked alongside Thoth, a god of wisdom, writing, knowledge, and medicine. He is also syncretised with the Greek deified mortal Asclepius[181] (Roman: Vejovis), and they were jointly worshipped in healing temples. He is also occasionally associated with Nefertem, the youthful son of Ptah and Sekhmet who is a god of healing and regeneration.

Imhotep is traditionally depicted in human form, never with the head of an animal like other gods. He is usually seated on a low stool or block. He wears a simple, tight-fitting robe (like a priest or a scholar). His hair is shaven or closely cropped (typical of scribes or priests). He has a papyrus scroll or an open tablet resting on his knees. His expression is calm, serious, and wise. Sometimes he is wearing a cap or skullcap, but usually bareheaded. He sometimes wears the short stylised beard of a nobleman or deity.

Imhotep was worshipped at the Saqqara Necropolis near Memphis. He was also worshipped alongside another deified mortal, Amenhotep son of Hapu[182] [183], at Deir el-Bahari (Thebes) on the

---

[178] Kemp, B.J. (2005). Ancient Egypt. Routledge. p. 159.
[179] Ranke, Hermann (1935). Die Ägyptischen Personennamen [Egyptian Personal Names] (PDF) (in German). Vol. 1: Verzeichnis der Namen. Glückstadt: J. J. Augustin. p. 9. Retrieved 24 July 2020.
[180] Lichtheim, M. (1980). Ancient Egyptian Literature. The University of California Press. ISBN 0-520-04020-1.
[181] Pinch, Geraldine (2002). Handbook of Egyptian Mythology. World Mythology. Santa Barbara, CA: ABC-Clio. ISBN 9781576072424. OCLC 52716451.
[182] Boylan, Patrick (1922). Thoth or the Hermes of Egypt: A study of some aspects of theological thought in ancient Egypt. Oxford University Press. pp. 166–168.
[183] Lichtheim, M. (1980). Ancient Egyptian Literature. The University of California Press. ISBN 0-520-04020-1.

West Bank of the Nile across from Luxor in Upper Egypt. He was worshipped alongside the Greek god Asclepius[184] at Philae Island, a major Greco-Roman religious complex.

Imhotep, Wikipedia Creative Commons, Public Domain

The Old Kingdom: Imhotep is a living historical figure, chancellor and high priest of Heliopolis under Pharaoh Djoser (3rd Dynasty). He designs the Step Pyramid at Saqqara. He is respected as a brilliant court official and a genius.

The Middle Kingdom: Imhotep's reputation as a wise man begins to grow. He is remembered in literary texts and proverbs. He is mentioned as a symbol of wisdom and knowledge.

The New Kingdom: He begins to be venerated alongside Amenhotep son of Hapu, another deified wise man. Statues and stelae (inscribed stone or wooden slabs) show offerings made to him. He is mentioned in temple inscriptions as a wise man and a healer[185] [186]. He is an honoured figure of cultic respect; proto-deification begins.

The Third Intermediate Period: There are growing local cults of Imhotep, especially in Memphis (Saqqara) and Thebes. He is viewed as a protector of the sick, and invoked in healing contexts. He is semi-divine, and popular with healers and priests[187].

The Late Period: Imhotep is fully deified and worshipped as a god of healing, wisdom, and architecture. Major cult centres are established at Saqqara, Deir al-Bahari, and the temple of the syncretic Greco-Roman god Serapis. He appears in inscriptions as 'Son of Ptah', and 'He Who Heals'. Pilgrims leave votive offerings and sleep in temples seeking healing dreams. He is fully divine and worshipped nationwide as a healing god.

The Ptolemaic Period: Imhotep is syncretised with the Greek god Asclepius (Roman: Vejovis). He is worshipped in Greek-Egyptian healing sanctuaries (e.g. Philae Island and Alexandria). He is seen as a universal healer, invoked by both Egyptians and Greeks. Dream healing (incubation) becomes common at his temples. He is a major healing deity of both Egyptian and Hellenistic religion.

The Roman Period: His worship continues, particularly in Upper Egypt. Roman-era texts and inscriptions still refer to him as a healer. He is revered in the context of Greco-Roman temple religion.

The Byzantine Period: Worship of Imhotep (and all Egyptian gods) ends with the rise of Christianity. Temples are closed, and cults are suppressed. Imhotep's legacy survives in memory, remembered in history and later in legend.

As a deified mortal of medicine and healing, Imhotep is comparable to the Greek / Roman god Asclepius / Aesculapius / Vejovis, also a god of medicine and healing, whose temples served as hospitals. As a god of wisdom, intellect, and invention, he is comparable to Hermes / Mercury, and the syncretised Thoth-Hermes Trismegistus. People could pray to Imhotep for healing of the body and mind, wisdom and creative inspiration, success in studies or design, peace, harmony, and protection.

---

[184] Allen, James Peter (2005). The Art of Medicine in Ancient Egypt. Yale University Press. p. 12. ISBN 9780300107289. Retrieved 17 August 2016.
[185] Baud, M. (2002). Djéser et la IIIe dynastie [Djoser and the Third Dynasty] (in French). p. 125.
[186] Wildung, D. (1977). Egyptian Saints: Deification in pharaonic Egypt. New York University Press. p. 34. ISBN 978-0-8147-9169-1.
[187] Hurry, Jamieson B. (2014) [1926]. Imhotep: The Egyptian god of medicine (reprint ed.). Oxford, UK: Traffic Output. pp. 47–48. ISBN 978-0-404-13285-9.

Isis: Goddess of Magic, Protection, and Healing

Left: Two variations of 'Isis' in hieroglyphs

Isis is a goddess of magic, healing, motherhood, fertility, protection, queenship, marriage, nature, the throne, the dead, resurrection, wisdom, divination, and the moon. Her name means 'She of the Throne' or simply 'Throne'. She is the most powerful magician among the gods. She uses her magic to protect her son Horus, healing him when he is harmed by scorpions or snakes. She protects the living and the dead, the vulnerable and the oppressed, and women and children. She also guards the pharaoh and supports his divine right to rule. She guides souls to the afterlife and has the power to heal the sick and bring the dead back to life[188], including her husband Osiris. In later times, under Greek and Roman influence, Isis becomes a cosmic goddess who rules the heavens, earth, and underworld, with power over fate, the stars, the seas, and even time itself.

In the Osiris Myth[189], her husband Osiris is murdered and dismembered by his jealous brother Set, and Isis searches all over Egypt to find his body parts. Using her magic and wisdom she puts him back together and becomes the first to mummify a body[190]. She then uses her magic to bring Osiris back to life for a short time, during which they conceive their son, Horus. Osiris becomes the ruler of the underworld[191] while Isis raises Horus in secret to keep him safe from Set. In time, Horus defeats Set and becomes the rightful king of Egypt, completing the cycle of divine kingship.

In the Tale of Isis and the Name of Ra, Isis wants to gain more power and knowledge, especially the secret name of Ra, the sun god. She creates a magical serpent that bites Ra, making him weak. Isis offers to heal him, but only if he tells her his true name, which holds great cosmic power. Ra is forced to give in, and by learning his secret name, Isis becomes the most powerful magician among the gods. Isis is associated with Hathor, as both goddesses are associated with motherhood, love, fertility, and music. In many temples, Isis takes on the role and titles of Hathor, particularly in depictions of Isis as a mother and protector. Isis is sometimes called 'Isis-Hathor', especially in Ptolemaic temples like Philae Island.

---

[188] Assmann, Jan (2005) [German edition 2001]. Death and Salvation in Ancient Egypt. Translated by David Lorton. Cornell University Press. ISBN 978-0-8014-4241-4.
[189] Wilkinson, Richard H. (2003). The Complete Gods and Goddesses of Ancient Egypt. Thames & Hudson. ISBN 978-0-500-05120-7.
[190] Pinch, Geraldine (2002). Egyptian Mythology: A Guide to the Gods, Goddesses, and Traditions of Ancient Egypt. Oxford University Press. ISBN 978-0-19-517024-5.
[191] Assmann, Jan (2001) [German edition 1984]. The Search for God in Ancient Egypt. Translated by David Lorton. Cornell University Press. ISBN 978-0-8014-3786-1.

Isis is usually shown as a woman wearing a throne-shaped crown. She can also have cow horns with a sun disk on her head. Sometimes, she is seen nursing baby Horus or with large outstretched wings. She often holds an ankh and a was-sceptre. In Greek and Roman times, she is shown in flowing robes, holding a sistrum, a situla, a steering rudder, or a cornucopia (a 'horn of plenty' representing abundance). The most famous temple of Isis is on Philae Island. It is an important religious centre during Ptolemaic and Roman times and was the last ancient Egyptian temple used up until the 6th century CE.

Isis, Wikipedia Creative Commons, Public Domain

The Old Kingdom: The earliest mentions of Isis appear in the Pyramid Texts[192] as a mourner of Osiris, a divine mother, and a protector of the pharaoh.

The Middle Kingdom: In the Coffin Texts, Isis becomes more important in magic and religion. Her roles as a mother and protector grow stronger. There are still no temples dedicated to her at this time, but she appears more often in tombs and magical spells.

The New Kingdom: Isis becomes widely worshipped by both the Egyptian elite and the common people. In the Book of the Dead, she appears as a guide and protector of the soul in the afterlife. She is often shown nursing her son Horus. Her worship also spreads to Nubia and other lands under Egyptian control.

The Third Intermediate Period: Her cult remains strong, especially at Abydos, where she is closely connected with Osiris. Greater emphasis is placed on her magical abilities. She also begins to merge with other goddesses such as Hathor..

The Late Period: The rise of formal temples to Isis begins. The temple at Behbeit el-Hagar in the Nile Delta is built. Isis's independent cult becomes prominent, not just as a consort to Osiris.

The Ptolemaic Period: Under Greek rule, Isis's worship explodes in popularity. A major temple is built at Philae Island, which becomes the centre of her cult. Isis becomes a cosmic mother and ruler of the universe. Her cult spreads through the eastern Mediterranean (e.g. Delos, Rhodes, Athens, etc.).

The Roman and Byzantine Periods: The Cult of Isis spreads throughout the Roman Empire, with temples built in cities like Pompeii, Rome, Paris, and London. Isis becomes part of Roman mystery religions and is worshipped as Isis-Panthea, meaning 'Isis of All Gods'. In 394 CE, Emperor Theodosius I officially closes the Temple of Isis at Philae Island. Worship of Isis fades as Christianity replaces pagan religion across Egypt and the Roman world.

Isis shares attributes with several Greek / Roman goddesses like Demeter / Ceres (motherhood and farming), Aphrodite / Venus (love and fertility), Artemis / Diana (protector of women and children), Tyche / Fortuna (luck and fate), and Cybele / Magna Mater (great mother goddess)[193]. People could pray to Isis for protection, healing, safety, fertility, childbirth, family well-being, resurrection, eternal life, divine justice and royal favour, guidance, salvation, and inner strength.

---

[192] Pinch, Geraldine (2002). Egyptian Mythology: A Guide to the Gods, Goddesses, and Traditions of Ancient Egypt. Oxford University Press. ISBN 978-0-19-517024-5.
[193] Dunand, Françoise; Zivie-Coche, Christiane (2004) [French edition 1991]. Gods and Men in Egypt: 3000 BCE to 395 CE. Translated by David Lorton. Cornell University Press. ISBN 978-0-8014-8853-5.

Kauket: Primordial Goddess of Darkness

Left: 'Kauket' in hieroglyphs

Kauket is a goddess of darkness, night, primordial chaos, the unknown, and the hidden forces before creation[194]. She is a key figure in the Ogdoad. As the female counterpart to Kek, the male force of night, she embodies the unseen, the quiet void, and the transitional state between nonexistence and creation. Her name derives from the ancient Egyptian root '*kk*', meaning darkness or obscurity. The feminine suffix '-*et*' or '-*it*' denotes her gender. Therefore, Kauket roughly translates to "the Dark One (feminine)" or "She of Darkness". She is also referred to as the 'riser up of the night' and 'the bringer in of the night'[195].

Kauket serves a cosmic, symbolic function. She does not act as a character in mythological narratives but instead embodies the concept of primordial night. Her presence is essential to Egyptian creation mythology, as she helps maintain the cycle of day and night and the hidden structure of the universe. She is sometimes symbolically involved in the sun god Ra's nightly journey through the underworld, as the concealing darkness before dawn. Her qualities of darkness, the unseen, and transformation align loosely with other goddesses who have associations with the underworld or mystery. However, no official syncretism or merging with other deities is attested in texts.

Kauket is depicted in various symbolic forms: as a woman, either standing or striding in profile, as a frog-headed woman (like her male counterpart Kek, who is sometimes shown with a frog's head), or as a serpent or serpent-headed woman[196], another common form for Ogdoad deities. In temple art, she is sometimes shown in paired reliefs with Kek, both representing dual aspects of darkness. She is also depicted in stylised cosmic or watery environments, often linked to the primordial flood. Kauket's primary centre of reverence was Hermopolis (*Khmunu*), the intellectual and theological centre of the Ogdoad creation myth. Priests and scholars honour the eight deities as symbolic forces in temple rituals and cosmological teachings. Unlike major deities with active cults and temples, Kauket had no individual cult or widespread worship outside Hermopolis.

The Pre-Dynastic Period: The roots of primordial cosmology and dual concepts such as darkness and chaos are likely to have developed during this period, laying the groundwork for later Ogdoad theology. There is no direct evidence of Kauket yet, but early religious ideas about night and chaos evolve.

---

[194] Ferris, C. (2024, June 25). Kauket: Egyptian Deity Of Darkness And Chaos. Retrieved July 4, 2025, from https://mysteryinhistory.com/kauket/
[195] Hill, J. (n.d.). Kauket. Retrieved July 4, 2025, from https://ancientegyptonline.co.uk/kuaket/
[196] Ferris, C. (2024, June 25).

Kauket, Wikipedia Creative Commons, Public Domain

The Early Dynastic Period: Foundational religious ideas are taking shape, but Kauket is not yet directly referenced in any known records at this time.

The Old Kingdom: There are early references to primordial forces appearing in Pyramid Texts (the oldest religious texts), including abstract concepts linked to darkness and the underworld. The formal concept of the Ogdoad, including Kauket, begins to emerge in religious thought, though she is not yet prominently depicted.

The First Intermediate Period: Religious decentralisation limits available evidence, but localised theological development in Hermopolis is likely to have continued.

The Middle Kingdom: There is increased textual evidence of the Ogdoad appearing in Coffin Texts and funerary literature. Kauket, as part of the Ogdoad, is referenced symbolically in cosmological contexts related to creation myths and the journey through the underworld. Hermopolis (Khmunu) rises as a significant religious centre where the Ogdoad is venerated.

The Second Intermediate Period: Foreign influence and political fragmentation limit religious expansion, but existing Hermopolitan theology, including Kauket's role, persists.

The New Kingdom: The Ogdoad, including Kauket, features more prominently in temple inscriptions and cosmological texts, especially in Hermopolis and in temples devoted to Thoth and creation. Artistic depictions of Kauket appear occasionally, often alongside Kek, in temple reliefs and religious iconography.

The Third Intermediate Period: Local priesthoods maintain traditional theologies. While Kauket is not prominent, references to the Ogdoad continue in theological writings.

The Late Period: There is continued reverence for the Ogdoad deities in religious texts and temple rituals, though emphasis begins to shift toward more popular gods like Isis, Osiris, and Amun. Kauket remains a symbolic figure within Hermopolitan theology and creation narratives.

The Ptolemaic Period: Egyptian religious traditions, including the Ogdoad, persist alongside Hellenistic influences. Kauket and the Ogdoad are still acknowledged in temple art and writings, particularly in Hermopolis, though largely as part of ancient cosmology rather than active popular worship.

The Roman and Byzantine Periods: Kauket and the Ogdoad retain symbolic significance in a limited capacity. The rise of Greco-Roman religious systems leads to the decline of traditional Egyptian theology. With the spread of Christianity and the closing of Egyptian temples, the worship and knowledge of Kauket fades, surviving only in archaeological and written records.

Kauket is perhaps comparable to the Greek / Roman goddess Nyx / Nox, the goddess and personification of the night, or Erebus, the god and personification of deep darkness. Kauket is more abstract and primordial, and therefore would not be prayed to in the same way other goddesses might be. However, she could be invoked and acknowledged for her role in creation, cosmic balance, transitions, hidden potential, the darkness before the light, and cyclical renewal.

Kek: Primordial God of Darkness

Kek is a god of darkness[197], chaos, primordial night, obscurity, the void, time before creation, transition, the darkness before the dawn, and unseen forces. His name comes from the ancient Egyptian root 'kk' or 'k3k', which is closely associated with darkness[198] or the absence of light, and means 'Darkness' or 'The Dark One'.

He is also referred to as 'Bringer-in-of-the-Light', 'Raiser-up-of-the-Light'[199], 'The Darkness That Precedes the Light', 'He Who Dwells in the Shadow', 'Lord of the Hours of the Night', 'The Hidden One of the Night', 'He Who Opens the Dawn', 'The Unknown', or 'The Unseeable One'.

He plays a specific role in Egyptian cosmology, particularly in the Ogdoad. He personifies primordial darkness, the state of total obscurity and non-existence before creation. He is the darkness before the dawn, representing the mystery and uncertainty that exists before the ordered world. His female counterpart is Kauket[200] [201] with whom he shares the male / female aspects of cosmic darkness.

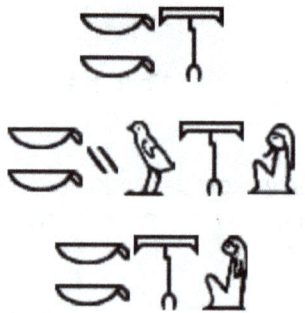

Left: Three variations of 'Kauket' in hieroglyphs

Although he is associated with darkness, he also assists in guiding the solar barque of Ra through the underworld during the night, helping Ra to emerge at dawn. Kek acts as a liminal or boundary force that exists in a state of in-betweenness, facilitating transformation from night to day, from chaos to order.

Though not directly allied, Kek and Apophis (Apep) both represent aspects of chaos and darkness, but they are very different in character: Apep is the embodiment of malicious chaos and an enemy of Ra. Kek represents primordial darkness in a neutral or even constructive role, necessary for creation.

In earlier or more symbolic contexts, Kek is depicted as a human man, wearing a nemes headdress, a double-plumed crown, holding a was-sceptre, and holding an ankh. In later periods, Kek is depicted with as a man with the head of a frog, wearing a shendyt (kilt). When depicted as part of the Ogdoad, the male gods have the head of a frog, whereas the female goddesses have the head of a serpent[202]. Frogs were abundant after the annual flooding of the Nile, and were associated with birth, life emerging from the waters, creation, fertility, and transformation.

---

[197] Hornung, E. (1965). "Licht und Finsternis in der Vorstellungswelt Altägyptens". Studium Generale. 8: 72–83.
[198] Budge, E. A. Wallis (1904a). The Gods of the Egyptians: Or, Studies in Egyptian Mythology. Vol. 1. Methuen & Co. pp. 241, 283–286.
[199] Budge, E. A. Wallis (1904a).
[200] Budge, E. A. Wallis (1904a).
[201] Steindorff, Georg (1905). The Religion of the Ancient Egyptians. G. P. Putnam's Sons. p. 50.
[202] Smith, Mark (2002), On the Primaeval Ocean, p. 38

Kek's primary centre of worship is Hermopolis, the intellectual and theological centre of the Ogdoad creation myth. Priests and scholars honour the eight deities as symbolic forces in temple rituals and cosmological teachings. Unlike major deities with active cults and temples, Kek had no individual cult or widespread worship outside of Hermopolis.

Kek, Wikipedia Creative Commons, Public Domain

The Pre-Dynastic Period: There are no known references to Kek at this point. Religious focus was local and animistic (all things have a spiritual essence and agency). The concept of primordial chaos exists, but the Ogdoad system had not yet fully emerged.

The Old Kingdom: Kek is not directly attested by name in this period. However, ideas of primordial darkness and creation emerging from chaos begin to appear in pyramid texts in the context of Nu and cosmic waters.

The Middle Kingdom: The first clear references to Kek emerge as part of the Odgoad. He is found in Coffin Texts and in spells in the Book of the Dead. He is associated with primordial darkness, duality, and cosmic transition from night to dawn. There are no temples dedicated to Kek, but he is included in temple mythology, especially in Hermopolis (Ashmunein) and in cosmological writings.

The Third Intermediate Period: Worship of Kek continues as part of esoteric cosmology in priestly and temple contexts. He is seen in ritual texts, solar hymns, and books about the underworld. The Ogdoad remains a symbolic system, not a living cult.

The Late Period: Kek appears more frequently in religious texts and tomb decorations, often depicted as a frog-headed man. There is greater theological interest in cosmic origins and Neoplatonic style dualities, which boosts interest in Ogdoad deities like Kek. There are some occasional artistic representations of Kek and Kauket in this period.

The Ptolemaic Period: Under Greek rule, Egyptian theology becomes more systematised and preserved. Kek is still part of the Hermopolitan cosmology and appears in temple inscriptions (e.g. at Esna and Dendera). He is often shown as part of paired male-female deities.

The Roman Period: Kek continues to appear in temple art and late magical texts (e.g. Greco-Egyptian papyri). Some syncretic interpretations emerge, but Kek is not widely worshipped as an individual god. Interest in primordial forces aligns with Hellenistic mystical traditions.

As the personification of darkness and the primordial void, Kek is comparable to the Greek / Roman god Erebus / Scotus. As a symbol of the darkness before the dawn giving way to light, he is comparable to Nyx / Nox giving way to Hemera / Dies, the goddess of the day, or Eos / Aurora, the light of the dawn. As the unformed void that precedes creation, he is comparable to Chaos. As a symbol of transformation and emergence from nothingness, he is comparable to Phanes or Eros Protogonos, born from darkness as the first light.

Kek is more of a cosmic principle than an anthropomorphised god, he is not worshipped in the same way as other gods. However, priests, magicians, and theologians could invoke him in rituals concerning rebirth, renewal, the return of light after darkness, and the transformation from chaos to order.

Khepri: Scarab-Headed God of the Morning Sun

Left: 'Khepri' in hieroglyphs

Khepri is a god of the rising sun, creation, renewal, and resurrection. He embodies the concept of the sun reborn each dawn and the self-creating principle of life[203]. His name derives from the verb '$ḫpr$', meaning 'to develop', 'to become', or 'to come into being'[204] [205]. He is often referred to as the 'Emerging One', 'The Being', or 'The Extant'. Each day Khepri pushes or rolls the sun across the horizon, paralleling a scarab beetle rolling its dung ball. This action symbolises the sun's resurrection, the eternal cycle of life, and the transition from darkness to light. He also functions as a self-created creator god, sometimes credited with bringing forth the first gods.

While no standalone myth centres on Khepri, cosmological texts such as the Pyramid Texts, Book of the Dead, and Amduat depict him guiding Ra's barque through the underworld: in the final hours of the Amduat (the journey that Ra takes from the time the sun sets in the west and then rises in the east) he helms the solar barque emerging into dawn[206] [207]. He is regarded as an aspect of Ra (i.e. the morning sun) and is connected to Atum (the evening sun). In later symbolism, Khepri is sometimes merged with Osiris to emphasise resurrection themes. Khepri is variously depicted as a scarab beetle, often pushing a solar disk, a man with a scarab head, holding a was-scepter and an ankh[208], a ram's head on a beetle's body, or wearing the Atef crown, blending solar and underworld symbolism. Though no temples are dedicated solely to him, Khepri was honoured in Heliopolis[209], the major centre of solar worship. Scarabs and statues appear in most temples, and archaeological evidence shows widespread use of heart-scarab amulets.

The Pre-Dynastic Period: While there is no direct mention of Khepri by name, early reverence for the scarab beetle (dung beetle) is evident. Scarab-shaped amulets and imagery begin appearing in burials, connected to solar and rebirth symbolism that would later be embodied by Khepri.

---

[203] van Ryneveld, Maria M. The Presence and Significance of Khepri in Egyptian Religion and Art, University of Pretoria (South Africa), Ann Arbor, 1992. ProQuest 304016142.
[204] Wilkinson, Richard H. (2003). The Complete Gods and Goddesses of Ancient Egypt. Thames & Hudson. pp. 230–233
[205] Liszka, Kate. "Scarab Amulets in the Egyptian Collection of the Princeton University Art Museum". Record of the Art Museum, Princeton University, vol. 74, 2015, pp. 4–19. JSTOR, www.jstor.org/stable/26388759. Accessed 1 Dec. 2020
[206] Hornung, Erik; Baines, John (1996). Conceptions of God in Ancient Egypt: The One and the Many. Ithaca, N.Y: Cornell University Press, pp. 155-156. ISBN 978-0-8014-8384-4.
[207] Schweizer, Andreas; Lorton, David; Hornung, Erik (2010). The Sungod's Journey Through the Netherworld: Reading the Ancient Egyptian Amduat. Ithaca, N.Y: Cornell University Press, pp. 19-20. ISBN 978-0-8014-4875-1.
[208] Studies in Aegean Art and Culture: A New York Aegean Bronze Age Colloquium in Memory of Ellen N. Davis. INSTAP Academic Press. 2016. doi:10.2307/j.ctt1kk66gk. ISBN 978-1-931534-86-4. JSTOR j.ctt1kk66gk.
[209] van Ryneveld, Maria M. 1992.

The Early Dynastic Period: Religious concepts around solar deities begin forming, especially in Heliopolis, a major cult centre of sun worship. Khepri is not yet firmly attested but may have existed in proto-forms or as a conceptual aspect of solar emergence.

Khepri, Wikipedia Creative Commons, Public Domain

The Old Kingdom: Khepri first appears in written texts, particularly the Pyramid Texts, as a form of the sun god associated with rebirth and morning light. Depicted as a scarab-headed man, Khepri becomes part of the solar triad: Khepri (the morning sun), Ra (the midday sun), and Atum (the setting sun).

The First Intermediate Period: Political fragmentation leads to reduced state-sponsored religious activity, but local devotion to solar forms like Khepri continues. Scarab amulets remain in use in elite burials, suggesting a sustained symbolic value.

The Middle Kingdom: Khepri's role as a creator and solar god is solidified in religious literature such as the Coffin Texts. Scarabs become extremely popular as amulets, seals, and funerary tokens, symbolising protection, rebirth, and the sun's daily renewal. The scarab becomes a widespread magical emblem across social classes.

The Second Intermediate Period: Even under Hyksos rule in parts of Egypt, Khepri's imagery continues, especially in amulet production, showing continued belief in Khepri's protective powers.

The New Kingdom: Khepri appears prominently in funerary texts such as the Amduat, the Book of the Dead, and the Book of Gates. He is depicted steering the solar barque through the underworld before sunrise. There is widespread use of heart-scarab amulets in burials (especially from the 18th Dynasty onward). He is incorporated into solar cults alongside Ra and Amun-Ra in state temples.

The Third Intermediate Period: Khepri has continued presence in priestly traditions and temple inscriptions. Scarab iconography remains a key funerary and magical motif. Khepri retains relevance, although overshadowed by political instability and localised religious centres.

The Late Period: Renewed interest in older traditions sees Khepri featured in temple inscriptions, especially at Esna and Edfu. Baboons and solar disks linked to Khepri appear in temple art.

The Ptolemaic Period: Khepri is included in temple reliefs and sacred texts written in Demotic and hieroglyphs, as part of traditional Egyptian religion maintained under Greek rule. There is continued fusion with solar deities, and strong emphasis on resurrection motifs in temple and tomb art.

The Roman and Byzantine Periods: Khepri is still depicted in funerary materials. The scarab motif remains common in Roman-Egyptian jewellery and grave goods. With the rise of Christianity and the closure of pagan temples, public worship of Khepri ends. His image survives only in archaeological artefacts, such as scarab amulets and temple carvings.

Khepri is comparable to the Greek / Roman god Helios / Sol (the sun's daily rebirth), Apollo (light, vitality, and creative force), and Phanes / Protogonos (emergence of life from primordial darkness). He could be prayed to for rebirth, renewal, new beginnings, transformation, creative energy, resurrection in the afterlife, strength, and perseverance.

Khnum: The Divine Potter

Left: 'Khnum' in hieroglyphs

Khnum is a creator god and a fertility deity, closely associated with the waters of the Nile and the formative underworld waters that give life and clay. His name stems from the verb '*khnem,*' meaning 'to mould', 'to unite', or 'build', and may also echo the word for 'spring' or 'source'. He is often called the 'Divine Potter', 'Father of Fathers and Mother of Mothers', and in later forms, Khnum-Ra. Khnum fashions human souls and bodies on his potter's wheel, moulding clay into newborns and even other deities, and bestows their vital spirit ('*ka*'). He also regulates the Nile's flood, ensuring fertility of the land.

In the Famine Stela (an inscription written in hieroglyphs located on Sehel Island, Third Dynasty, Djoser)[210], Khnum appears in a vision to Imhotep, promising to end a seven-year drought once his temple is restored. In the Westcar Papyrus (Second Intermediate Period) he blesses the birth and health of future pharaohs. In some traditions, he is merged with Ra as Khnum-Ra or considered an agent of Ptah in fashioning life. He is also one of the Elephantine Triad, along with Satis and Anuket, goddesses of the Nile and fertility. In Esna[211][212], he is linked with goddesses Neith, Menhit, or Nebtu, and is sometimes associated with Heka or even Osiris, reflecting his roles in magic and death.

Khnum is depicted as a ram-headed man or full ram, with horns that evolve from corkscrew to curved (like later depictions of Amun). He is frequently shown at a potter's wheel, moulding humans or gods[213][214][215]. He is occasionally shown wearing the Atef crown or the Hedjet crown[216][217], holding a was-sceptre, ankh, or a situla. He is also rarely shown in four-headed form (Sheft-hat) merging aspects of Ra, Shu, Geb, and Osiris. The primary and oldest cult centre of Khnum is at Elephantine Island, located at the first cataract where ancient Egyptians believe the Nile begins. He is referred to there as 'Lord of the Cataract', the guardian of the Nile's source. In Esna (Latopolis), the Temple of Khnum includes rich inscriptions and detailed ceilings referencing Khnum's role in creation, magic, and

---

[210] Miriam Lichtheim: Ancient Egyptian Literature: The Late Period. University of California Press, Berkeley 2006, ISBN 0-520-24844-9, page 94-100.
[211] Redford, Donald B. (2001). "Khnum". The Oxford Encyclopedia of Ancient Egypt. Oxford University Press. ISBN 9780195102345.
[212] Hallof, Jochen (2011-10-27). "Esna" (PDF). UCLA Encyclopedia of Egyptology. 1602 (1). Los Angeles: UCLA: 1–15.
[213] Velde, H. te (1980). "A Few Remarks upon the Religious Significance of Animals in Ancient Egypt". Numen. 27 (1): 76–82. doi:10.2307/3269982. ISSN 0029-5973. JSTOR 3269982.
[214] Hart, George (2005). The Routledge dictionary of Egyptian gods and goddesses (2 ed.). London: Routledge. ISBN 978-0-415-36116-3.
[215] Pinch, Geraldine (2004). Egyptian Mythology: A Guide to the Gods, Goddesses, and Traditions of ancient Egypt. USA: Oxford University Press
[216] Ali, Mona Ezz (2020). "God Heryshef" (PDF). Journal of Association of Arab Universities for Tourism and Hospitality. 18 (2): 27.
[217] Treasure, Matthew (2021-01-31). ""Four Faces on One Neck": The Tetracephalic Ram as an Iconographic Form in the Late New Kingdom". Theses and Dissertations.

divine kingship. Khnum was also worshipped at Memphis and Heliopolis in syncretic forms, and acknowledged in major theological centres as part of creation myths.

Khnum, Wikipedia Creative Commons, Public Domain

The Pre-Dynastic Period: There are no direct references to Khnum by name. Ram symbolism linked to virility and strength begins appearing in early iconography, laying the groundwork for Khnum's later form. Proto-forms of Nile-related deities may have existed in southern Upper Egypt, especially near the First Cataract.

The Early Dynastic Period: Elephantine Island becomes an early cult centre for Khnum. He emerges as a guardian of the Nile's source and is venerated alongside local water deities Satis and Anuket.

The Old Kingdom: Khnum is increasingly incorporated into royal theology. The Famine Stela (although inscribed later) attributes a myth to this period: Khnum halts a drought during Djoser's reign in exchange for temple restoration. He is revered as a creator god, fashioning humans and gods on a potter's wheel.

The Middle Kingdom: Khnum's identity as a divine potter is emphasised. He is featured in the Westcar Papyrus, where he blesses royal births. His cult gains increased prominence in funerary practices and temple inscriptions.

The New Kingdom: Khnum is honoured in major temple complexes and royal theology. He appears in divine birth scenes (e.g., in the mortuary temple of Hatshepsut), where he forms the pharaoh on his wheel. He is commonly shown in the Book of the Dead and other religious texts as a creator and a fertility god. Worship at Elephantine Island and Esna expands.

The Late Period: There is a revival of traditional religion and temple building, which includes construction and restoration of Khnum temples at Esna. Ram-headed imagery becomes even more symbolic of divine power and creation.

The Ptolemaic Period: The Temple of Khnum at Esna is expanded and richly decorated. Khnum is revered in syncretic forms, such as Khnum-Ra, merging his creative power with solar theology. There is a continued emphasis on his role in royal legitimacy, creation myths, and Nile flooding.

The Roman Period: The worship of Khnum continues under Roman rule. Emperors depict themselves making offerings to Khnum in temple reliefs[218]. Religious imagery and rituals associated with Khnum remain state-sanctioned. Temples at Esna and Elephantine Island remain active religious centres.

The Byzantine Period: The Christianisation of Egypt leads to the decline of Khnum's cult. Pagan temples are closed or re-purposed. Khnum's public worship ends. His legacy survives in inscriptions, architecture, and amulets.

Khnum is comparable to the Greek / Roman god Prometheus, who in some traditions created humans out of clay. People could pray to Khnum for fertility, conception, safe childbirth, abundant Nile floods, agricultural prosperity, skill and inspiration in craftsmanship, spiritual rebirth, and renewal in the afterlife.

---

[218] Wilkinson, Richard H. The Complete Temples of Ancient Egypt. Thames and Hudson. ISBN 0-500-05100-3

Khonsu: God of the Moon

Left: 'Khonsu' in hieroglyphs

Khonsu is a moon god and a deity of time, healing, protection, fertility, and navigation across the night sky. His name means 'traveller' or 'wanderer', evoking the moon's nightly journey across the heavens. He is also referred to as 'Khonsu-neferhotep' ('Khonsu, Lord of *Ma'at* in Karnak'), 'Khonsu pa-khered' ('Khonsu the Child'), and 'Khonsu heseb-ahau' ('Khonsu, Decider of the Lifespan').

Khonsu guides the lunar barque, marks the passage of time, heals the sick, protects travellers, influences fertility, and enforces rebirth and cosmic order. He is also associated with baboons[219]. In the Old Kingdom Pyramid Texts, Khonsu appears in the Cannibal Hymn, wielding fierce power to aid the deceased king. In the Bentresh Stela, he heals a princess in foreign lands. A lunar myth credits him with adding five extra days to the calendar so Nut could bear her children.

Khonsu is part of the Theban Triad (son of Amun and Mut). He is linked with Thoth[220] (as 'Khonsu-Djehuti'), Ra, Shu, Min, Horus, and Osiris in different contexts. He is variously depicted as a mummiform youth with a sidelock, curved beard, and lunar disk above a crescent. He is sometimes depicted as a falcon-headed god with lunar symbols[221]. He is occasionally shown with crook, flail, was-sceptre, djed staff, or playing senet (board game) with Thoth. Khonsu was mainly worshipped at Karnak (Thebes) at a major temple constructed under Ramesses III and expanded during the Ptolemaic dynasty. Khonsu was also worshipped as part of the Theban Triad with Amun and Mut. He has additional cult sites in Memphis, Hibis (Dakhla Oasis), and Edfu[222].

The Pre-Dynastic Period: There is no direct evidence of Khonsu's worship in this period. However, lunar symbolism and the cultic importance of celestial cycles (especially the moon) are emerging, laying conceptual groundwork for future lunar deities like Khonsu.

The Early Dynastic Period: Khonsu does not yet appear as a fully formed deity. Lunar deities exist in localised or proto-forms, but Khonsu's name and role has not yet solidified.

The Old Kingdom: One of the earliest references to Khonsu is found in the Pyramid Texts, specifically the Cannibal Hymn, where he is portrayed as a fierce and powerful being capable of

---

[219] "Khonsu | Egyptian Moon God, Mythology, & Depiction | Britannica". www.britannica.com. Retrieved 2024-12-04.
[220] Goyon, Jean-Claude (2013).Thèbes : Khonsou, Thot et la monarchie pharaonique après la Troisième Période de Transition. La fête de Thot du 19 du premier mois de l'année et les rites de confirmation du pouvoir royal à Karnak, Edfou et Philean.In Thiers, Christophe (ed.). Documents de Théologies Thébaines Tardives. Université Paul Valéry.p.40.
[221] Redford, Donald B., ed. (2003). The Oxford Guide: Essential Guide to Egyptian Mythology. Berkley. pp. 186–187. ISBN 0-425-19096-X.
[222] Redford, Donald B., ed. (2003).

decapitating other gods to nourish the king in the afterlife[223]. At this stage, he is more a celestial force of aggression than a benevolent lunar god.

Khonsu, Wikipedia Creative Commons, Public Domain

The First Intermediate Period: During this time of political decentralisation, cult centres like Thebes begin rising in prominence. Khonsu's lunar associations remain intact, but his worship is localised and not highly organised.

The Middle Kingdom: Khonsu's benevolent aspects begin to emerge more clearly. His role as a healer and protector, especially of children and travellers, becomes more emphasised. He may start to be included more formally as part of Theban theology during this period.

The Second Intermediate Period: Despite foreign rule in the north, Theban traditions and local deities like Khonsu remain respected in Upper Egypt. His growing association with Amun and Mut possibly begin forming in this period.

The New Kingdom: The high point of Khonsu's worship. Khonsu is fully integrated into the Theban Triad with Amun and Mut, and recognised as their divine son. Major construction at the Temple of Khonsu at Karnak (Thebes), especially under Ramesses III, shows his elevated status. Khonsu becomes strongly associated with healing, lunar timekeeping, fertility, and protection. His image appears frequently in royal temples and tombs. Worship expands beyond Thebes, with national recognition.

The Third Intermediate Period: Though Egypt is politically fragmented, Khonsu continues to be widely revered, especially in Thebes. The priesthood of Khonsu in Thebes gains prominence.

The Late Period: Traditional religion experiences a revival. Khonsu continues to be honoured in restored or newly embellished temples. Depictions emphasise his role as time-keeper and healer, sometimes combining aspects of Thoth.

The Ptolemaic Period: Hellenistic rulers actively support Egyptian temples and religion. The Bentresh Stela, a Ptolemaic legend, highlights Khonsu's miraculous healing powers in a narrative involving the king of Bakhtan and his sick daughter. His temple at Karnak (Thebes) is refurbished and remains an important religious site. Khonsu becomes associated with syncretic lunar deities and gains appeal beyond Egypt.

The Roman and Byzantine Periods: The Roman state continues to sponsor major temples, including those of Khonsu. Roman emperors are depicted in Egyptian style making offerings to Khonsu in temples. The rise of Christianity leads to the closure of pagan temples. The cult of Khonsu disappears from official religious practice. Knowledge of Khonsu is preserved only through temple inscriptions, amulets, and later historical texts.

Khonsu is comparable to the Greek / Roman goddess Selene / Luna, or Artemis / Diana who are strongly associated with the moon. People could pray to Khonsu for healing, protection, safe travel by night or over long distances, guidance through uncertainty, health, vitality, renewal, and harmony with lunar and cosmic cycles.

---

[223] Adel Zaki Nasr, Youmna (December 12, 2022). "Apotropaic Roles of Khonsu in the Ancient Egyptian Religion during the Dynastic Period" (PDF). Research Journal of the Faculty of Tourism and Hotels (12). Mansoura University: 288–290.

Maahes: The Lion-Headed Warrior and Protector

Left: 'Maahes' in hieroglyphs

Maahes is a lion-headed god of war[224], protection, strength, ferocity, lions, weather, knives, and punishment. His name means 'The Lion' or 'He who is true beside her', referring to his role as a protector, especially when standing beside a goddess like Bastet or Sekhmet. He is also referred to as 'Lord of Slaughter'[225], Wielder of the Knife', 'Avenger of Wrongs', 'The Scarlet Lord', 'Son of Bastet', or 'Son of Sekhmet'.

Maahes is a fierce protector of *ma'at*. He punishes those who do evil or threaten cosmic balance. As a guardian of truth and justice, he uses force when needed to uphold divine law. He acts as an executioner of the gods' enemies, especially those of Ra[226], fighting demons and chaotic forces. A warrior god, Maahes leads in battle and stands for bravery, fury, and strength. He is called upon for protection in war and to bring victory. He also protects the pharaoh, both physically and spiritually, and represents royal vengeance. In some beliefs, Maahes controls weather and storms, especially fiery heat. He is also a god of knives and execution, often shown with blades, symbolising precise and deadly force against evil. Depending on the region, he is seen as the son of Bastet or Sekhmet, and sometimes merged with other lion gods like Nefertum and Shezmu.

Maahes has a human body and a lion's head, symbolising strength, power, and royalty. Lions are sacred in ancient Egypt and stand for both the sun and royal protection. He often wears a solar disk and a uraeus on his head. He is usually shown holding a knife or sword, and sometimes a lotus flower, which connects him to the god Nefertum, who may be his brother. Maahes wears a kilt or military-style clothing, and often a striped nemes headdress. In artwork, he is sometimes shown with real lions, showing his control over them. In more symbolic images, he may appear as a full lion.

Maahes's main centre of worship is Leontopolis, where sacred lions are kept within the temple precincts and are considered living manifestations of Maahes, the lion-headed god of war, protection, and royal power. Maahes was also worshipped at Bubastis (Per-Bastet) on the eastern Nile Delta. Bastet is considered to be Maahes's mother in local theology. As a lion / feline deity, Maahes is honoured alongside Bastet during festivals and ceremonies. He is seen as a guardian and divine enforcer connected to the feline cult. He was also worshipped at Memphis near modern day Cairo, the capital of the Old Kingdom of Egypt. Maahes is considered to be the son of Sekhmet and Ptah there. He is a part of some versions of the Memphite Triad (Ptah, Sekhmet, and Maahes, or Ptah, Sekhmet, and Nefertum). Here worship focuses on Maahes's role as a punisher of wrongdoers and a divine warrior. In Thebes in Upper Egypt, Maahes was venerated alongside Sekhmet, a prominent goddess

---

[224] Manfred Lurker (1987). Dictionary of Gods and Goddesses, Devils and Demons. Routledge. p. 215. ISBN 978-0-7102-0877-4.
[225] Manfred Lurker (1987).
[226] Wilkinson, Richard H. (2003). The Complete Gods and Goddesses of Ancient Egypt. Thames & Hudson. pp. 178–179

in Thebes. He was worshipped as a protective deity, invoked in contexts relating to healing, war, and ritual vengeance.

Maahes, Wikipedia Creative Commons, Public Domain

The Early Dynastic Period: Maahes does not yet appear in known records. The worship of lion deities begins to emerge, but Maahes as a distinct god is not yet developed at this time. He is perhaps a local or emerging aspect of another deity like Sekhmet or Bastet.

The Old Kingdom: There is no direct evidence of Maahes worship yet. However, lion symbolism begins to grow in importance. Sekhmet and Bastet (both of whom are considered to be Maahes's mothers in different regions) are already significant by this time.

The Middle Kingdom: There is still limited evidence of Maahes as a separate deity. Some scholars believe his cult begins forming in this period, possibly as a local lion god associated with solar worship and protection. He may have begun as a regional aspect of Nefertum or Shezmu.

The New Kingdom: The peak of Maahes worship. Maahes becomes fully recognised as a distinct deity. He is linked to Sekhmet at Memphis, and Bastet at Bubastis. Leontopolis rises as his main cult centre, where live lions are kept and revered as living embodiments of Maahes[227]. He is often mentioned in inscriptions and temple reliefs as 'Lord of the Knife' or 'Avenger of Wrongs'. He is connected to the Memphite Triad as the son of Sekhmet and Ptah, and the brother of Nefertum. Some Egyptologists suggest that Maahes is of foreign origin[228].

The Third Intermediate Period: Worship of Maahes continues, especially in Lower Egypt. Leontopolis remains active, with evidence of lion burials and temples. Maahes remains invoked in protective and funerary contexts.

The Late and Ptolemaic Periods: There is continued worship of Maahes, although he has been eclipsed in prominence by other major deities. He is still honoured in temples and depicted in artwork, especially in the Nile Delta region. Greek visitors refer to Leontopolis and describe sacred lions kept in enclosures, identifying Maahes with Apedemak[229] (a lion-headed Nubian god) or Heracles (Roman: Hercules). Maahes worship persists under Greek rule. Worship becomes more symbolic and localised.

The Roman and Byzantine Periods: Maahes's cult gradually declines as traditional Egyptian religion is replaced by Hellenistic and later Christian beliefs. Leontopolis and Bubastis fade as religious centres.

As a god of physical power, protection, and heroism, Maahes is comparable to the Greek / Roman god Heracles / Hercules, who interestingly is depicted with a lion's head as a helmet (specifically the Nemean Lion, who he defeats in his most famous myth, the First Labour of Hercules). Maahes could be prayed to for protection and victory, vitality and strength, royal authority, natural order and fertility.

---

[227] Seawright, Caroline. "Maahes, God of War and Protection, The Leonine Lord of Slaughter". Archived from the original on 4 November 2019.
[228] Walter Yust ed., Encyclopædia Britannica: A New Survey of Universal Knowledge, 1956, p.54
[229] The Ancient World : Extraordinary People in Extraordinary Societies. Michael Shally-Jensen. Ipswich, Mass.: Salem Press. 2017. ISBN 978-1-68217-190-5. OCLC 975044922.

Ma'at: Goddess of Truth, Justice, and Order

Above: Eight variations of 'Ma'at' in hieroglyphs

Ma'at is the ancient Egyptian concept of balance, cosmic order, justice, and truth. Ma'at is also the name of the goddess who personifies this concept. She is usually depicted wearing a large blue ostrich feather on her head. This feather is called the 'Feather of Ma'at', which sometimes appears on its own representing the goddess Ma'at, the concept of *ma'at*, or both.

The Feather of Ma'at is central to the Weighing of the Heart ceremony, as described in the Book of the Dead. The heart of the deceased is weighed against the Feather of Ma'at. Anubis leads the deceased into the Hall of Ma'at. Osiris presides over the judgement as the ultimate authority, admitting successful souls into the afterlife (the Field of Reeds). Thoth records the outcome of the weighing on a tablet as a cosmic notary, confirming the soul's fate. Unsuccessful souls have their hearts devoured by Ammit, resulting in a 'second death', denying the soul eternal life. Ma'at maintains the balance of the universe and opposes chaos. Without *ma'at*, everything collapses into *isfet* (chaos, injustice, violence, and falsehood)[230].

Ma'at accompanies the sun god Ra on his daily journey across the sky and through the underworld. She rides in Ra's solar barque, helping him maintain stability against the forces of chaos, particularly during his nightly battle with the serpent Apophis. Ma'at ensures that creation remains in balance, allowing Ra to rise each morning and illuminate the world.

The Pharaoh's primary role is to uphold *ma'at*, ensuring law, fairness, and cosmic stability[231]. In rituals, iconography, and symbols, Egyptian pharaohs offered the concept of *ma'at* to the gods.

While Ma'at did not have large temples dedicated solely to her, she was widely venerated throughout ancient Egypt in temples, courts, tombs, and royal contexts where her role was of particular importance. At the Karnak and Luxor Temple Complexes in Thebes, reliefs show pharaohs offering *ma'at* to the gods. At Abydos, a major cult centre of Osiris, Ma'at is depicted in scenes relating to judgment and the afterlife. At Hermopolis, and Panopolis, both centres of Thoth worship, Ma'at is Thoth's divine counterpart in justice and truth. At Heliopolis, a centre of solar worship, Ma'at is closely

---

[230] Assmann, Jan (2006). Religion and Cultural Memory: Ten Studies. Translated by Rodney Livingstone. Stanford University Press. ISBN 0-8047-4523-4.
[231] McCall, Henrietta (1990). Mesopotamian myths. University of Texas Press. ISBN 0-292-72076-9.

associated with Ra. Ma'at was highly revered at Memphis and is present in legal proceedings and the court system.

Ma'at, Wikipedia Creative Commons, Public Domain

The Early Dynastic Period: *Ma'at* (cosmic order) appears conceptually as a foundational principle of kingship and law. Earliest references are indirect: pharaohs claim to 'uphold *ma'at*', even before she is personified as a goddess. The ideal order vs. chaos (*ma'at* vs. *isfet*) becomes a core part of state ideology.

The Old Kingdom: Ma'at is personified and recognised as a goddess[232]. Pharaohs are described as 'living by *ma'at*' and offering her to the gods. She appears in Pyramid Texts[233], especially in royal funerary contexts. Judges and advisors are called 'priests of Ma'at'[234].

The First Intermediate Period: Centralised worship declines, but Ma'at remains important in local court and temple inscriptions. Concepts of personal morality and judgement after death begin to expand beyond royalty.

The Middle Kingdom: Revival of state order brings Ma'at back to prominence. Coffin Texts emphasise personal judgement and ethical conduct, Ma'at becomes key to all individuals, not just kings. She is associated more closely with Thoth and the development of divine judgement scenes.

The New Kingdom: Ma'at is extensively featured in the Book of the Dead, especially in Spell 125, the Weighing of the Heart. She is depicted in temple reliefs at Karnak and Luxor (Thebes), and Abydos. Pharaohs depict themselves offering *ma'at* to the gods as a symbol of legitimate rule. Tomb scenes show the Feather of Ma'at as the standard for moral judgement in the afterlife.

The Third Intermediate Period: Despite political and religious fragmentation, Ma'at remains vital in theology and morality. Smaller temples and local priesthoods continue to invoke her in judicial and funerary roles.

The Late Period: An increased emphasis on reviving Old Kingdom traditions brings renewed references to Ma'at. Temples still feature Ma'at in inscriptions.

The Ptolemaic Period: Ma'at is still present in temple rituals, equated with Greek goddesses Dike (justice) or Themis (divine law). There is continued use of judgement scenes in tombs and papyri.

The Roman and Byzantine Periods: Egyptian religion declines under Roman rule and Christianisation. Ma'at's symbolic legacy continues, though overt worship fades. Her influence remains embedded in Egyptian moral and religious concepts that survive into Greco-Roman and early Christian philosophical thought.

Ma'at as truth and justice is equivalent to the Greek / Roman goddess Themis / Justitia. As the concept of cosmic balance, she is equivalent to Dike / Justitia. Ma'at could be prayed to for justice and fairness, stability and harmony, moral guidance, and success in the afterlife.

---

[232] Redford, Donald B., ed. (2003). The Oxford Essential Guide to Egyptian Mythology. Berkley Publishing. ISBN 0-425-19096-X.
[233] Morenz, Siegfried (1973). Egyptian Religion. Cornell University Press. ISBN 978-0-8014-8029-4.
[234] Morenz, Siegfried (1973).

Menhit: Goddess of War and Protection

Left: 'Menhit' in hieroglyphs

Menhit is a goddess of war, battle, conquest, protection, solar power, divine wrath, kingship, Nubia, and lionesses. Her name means 'she who sacrifices', or 'she who massacres'[235]. Menhit serves as a fierce protector and embodiment of divine wrath. Often associated with Nubia, she leads and defends the pharaoh's armies in battle, using her fiery, solar energy to annihilate enemies and uphold *ma'at*. As a consort to war gods like Khnum and a manifestation of the Eye of Ra, Menhit plays a vital role in warfare, blazing across the battlefield with the destructive power of the sun[236].

In the Eye of Ra Myth Cycle, Menhit is sometimes identified with or considered an aspect of the Eye of Ra, the fierce solar goddess sent to punish humanity or enemies of the gods. In these stories, the Eye takes the form of a lion-headed goddess. While the core myth often features Sekhmet, Menhit may be a localised or alternate version in Nubian or southern Egyptian regions. In inscriptions and texts (such as those from Esna and Nubia), Menhit is depicted as a protective goddess who marches before the pharaoh in battle, annihilating his enemies with fiery force[237]. These are symbolic portrayals of divine action in service of kingship. In some regions, Menhit is part of a triad with Khnum (her consort) and Heka (her child, god of magic). Menhit is associated with the goddesses Sekhmet, Tefnut, and early versions of Bastet. They are all feline, leonine, or lion-headed goddesses who have solar and protective functions, particularly in the Eye of Ra myth. In the broader Eye of Ra mythology, lioness goddesses like Menhit often merge or overlap with Hathor (in her wrathful form) and Mut (another lion-headed goddess in certain contexts). Menhit is also paired as the consort of Khnum, the ram-headed creator god of Elephantine Island and Esna. Menhit, together with Khnum, and their son Heka (god of magic) form a divine triad in some local theologies. As the mother of Heka, Mehnit has associations with divine authority and cosmic order.

Menhit is depicted as a woman with the head of a lioness, with a solar disk and uraeus above her head[238] [239]. She is sometimes depicted holding a spear or knife, and sometimes an ankh or a sceptre. Menhit was worshipped at Esna (Latopolis) in Upper Egypt. In the Temple of Esna, reliefs and inscriptions depict Menhit prominently, often alongside Khnum in creation and protection contexts. At Elephantine Island on the southern border of Egypt near Nubia, Menhit was invoked as a goddess of

---

[235] Farid, Mona; Fekri, Magdi Mohamed; Abd-elaal, Magdi Ismail (Hesham Ezz-eldin). "Archeological Study of Wild Animals in the New Kingdom". University of Sadat. ResearchGate. Retrieved 2023-09-07

[236] Wilkinson, Richard H. (2017). The Complete Gods and Goddesses of Ancient Egypt. Thames & Hudson. p. 179. ISBN 978-0-500-28424-7.

[237] Hans Bonnet: Menhit, in: Lexikon der ägyptischen Religionsgeschichte (English: Lexicon of Egyptian History of Religion) p.451f

[238] Wilkinson, Richard H. (2017). The Complete Gods and Goddesses of Ancient Egypt. Thames & Hudson. p. 179. ISBN 978-0-500-28424-7.

[239] Budge, E. A. Wallis (2018-08-28). The Ancient Egyptian Book of the Dead: Prayers, Incantations, and Other Texts from the Book of the Dead. Crestline Books. ISBN 978-0-7603-6443-7.

war, protection, and border defence. In Nubia, especially Lower Nubia where Menhit is believed to have originated, evidence of her worship appears in inscriptions and temple ruins in Nubian sites such as Toshka, Qasr Ibrim, and Kalabsha.

Menhit, Wikipedia Creative Commons, Public Domain

The Pre-Dynastic Period: Menhit originates as a lioness war goddess in Nubia. Her attributes suggest early local veneration in the southern Nile Valley.

The Early Dynastic Period: Menhit is absorbed into Egyptian religion through cultural exchange with Nubia. Her characteristics align with early lioness goddesses who protect the pharaohs.

The Old Kingdom: Royal iconography features protective lioness deities. Menhit is perhaps a regional form of Sekhmet or a protective goddess on Egypt's southern frontier.

The Middle Kingdom: Growing military activity in Nubia elevates Menhit's role as a protective war goddess. Increased interaction between Egypt and Nubia encourages her integration into Egyptian cults.

The New Kingdom: Menhit becomes more clearly identified in inscriptions and texts, especially in Nubian and southern Egyptian temples. She is associated with Khnum (as consort), Heka (as mother), and The Eye of Ra (as a lioness-warrior). She appears in temples at Elephantine Island and Lower Nubia (Toshka and Qasr Ibrim).

The Third Intermediate Period: Her worship continues regionally as Egypt faces political fragmentation. She remains a symbol of border protection and may be invoked in royal or military texts.

The Late Period: Menhit's cult is formalised in Esna, where she becomes part of the local triad with Khnum and Heka. Her identity is sometimes merged or paralleled with Sekhmet and other leonine goddesses.

The Ptolemaic Period: Menhit continues to be worshiped in Esna and southern Egypt. Greek influence increases syncretism, but local cults persist.

The Roman Period: Menhit's cult declines along with traditional Egyptian religion. Some temples, like Esna, remain in use, but Menhit becomes largely symbolic. Menhit is eventually supplanted by Christianity and the decline of temple-based worship.

The Byzantine Period: By the Byzantine period, Menhit's worship is essentially defunct in Egypt. She survives only in memory, inscriptions, or as part of older temple iconography, rather than as a living religious practice. Any 'worship' takes place privately, hidden, or symbolically rather than in an organized form.

As a warrior goddess, Menhit is perhaps closest to the Greek / Roman goddess Athena / Minerva, also a goddess of battle, a protector of cities and kings, and embodying strategic warfare and courage. People could pray to Menhit for victory in battle, protection from enemies, courage, and the maintenance of order.

Min: God of Fertility

Left: Min' in hieroglyphs

Min is a god of fertility, male potency, reproduction, virility, procreation, agriculture, harvest, growth, and regeneration. His name means 'firmness', 'endurance', or 'permanence'. He is also known as 'The Mighty Bull', 'Lord of the Eastern Desert' 'Min of Coptos', 'Min the Strong', 'Protector of the Pharaoh', 'Lord of Heaven', 'He Who Bestows Seed', and 'Min the Fertile'.

He is responsible for ensuring the reproduction of humans, animals, and the abundance of crops. He plays a crucial role in agricultural cycles as a patron of planting and harvest, and is closely associated with the vitality and strength of the pharaoh, whom he protects and empowers through ritual. He also serves as a guardian of desert trade routes and mining expeditions, particularly in the Eastern Desert.

He embodies the forces of regeneration, creation, and cosmic permanence in nature and kingship. In the 'Festival of the Coming Forth of Min'[240] the pharaoh would offer a ceremonial cutting of grain to Min.

In later periods, Min is syncretised with other gods, such as Amun-Min (combining his fertility aspect with Amun's cosmic power) and Min-Kamutef ('Min, Bull of His Mother')[241], emphasising his role in divine self-regeneration as a concept. The Greeks identified Min with Pan and Priapus, reflecting similar fertility roles.

Min is depicted standing upright with his legs bandaged[242], his arm is raised, holding a nekhekh (flail) over his head, a symbol of fertility, power, and kingship. He is shown as ithyphallic (with an erect phallus), symbolising potency, fertility and creation. He wears the Hedjet crown often adorned with two tall plumes, sometimes known as the Atef crown. He has a long ceremonial beard, and he is usually dressed in white, sometimes wearing a short kilt (shendyt). His skin is sometimes show as reddish brown, or sometimes black to represent the fertility of the soil of the Nile[243][244][245]. Sometimes a lettuce is placed near to him or used in offerings, which is considered an aphrodisiac and sacred to him[246].

---

[240] "Min". Encyclopædia Britannica. Encyclopædia Britannica Online. 2020. Retrieved 2024-09-01.
[241] Wilkinson, Richard H. (2003). The Complete Gods and Goddesses of Ancient Egypt. London: Thames & Hudson. p. 93. Retrieved 9 October 2022.
[242] Christiane, Zivie-Coche (2004). Gods and men in Egypt: 3000 BCE to 395 CE. Ithaca, NY: Cornell Univ. Press. pp. 17–18. ISBN 978-0-8014-4165-3. OCLC 845667204.
[243] Orlin, Eric (2015-11-19). Routledge Encyclopedia of Ancient Mediterranean Religions. Routledge. ISBN 978-1-134-62552-9.
[244] Power, Mick (2012-01-06). Adieu to God: Why Psychology Leads to Atheism. John Wiley & Sons. ISBN 978-1-119-97995-1.
[245] Sabbahy, Lisa K. (2019-04-24). All Things Ancient Egypt: An Encyclopedia of the Ancient Egyptian World [2 volumes]. ABC-CLIO. ISBN 978-1-4408-5513-9.
[246] Najovits, Simson R. (2004). Egypt, trunk of the tree: a modern survey of an ancient land. Algora Pub. pp. 68, 93. ISBN 978-0-87586-222-4. OCLC 51647593.

The main centre of the worship of Min, especially in later periods, is at Akhmim. It is known as Khent-Min meaning 'Foremost of Min'. A major temple complex is dedicated to him featuring many large ithyphallic statues. An early and important centre for the worship of Min, particularly in the Old and Middle Kingdoms was at Coptos[247], often associated with desert trade routes and mining expeditions. It was also the site of the 'Festival of the Coming Forth of Min'. As Amun-Min he was also worshipped at Thebes (Luxor).

Min, Wikipedia Creative Commons, Public Domain

The Pre-Dynastic Period: The earliest origins of Min trace back to prehistoric fertility cults in Upper Egypt[248] [249]. Fertility and virility were vital concepts in early agricultural society. Early votive items and symbols (possibly ithyphallic figurines) suggest that his proto-form existed in this area.

The Early Dynastic Period: Min becomes fully integrated into the state religion. His cult is established at Coptos and Akhmim. He is associated with royal power and the pharaoh's potency.

The Old Kingdom: Min's prominence increases, especially in state rituals tied to fertility and harvest. Pharaohs participate in the 'Coming Forth of Min' festival. Min is depicted in pyramid temples and funerary texts. He is known as 'Min the Powerful' or 'Min of Coptos'.

The Middle Kingdom: There is continued strong worship of Min, particularly in agricultural contexts. The expansion of desert trade routes sees Min invoked as a protector of miners and desert travellers. Temples to Min are maintained and expanded.

The New Kingdom: Min becomes closely associated with Amun, forming the hybrid deity Amun-Min. Worship becomes more elaborate, with rich temple reliefs (e.g. in Karnak, Luxor, Thebes). Pharaohs invoke Min in rituals demonstrating royal fertility and cosmic order. The Festival of Min continues as a major public religious event.

The Late Period: Min's cult remains active, and he retains status as a fertility and desert god. Depictions and inscriptions from this time still show him as ithyphallic, holding the flail, and protecting mining expeditions.

The Ptolemaic Period: Under Greek rule, Min is equated with Pan and Priapus, due to his fertility symbolism. Temples are renovated and re-dedicated, especially in Akhmim (Panopolis). Cult imagery becomes more hybridised, blending Egyptian and Hellenistic styles.

The Roman and Byzantine Periods: Worship continues, but gradually declines with the spread of Christianity. Some temples dedicated to Min are closed or converted. Min's cult disappears, but echoes survive in Greco-Roman fertility traditions and local folklore.

As a symbol of male fertility and virility, Min is comparable to the Greek / Roman god Priapus. As a god of agricultural abundance, he is comparable to Dionysus / Bacchus. People could pray to Min for fertility, potency, abundance, and life energy.

---

[247] Manchip, White, J. E. (2013). Ancient Egypt: Its Culture and History. Dover Publications. ISBN 978-0-486-22548-7. OCLC 868271431.
[248] "Min". Encyclopædia Britannica. Encyclopædia Britannica Online. 2020. Retrieved 2024-09-01.
[249] Alan., Lothian (2012). Ancient Egypt's myths and beliefs. Rosen Pub. ISBN 978-1-4488-5994-8. OCLC 748941784.

Montu: God of War and the Sun

Left: 'Montu' in hieroglyphs

Montu is a god of war[250], sun, valour, strength, kingship, military conquest, raging bulls, protective power, and the destructive power of the sun. His name means 'nomad' or 'the Nomadic One' ('*mnṯw*', 'wandering' or 'movement')[251].

He was known as 'Lord of Thebes', 'Mighty Bull', 'Lord of the Sword', 'Wielder of the Strong Arm'[252], 'Lord of Destruction', 'He Who Slaughters the Rebels', 'Raging One', and 'Avenger of the Gods'. He embodies the fierce, destructive power of the sun in battle, leading armies, inspiring warriors, and protecting the pharaoh. As a solar warrior and personification of military might, he enforces *ma'at*, slaughters enemies, and defends the cosmos against chaos in the name of Ra.

Montu is frequently invoked in temple reliefs and pharaoh propaganda as the divine embodiment of military strength[253], often described as a raging bull or a fierce warrior fighting alongside or as the manifestation of the sun god Ra.

Montu is closely associated with several other gods through syncretism and shared attributes. He is often identified with Ra, the sun god, as his warlike aspect, sometimes appearing as Montu-Ra. Montu is also linked to Horus, the falcon-headed sky god and patron of kingship, due to their shared roles as divine protectors of the pharaoh in battle. In some contexts, he is compared to or aligned with Set, another warrior god, particularly in his more protective and combative aspects. Montu's mythological role is also reinforced by his association with Amun, the chief god of Thebes[254], especially during the New Kingdom when Montu was worshipped in major Theban temples alongside Amun.

Montu is typically depicted as a man with the head of a falcon, often crowned with a solar disk surrounded by a uraeus[255] and two tall feathers. Sometimes, he is shown as a bull or with bull-like features. In art and temple reliefs, Montu is frequently portrayed wearing a traditional warrior's kilt and carrying weapons such as a spear or a curved sword[256].

---

[250] Pinch, Geraldine. Egyptian Mythology: A Guide to the Gods, Goddesses, and Traditions of Ancient Egypt. Oxford University Press, 2004. ISBN 978-0-19-517024-5. p. 165.
[251] Ruiz, Ana (2001). The Spirit of Ancient Egypt. Algora Publishing. p. 115. ISBN 9781892941688. montu nomad.
[252] Wilkinson, Richard H. (2003). The Complete Gods and Goddesses of Ancient Egypt. Thames & Hudson. pp. 203–4.
[253] Hart, George, A Dictionary of Egyptian Gods and Goddesses, Routledge, 1986, ISBN 0-415-05909-7. p. 126.
[254] Rachet, Guy (1994). Dizionario della civiltà egizia. Rome: Gremese Editore. ISBN 88-7605-818-4. p. 208.
[255] "Egypt: Montu, Solar and Warrior God". www.touregypt.net. Retrieved 2023-05-30.
[256] "Gods of Ancient Egypt: Montu". www.ancientegyptonline.co.uk. Retrieved 2018-05-03.

Montu, Wikipedia Creative Commons, Public Domain

The main centres of worship for Montu are primarily located in Upper Egypt, with Thebes (Luxor) being the most prominent cult city. Other significant cult centres included Armant, where a major temple dedicated to him stood, and Medamud (5km east of Karnak)[257], home to an important Montu sanctuary featuring grand temples and ritual sites. Additionally, Montu was worshipped at Tod (15km Southwest of Thebes) and Hermonthis (Armant), which were also important religious hubs linked to his bull symbolism. These centres were not only religious sites but also military and political strongholds where Montu's role as a god of war and kingship was especially emphasised, with temples that hosted festivals, rituals, and the veneration of sacred bulls believed to embody his spirit.

The Old Kingdom: Montu is first attested as a local war and solar deity in Upper Egypt. Early mentions appear in royal inscriptions and tombs, especially in the Theban region.

The First Intermediate Period and Middle Kingdom: Montu's cult grows stronger in Thebes and surrounding areas like Armant and Medamud. He becomes closely associated with the rising political power of Thebes. Pharaohs begin invoking Montu's martial power for legitimising their rule[258].

The New Kingdom: Montu reaches peak prominence, especially under the 18th Dynasty pharaohs like Thutmose III and Ramesses II, who heavily emphasise his warrior aspect. Major temples are built or expanded at Thebes, Armant, and Medamud. Pharaohs often depict themselves as incarnations of Montu in battle, and Montu is deeply integrated into royal ideology. Montu is sometimes syncretised with Amun and Ra, reinforcing his solar and warlike roles.

The Third Intermediate and Late Periods: Montu's worship continues but gradually declines as Amun becomes the dominant deity of Thebes. Temples and cults persist, but with reduced royal patronage. Montu remains venerated in traditional cult centres, though his influence diminishes further. The cult of the sacred bull Buchis[259], associated with Montu, continues to be important.

The Ptolemaic Period: Montu is still worshipped, often merged with Greek gods or in syncretic forms. Temples like those at Armant continue to be active religious sites. The Greeks associate Montu with the war god Ares (Roman: Mars), but because of his solar aspect he is assimilated to Apollo[260].

The Roman Period and Byzantine Periods: Montu's worship fades as Egyptian religion declines with the spread of Christianity and later Islam in Egypt.

As a god of war and valour, Montu is comparable with the Greek / Roman god Ares / Mars, as both are gods of war and martial strength, protectors of warriors, and of military success. In his solar and sky aspects, he is comparable with Apollo or Helios / Sol. Montu could be prated to for victory, protection, courage, and martial strength.

---

[257] Fletcher, Joann. (2011) Cleopatra the Great: The Woman Behind the Legend. HarperCollins, ISBN 978-0-06-210605-6. pp. 114ss.
[258] Gae Callender: The Middle Kingdom Renaissance, In: Ian Shaw (ed): The Oxford History of Ancient Egypt, Oxford University Press, Oxford, 2000, ISBN 0-19-815034-2, pp. 148-183.
[259] Pinch, Geraldine. Egyptian Mythology: A Guide to the Gods, Goddesses, and Traditions of Ancient Egypt. Oxford University Press, 2004. ISBN 978-0-19-517024-5. p. 165.
[260] Wilkinson, Richard H. (2003). The Complete Gods and Goddesses of Ancient Egypt. Thames & Hudson. pp. 203–4.

Mut: Goddess of Motherhood and the Sky

Left: Two variations of 'Mut' in hieroglyphs

Mut (*Maut, Mout*) is a major ancient Egyptian goddess. Her name literally means "mother" in ancient Egyptian[261]. She is primarily known as a goddess of motherhood, creation, and protection, and is also called the 'Eye of Ra', the 'Lady of Heaven', and 'Mistress of All the Gods'. Mut is sometimes equated with goddesses like Sekhmet, Tefnut, Bastet, and Hathor, due to shared attributes and mythology.

Mut is considered a primal mother figure, associated with the primordial waters of Nu, from which all life emerges. In some myths, she gives birth to the world without a male partner. More commonly, she is portrayed as the wife of the creator god Amun-Ra and the mother of Khonsu, the moon god[262]. She protects young women[263], is invoked for fertility and childbirth, and plays a central role in state rituals, festivals, and divine succession.

Mut features prominently in the 'Eye of Ra' myth, where she appears as a wandering, angry lioness who must be calmed and returned to Egypt. In this tale, she transforms into various animals (cat, vulture, gazelle) and is eventually appeased by the god Thoth. After drinking from the Isheru lake and being soothed by music and rituals, she returns to Thebes and gives birth to Khonsu. In Theban mythology, she is also portrayed as a serpent emerging from the primordial waters, the mother-daughter-wife figure in divine triads, and the mother who gives birth to her own father, symbolising cyclical rebirth and divine unity[264].

Mut is part of the Theban Triad: Amun (her consort), Mut, and Khonsu (her son). She is not originally Amun's wife but later replaces earlier consorts like Amunet and Wosret[265] [266]. The integration of her identity with that of Tefnut, Sekhmet, Bastet, and Hathor reflects her fluid nature in mythology. She also embodies aspects of Ma'at and shares titles with male gods like Ra and Min, representing self-creation and divine inheritance.

Mut is most commonly shown as a woman wearing the Pschent crown of Upper and Lower Egypt, with the wings of a vulture, holding an ankh, and wearing a red or blue dress. She often has the feather of

---

[261] te Velde, Herman (2002), "Mut", in Redford, D. B. (ed.), The Ancient Gods Speak: A Guide to Egyptian Religion, New York: Oxford University Press, p. 238
[262] van Dijk, J. (2010). Onder Orchideeën. Nieuwe Oogst uit de Tuin der Geesteswetenschappen te Groningen. Barkhuis Publishing. p.72.
[263] van Dijk, J. (2010). pp.75-76.
[264] Sethe, Kurt Heinrich (1929). Amun und die acht Urgötter von Hermopolis eine Untersuchung über Ursprung und Wesen des aegyptischen Götterkönigs. Berlin: Verlag der Akademie und Wissenschaft. p.31.
[265] te Velde, Herman (1988). p.398.
[266] Wilkinson, Richard H. (2003). The Complete Gods and Goddesses of Ancient Egypt. Thames & Hudson. pp. 153–155, 169

Ma'at at her feet. Due to her merging with other goddesses, she can also appear as a lioness, cat, cobra, cow, or vulture. The main centre of Mut's worship is the Precinct of Mut at Karnak (Thebes). This temple complex includes the sacred Isheru lake, which plays a key role in rituals. Her worship extends to Jebel Barkal in Sudan, especially during the rule of the Kushite pharaohs. The Mut Temple is primarily administered by women, with the queen or her daughter serving as chief priestess. Pharaohs like Hatshepsut, Amenhotep III, Ramesses II, and even Roman emperors like Tiberius contribute to building or restoring her temples. The temple remains active into the Roman period before it eventually falls into disuse.

Mut, Wikipedia Creative Commons, Public Domain

The Early Dynastic Period: There is no clear evidence of Mut as a major deity in this era. Other mother goddesses like Neith or Hathor hold more prominent roles.

The Old Kingdom: Mut is not yet prominent in religious texts or monuments. The dominant mother goddesses remain Hathor or Neith. Mut may have existed as a local or minor goddess, but there is no strong archaeological evidence yet.

The Middle Kingdom: Mut begins to appear in Theban religious texts, possibly as a local mother deity. Theban theology is rising in influence, setting the stage for her elevation.

The New Kingdom: This is the height of Mut's prominence. As Thebes becomes Egypt's political and religious centre, Mut becomes the primary consort of Amun, the chief deity of Thebes. She forms the Theban Triad with Amun and their son Khonsu. A massive temple construction at Karnak (Thebes), especially the Precinct of Mut, shows her central role in state religion.

The Third Intermediate Period: Mut remains an important goddess, especially in Thebes. Priesthoods maintain her cult; she is still invoked as mother of the gods and protector of the pharaoh. Syncretism with other goddesses (like Isis and Sekhmet) becomes more pronounced.

The Late Period: Mut's worship continues but is increasingly blended with that of Isis and other goddesses. She is depicted more often with lion-headed forms, merging with warrior goddesses like Sekhmet and Bastet.

The Ptolemaic Period: Greek rulers adopt and adapt Egyptian religion. Mut is still worshipped, often syncretised with Greek goddesses like Hera (Juno) or Rhea (Ops). Her temple at Karnak (Thebes) remains active, though Isis becomes more dominant.

The Roman and Byzantine Periods: Mut's worship declines as Isis becomes the supreme mother goddess of both Egyptian and Greco-Roman worship. Some shrines and imagery of Mut persist, but she is no longer a major state deity. With the spread of Christianity and the eventual ban on pagan worship, Mut's temples fall into disuse. Her memory survives only in inscriptions, temple ruins, and mythological texts.

As a goddess of motherhood and creation, Mut is comparable to the Greek / Roman goddess Rhea / Ops, who is the mother of the Olympian gods, where Mut is the mother of the divine triad. Hera / Juno is also comparable as both are queens of the gods, and protectors of kingship and social order. Mut could be prayed to for motherhood, protection, royal authority, and stability.

Naunet: Primordial Goddess of the Waters

Left: 'Naunet' in hieroglyphs

Naunet is a goddess of the primordial waters, cosmic darkness, invisibility, and the unknown depths[267]. Her name is the feminine form of Nu[268], meaning 'primeval waters' or 'abyss'[269]. Naunet is also known as the Hidden One, the Lady of the Primeval Waters, and sometimes simply as the female counterpart of Nu.

Naunet functions as one of the eight deities in the Ogdoad. As the feminine aspect of Nu, she embodies the boundless, formless waters that existed before the world was formed. Naunet's role is not that of an active creator, but rather as a necessary cosmic presence, representing the chaotic potential from which creation emerges.

Naunet appears mainly in theological and cosmological texts rather than in stories or myths. Her presence is most prominent in the Hermopolitan creation myth, where the Ogdoad collectively initiates the birth of the sun and the ordered world.

Naunet is closely identified with Nu, her male counterpart, as well as with the broader concept of the primordial feminine in Egyptian cosmogony. She may be indirectly associated with other creator goddesses or elemental deities like Neith or Mut, who also represent aspects of cosmic origin, though Naunet's role remains more abstract and elemental. Her identity is primarily symbolic rather than syncretic.

Naunet is rarely depicted in Egyptian art, but when she is, she typically appears as a woman with the head of a snake or cobra[270], symbolising hidden danger, mystery, and the unknowable aspects of existence. Sometimes she is shown as a fully human woman wearing a vulture or modius headdress, in line with other primordial goddesses. Her cobra-headed form represents her link to protective, mysterious powers and her role in guarding the cosmic order before its manifestation.

Naunet was primarily venerated in Hermopolis, the major cult centre of the Ogdoad. This city was central to theological speculation and creation mythology, and Naunet was honoured as part of its priestly traditions. There are no known major temples exclusively dedicated to Naunet, but her worship would have occurred within the broader context of the Ogdoad and the theological practices of Hermopolitan cosmology.

---

[267] Wilkinson, Richard H. (2003). The Complete Gods and Goddesses of Ancient Egypt. Thames & Hudson. pp. 206–207. ISBN 0-500-05120-8.
[268] Budge, E. A. Wallis (1920). An Egyptian Hieroglyphic Dictionary. J. Murray. p. 350.
[269] Budge, E. A. Wallis (1904). The Gods of the Egyptians: Or, Studies in Egyptian Mythology. Vol. 1. Methuen & Company. p. 284.
[270] History, mystery in (24 June 2024). "Naunet: Ancient Egyptian Deity Of Chaos And Water". Retrieved 24 October 2025.

Naunet, Wikipedia Creative Commons, Public Domain

The Pre-Dynastic Period: There is no direct evidence of Naunet by name during this time. However, the concept of primeval waters (from which Naunet and Nu would later be derived) was likely already part of early religious thought and oral cosmologies.

The Early Dynastic Period: The formal Ogdoad of Hermopolis, including Naunet, may have begun to take shape in priestly circles. Naunet probably existed in oral tradition or temple philosophy, but was not yet a publicly recognised figure of worship.

The Old Kingdom: The Ogdoad becomes more defined in religious texts. Naunet appears indirectly in early religious ideas about the cosmos, especially in connection with Nu and the primordial abyss. Naunet may have been acknowledged in Memphite and Heliopolitan priestly traditions, though Hermopolis remains her spiritual home.

The Middle Kingdom: The Hermopolitan cosmology becomes more systematised. Naunet and the Ogdoad are fully integrated into temple theology at Hermopolis. She is paired with Nu as the female / male representation of primordial waters. No temples are built for her alone, but she would have been acknowledged in rituals and hymns alongside the other Ogdoad deities.

The New Kingdom: Naunet appears in cosmological texts, temple wall inscriptions, and funerary literature, such as the Book of the Dead and Coffin Texts, which describe the cosmic origins of the world. She is sometimes depicted as a cobra-headed goddess, a symbol of divine mystery and protection. She is still not worshipped personally, but revered as a concept in elite, theological settings.

The Third Intermediate Period: The Hermopolitan tradition continues, though national religious focus shifts more toward Theban deities (like Amun, Mut, Khonsu). Naunet remains relevant in priestly and theological circles, but continues to have no personal cult.

The Late Period: As Egyptian religion becomes more complex, the Ogdoad gains renewed interest, especially among temple priests and scholars. Naunet is viewed symbolically as part of the intellectual and spiritual heritage of ancient Egypt. There is still no evidence of public worship during this period.

The Ptolemaic and Roman Periods: The Ogdoad is sometimes merged with Greek philosophical ideas, especially in Hermopolis. Naunet remains a cosmic archetype, but is increasingly subsumed under other goddesses, such as Isis or Neith, in syncretic theology. Her role is preserved in esoteric texts and temple writings, but not in popular devotion.

The Byzantine Period: The worship of all ancient Egyptian deities, including Naunet, fades out with the rise of Christianity. Naunet's memory survives only in academic and archaeological records.

As a primordial water goddess, Naunet could be compared with the Greek goddess Nyx for her association with the mysterious and formless origins of creation, or perhaps Oceanus, the god of the pre-creation cosmic waters. Naunet could be prayed to for cosmic stability, fertility, renewal, and protective magical energy rooted in the origin of life.

Nefertem: The Healing God of the Lotus Flower

Left: 'Nefertem' in hieroglyphs

Nefertem is a god of healing, beauty, perfume, the lotus flower, the sunrise, and aromatherapy[271]. His name means 'Perfect One Who Has Completed' or 'Beautiful One Who Closes' (referring to the closing lotus blossom)[272]. He is also known as 'He Who is Beautiful', 'The Lotus Blossom at the Nose of Ra', and sometimes referred to as a solar or floral deity.

He is associated with the power of fragrant smells and rejuvenation. He represents the first sunlight and life emerging from the lotus flower. He brings pleasant aromas to the gods, and is often offered perfumes or aromatic oils in rituals. Nefertem also plays a role in medicine and magical healing, particularly using fragrant substances. His presence symbolises purity, rebirth, and the sweet beginning of the day. He also has protective aspects and is sometimes associated with defending or protecting the Two Lands (Upper and Lower Egypt), driving away darkness[273].

Nefertem is featured in the Heliopolitan creation myth. He emerges from the primeval waters of Nu as a lotus flower at the beginning of time[274]. In some myths, when the lotus flower opens, the sun god Ra rises from it[275] [276], linking Nefertem with the first sunrise. He is sometimes described as the son of Ptah and Sekhmet[277] (or Bastet in other traditions), forming a divine triad in Memphis.

Nefertem is often syncretised or associated with other deities. His solar and floral aspects link him symbolically with Ra and Horus, who are both solar deities. In later periods, he is also syncretised with Imhotep and Amenhotep son of Hapu in their roles as healing gods. His name also translates as 'Beautiful Atum', which suggests an identification or close association with Atum, especially in early creation ideas[278].

He is usually depicted as a young man wearing a blue lotus flower on his head, often with two plumes and sometimes a solar disk. Occasionally, he holds bouquets or perfume bottles. In some depictions,

---

[271] Alchin, L. (2015). Nefertum, god of Egypt. Land of Pyramids. Retrieved October 4, 2025, from https://www.landofpyramids.org/nefertum.htm
[272] Joshi, V., Mahabal , P., & Ghosh, D. (2025, January 1). Nefertem: Youthful God of Lotus blossom and Perfumes. Facts About Ancient Egyptians. Retrieved October 4, 2025, from https://ancientegyptianfacts.com/nefertem-youthful-god-of-lotus-blossom-and-perfumes.html
[273] Alchin, L. (2015)
[274] McDevitt, A. (2019, December 12). Nefertem. Ancient Egypt: The Mythology. Retrieved October 4, 2025, from http://www.egyptianmyths.net/nefertem.htm
[275] Alchin, L. (2015)
[276] Clayton, R. F. (2025). Gods and Goddesses of Ancient Egypt. PDF Coffee. Retrieved October 4, 2025, from https://pdfcoffee.com/gods-and-goddesses-of-ancient-egyptpdf-pdf-free.html
[277] Biesbroek, A. Nefertem. Alexander Ancient Art. Retrieved October 4, 2025, from https://www.alexanderancientart.com/nefertem.php
[278] Joshi, V., Mahabal , P., & Ghosh, D. (2025)

he appears with a lion's head, symbolising his connection to Sekhmet or Bastet and their fiercer aspects. He may also be shown riding a lion or with lion-like features.

Nefertem was primarily worshipped in Memphis, where he forms part of the Memphite Triad alongside Ptah and Sekhmet (or Bastet). He has a lasting presence in temples associated with healing and perfumery. Perfume-makers, physicians, and priests invoke him in healing rituals involving aromatic oils. In the Nile Delta at Buto he is sometimes said to be son of the cobra goddess Wadjet[279]. At Bubastis in some traditions, Bastet is his mother, and Nefertum has local cult associations there[280].

Nefertem, Wikipedia Creative Commons, Public Domain

The Old Kingdom: Nefertem begins to appear in the religious texts, particularly the Pyramid Texts, associated with perfume and the lotus. He is linked with Memphis and Ptah.

The First Intermediate Period: Worship continues on a more local level, especially around Memphis, but evidence is sparse due to general societal instability.

The Middle Kingdom: Nefertem grows in importance, often invoked in healing and beauty rituals. Depictions of him become more common in funerary texts and temples.

The Second Intermediate Period: Worship of Nefertem continues, especially in the north. His role as a healing god gains prominence during times of turmoil.

The New Kingdom: At the height of his popularity, he is frequently depicted in temples and tombs. He is seen as a comforting, rejuvenating presence in the afterlife. His lotus symbolism is tied deeply with rebirth and solar cycles.

The Third Intermediate Period: The cult of Nefertem remains strong. He is often represented in personal amulets and household shrines.

The Late Period: He continues to be venerated, often in combination with syncretic deities. He appears in invocations in healing temples alongside Imhotep.

The Ptolemaic Period: Worship of Nefertem remains localised but integrated into the Ptolemaic Greco-Egyptian religious worldview. His connection to perfume aligns with Hellenistic interests in aromatherapy and healing.

The Roman Period and Byzantine Periods: Nefertem is still honoured in healing contexts; and occasionally appears in magical texts and rituals. More syncretic representations of Nefertem begin to emerge. Later worship of traditional Egyptian gods, including Nefertem, largely declines with the rise of Christianity. He becomes a mythological figure rather than a living cult presence.

As a god of healing, perfume, and pleasant scent, Nefertem is comparable to the Greek deified hero Hyacinthus, as both are associated with fragrance, renewal, and the sun. More broadly, Nefertem is like a blend of Adonis (beauty), Apollo (healing, light), and Helios / Sol (sunrise, rebirth). People could pray to Nefertem for health and healing, renewal, rebirth, beauty and grace, and emotional healing and peace.

---

[279] Alchin, L. (2015)
[280] Alchin, L. (2015)

Neith: Goddess of War, Hunting, and Weaving

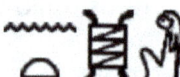

Left: Two variations of 'Neith' in hieroglyphs

Neith is a goddess of war, hunting, weaving, motherhood, wisdom, fate, creation, and protection. Her name has been interpreted in later esoteric sources to mean 'the terrifying one' because of her powerful and far-reaching nature. Her name is also linked to the Egyptian root '*nt*', which relates to weaving, and possibly to the name of the Deshret crown of Lower Egypt. She is also known as 'Mother of the Gods', 'Grandmother of the Gods', 'Great Goddess', 'Mistress of the Bow', 'Ruler of Arrows', and 'Nurse of Crocodiles'.

Neith plays many roles in Egyptian religion and mythology. She is a creator deity in some traditions, arising from the primeval waters (Nu), and being mother to gods such as Ra (the sun god) and Sobek (the crocodile god). She is also a goddess of war and hunting: she forges or blesses weapons, protects warriors, and is a patron of those who go to war or hunt.

As a goddess of weaving, she is connected with weaving the mummy bandages, domestic arts, cloth, and by extension protective, creative arts[281]. In funerary contexts, she protects the dead, watches over the mummy, is one of the goddesses guarding the canopic jars, protector of specific Sons of Horus (e.g. Duamutef, etc)[282]. She is also an arbitrator or judge among the gods in myths where she helps decide on rightful kingship.

In 'The Contendings of Horus and Set', Neith supports Horus in his dispute with Set over the rightful rule of Egypt. In some versions of the creation myths she is the mother of Ra and her spit into the waters of Nu produces Apophis, the enemy serpent of Ra. In cosmic myth she emerges from primeval waters. In her funerary role she helps guard the body of Osiris, and assists in the protection and resurrection of Osiris[283].

Neith is often identified or syncretised with several other deities. In her cosmic-creator aspect she is identified with Mehet-Weret, the Great Flooding Cow. In later periods, Neith takes on some of Hathor's and Nut's attributes with motherly or sky-cow imagery. In some traditions she is consort of Set[284]. In some temples (e.g. Esna) she is paired with Khnum as creator or consort[285].

---

[281] Mark, J. J. (2016, September 14). Neith. Retrieved October 4, 2025, from https://www.worldhistory.org/Neith/
[282] Egypt and Art. Neith. Retrieved October 4, 2025, from https://egyptartsite.com/neith.html
[283] Mark, J. J. (2016, September 14). Neith. Retrieved October 4, 2025, from https://www.worldhistory.org/Neith/
[284] Biesbroek, A. Neith. Alexander Ancient Art. Retrieved October 4, 2025, from https://www.alexanderancientart.com/nefertem.php
[285] Egypt and Art. Neith. Retrieved October 4, 2025, from https://egyptartsite.com/neith.html

Neith is usually depicted in human / anthropomorphic female form. She is often shown wearing the Deshret (the red crown of Lower Egypt)[286]. Sometimes she is depicted with crossed arrows over a shield, a bow and arrows, sometimes a bow-case on her head, or weaving in some contexts[287]. In later or cosmic images, she is sometimes depicted as a cow, or a celestial cow, occasionally nursing crocodiles[288]. Sometimes she is shown with a was-sceptre or an ankh[289]. Neith's main cult centres of worship included Sais in the western Nile Delta, Esna in Upper Egypt, and as she became more fully part of the national pantheon, Memphis.

Neith, Wikipedia Creative Commons, Public Domain

The Pre-Dynastic Period: Neith is already being worshipped and depicted with symbols (crossed arrows and shield etc.) appearing on early stelae (inscribed stone or wooden slabs). She is also being worshipped in Lower Egypt, especially Sais (or the region which became Sais), which is possibly the origin of her war / hunting attributes.

The Early Dynastic Period: Worship of Neith solidifies, with royalty adopting her name (e.g. Neith-hotep, Meret-Neith, etc.). She functions as a war goddess and is significant in the politics of Lower Egypt.

The Old Kingdom: Neith becomes integrated in funerary practices, appearing in Pyramid Texts as a protector of the dead. She also has the role of maintaining *ma'at*.

The Middle Kingdom: Neith continues to be worshipped in her dedicated temples. Her mythological role and identification with broader cosmic or creator aspects becomes more prominent.

The New Kingdom: Neith is strongly represented in mythic literature, and becomes more fully part of national pantheon, with increasing depictions of her appearing in temple art, showing her as a judge, protector, and a cosmic mother.

The Late Period: Neith becomes especially prominent in Sais. During the 26th Dynasty (the Saite Period), Sais is politically important, resulting in temple building, and a cult revival tied with the political identity of Saite pharaohs.

The Ptolemaic and Roman Periods: Worship of Neith continues under Greek rule. She is sometimes identified with Greek deities such as Athena (Roman: Minerva). Her temples remain active and she is still worshipped and honoured in cult practice. Neith is still venerated under Roman administration. Her temples and shrines are still in use. Her images are still present, including in festivals.

The Byzantine Period: Traditional Egyptian religion is suppressed under increasing Christianisation. Worship of Neith is syncretised or subsumed with other traditions and begins to fade.

Neith is comparable to the Greek / Roman goddess Athena / Minerva, as both are warrior goddesses associated with weaving, crafts, and strategic warfare. People could pray to Neith for protection, victory, wisdom, creative inspiration, and the maintenance of *ma'at*.

---

[286] Britannica.com (n.d.). Neith. Retrieved October 4, 2025, from https://www.britannica.com/topic/Neith
[287] Mark, J. J. (2016, September 14). Neith. Retrieved October 4, 2025, from https://www.worldhistory.org/Neith/
[288] Rhys, D. (2023, April 6). Neith - Creator of the Universe. Retrieved October 4, 2025, from https://symbolsage.com/neith-egyptian-goddess//
[289] The Metropolitan Museum of Art (n.d.). Neith - Creator of the Universe. Retrieved October 4, 2025, from https://www.metmuseum.org/art/collection/search/553004

Nekhbet: Ancient Winged Mother and Protector

Left: 'Nekhbet' in hieroglyphs

Nekhbet is a goddess of protection, motherhood, childbirth, queenship, and creation. Her name means 'She of Nekheb'. She is also called the 'White One of Nekhen' or 'Hedjet', after the White Crown of Upper Egypt, as well as 'Lady of Nekheb' and 'Mother of Mothers'. She protects the pharaoh and Upper Egypt and looks after queens, royal children, and childbirth. She also guards rituals and funerals. In the battle between Horus and Set, Nekhbet often appears with Wadjet beside Horus, usually with wings, to help and protect him. She is shown in Pyramid Texts and funerary writings as a caring mother figure who guards the king and the dead. Nekhbet supports and defends the pharaoh's right to rule and stands for national unity[290] and protection.

Sometimes Nekhbet is shown taking serpent form or appearing in symbols around the sun disk or royal name. Her caring and nurturing traits later mix with those of mother goddesses like Hathor or Mut. The Greeks linked her to Eileithyia (Roman: Lucina), a goddess of childbirth.

Nekhbet is usually shown as a white vulture[291], either perched, in profile, or with wings spread wide to protect. Sometimes she appears as a woman with a vulture's head, or a woman wearing a vulture headdress with the White Crown of Upper Egypt[292]. She may hold symbols like the shen ring[293], the Feather of Ma'at, or the royal flail. In temples, her wings are often painted overhead to protect rituals and royal ceremonies. Nekhbet's main centre of worship was Nekheb. Her name comes from the name of the city.

The Pre-Dynastic Period: Nekhbet is already an important deity in Upper Egypt, particularly worshipped at Nekheb. Her association with vultures and her maternal and protective symbolism develops early in Egyptian religious tradition.

The Early Dynastic Period: Nekhbet becomes closely integrated with royal authority in Upper Egypt. The merging of the Nekheb and Nekhen cult spheres elevates her status, and she is incorporated into the early concept of the 'Two Ladies'[294], paired with Wadjet to symbolise the king's rule over a unified Egypt.

---

[290] Wilkinson, Richard H. (2003). The Complete Gods and Goddesses of Ancient Egypt. Thames & Hudson. pp. 213–214
[291] Bailleul-LeSuer, Rozenn (ed), Between Heaven and Earth: Birds in Ancient Egypt. The Oriental Institute of the University of Chicago. pp. 61–62, 138
[292] Christiansen, S. U. 2023 What do the Figurines of "Bird Ladies" in Pre-Dynastic Egypt represent? (OAJAA)
[293] Wilkinson, Richard H. (2003).
[294] Wilkinson, Richard H. (2003).

The Egyptian Gods An Illustrated Introduction

Nekhbet, Wikipedia Creative Commons, Public Domain

The Old Kingdom: Nekhbet appears in the Pyramid Texts in her protective and cosmic roles. Her vulture motif becomes a royal emblem and great royal wives often wear vulture headdresses.

The First Intermediate Period: Political fragmentation weakens centralised state cults, but local worship of Nekhbet persists in Upper Egypt, particularly at her traditional cult centre, Nekheb.

The Middle Kingdom: Nekhbet's cult and iconography remain active and respected, particularly in her Upper Egyptian heartland.

The Second Intermediate Period: Political fragmentation leads to a reduced national emphasis on Nekhbet within royal and state-sponsored religion. However, she continues to be worshipped in her local cult centre at Nekhab.

The New Kingdom: Nekhbet becomes deeply integrated into state ideology and royal iconography. She appears frequently in temple and tomb art, spreading her wings in protective embrace over pharaohs and sanctuaries.

The Third Intermediate Period: Nekhbet's worship endures even as theological blending (syncretism) intensifies. Her protective symbolism and visual motifs (especially in crowns and iconography) remain prominent.

The Late Period: During the Saite Period's cultural and religious revival, Nekhbet's traditional role as protector of Upper Egypt and royal authority is reaffirmed.

The Ptolemaic and Roman Periods: Nekhbet's role as one of the 'Two Ladies' remains ritually and politically important. Her protective imagery and symbolic roles remain present in temple architecture and reliefs.

The Byzantine Period: Christianity becomes dominant and traditional Egyptian religion is increasingly suppressed. Nekhbet's temples fall out of use, and her worship fades with the collapse of traditional Egyptian religion.

Nekhbet has no direct equivalent in the Greek / Roman tradition, but Hera / Juno captures her maternal authority, while Athena / Minerva or Nike / Victoria capture her protective aspects. People could pray to Nekhbet for protection (especially of rulers and mothers), divine favour, safe childbirth, and spiritual guardianship.

Neper: God of Grain

Left: Two variations of 'Neper' in hieroglyphs

Neper is a god of grain[295], barley, agricultural fertility, grain cycles, and the life-force within food. His name translates roughly to 'Grain', 'Seed', or 'Lord of the Mouth'. He is sometimes referred to simply as the 'Personification of Grain'. His female counterpart is Nepit, a goddess of grain. His consort may also be Tayt, a goddess of weaving. Neper embodies the life force within grain, symbolising not just food but the cyclical nature of growth, death, and rebirth. His divine role is to ensure the successful germination, growth, and harvesting of grain crops[296].

Neper represents the essence of grain as a vital sustainer of life and is invoked during agricultural rituals to secure abundance and protection of the harvest. His life is tied to the life of the grain, he 'dies' when it was harvested and is 'reborn' when it sprouts again.

Neper appears in hymns and funerary texts, especially in contexts relating to rebirth and nourishment. In the Pyramid Texts and Coffin Texts, he is often mentioned alongside his mother, Renenutet, a goddess of nourishment and harvest. These texts sometimes describe him being 'reaped' and 'reborn'.

Neper is closely identified with and sometimes syncretised with Osiris, particularly in the context of life-death-rebirth cycles. Like Osiris, Neper's death and rebirth mirror the agricultural processes. He is also associated with his mother Renenutet, and she plays a protective role over the harvest, complementing his existence. Occasionally, he shares aspects with Min, a fertility god, and Geb, the earth god, due to his grounding in agricultural functions.

Neper is usually depicted as a young man, sometimes with grain stalks sprouting from his body or in his hands, symbolising his connection to the harvest. In some artistic depictions, his body may be covered in barley or wheat motifs, emphasising his embodiment of grain itself. Occasionally, he is shown with hieroglyphs for grain or as a sheaf of grain personified.

There is limited information on specific major temples or cult centres dedicated exclusively to Neper, but he is likely to have been worshipped widely in farming communities throughout Egypt. His veneration is particularly important in Lower Egypt, where grain production is more prevalent. He is

---

[295] Pinch, Geraldine. Egyptian Mythology p.171., Oxford University Press, USA (April 8, 2004) ISBN 0-19-517024-5.
[296] Willcockx, S. (n.d.). Magic and Religion in Ancient Egypt, Part II: 81 Gods. Retrieved October 5, l2025, from https://www.egyptology.nl/2ndprevw.pdf

also honoured in funerary rituals across Egypt due to his symbolic ties to resurrection and sustenance in the afterlife[297].

Neper, Wikipedia Creative Commons, Public Domain

The Early Dynastic Period: Neper does not appear by name in surviving texts from this time, but agricultural cycles are central to society, suggesting early conceptual roots.

The Old Kingdom: Neper first appears in the Pyramid Texts as a personification of grain and is associated with death and resurrection.

The First Intermediate Period: During this politically fragmented era, religious expression becomes more localised. Neper continues to be worshipped in agricultural and funerary contexts, but there is limited textual evidence of any expansion or major development in his cult.

The Middle Kingdom: Neper's role is expanded in Coffin Texts, where he is often linked to Renenutet (his mother) and to rebirth in the afterlife. His agricultural symbolism becomes more refined, and he is more frequently invoked in non-royal funerary texts, suggesting broader appeal.

The Second Intermediate Period: Little is added to Neper's cult in this period. As with other deities, his worship is likely to have persisted on a localised level, especially in agricultural regions.

The New Kingdom: Neper appears more often in temple hymns and ritual texts. His symbolism overlaps more clearly with Osiris in themes of death and renewal. Though still a minor god, he gains more consistent mention in religious literature, including in The Book of the Dead.

The Third Intermediate and Late Periods: Neper continues to be acknowledged in agricultural and funerary traditions, often in syncretic roles. Neper's worship persists in traditional texts and rituals but is largely overshadowed by more prominent deities like Osiris, Min, and Renenutet. He is retained in conservative religious contexts, especially where grain and agricultural symbolism are still emphasised.

The Ptolemaic Period: Under Greek rule, Egyptian religion sees increased syncretism. Neper is occasionally referenced in temple inscriptions (e.g., Edfu), but he is not the focus of any new cult developments. His function is largely symbolic and tied to grain offerings and fertility.

The Roman Period: Neper's worship continues in declining form, primarily as a symbolic figure in older temple rituals. His identity is often merged with other grain or fertility deities. There is no evidence of an active, independent cult during this time.

The Byzantine Period: By this time, Christianity has spread throughout Egypt, leading to the decline of traditional Egyptian religion. Neper, like most native deities, falls out of worship entirely and disappears from religious practice.

As a god of grain, Neper is comparable to the Greek / Roman goddess Demeter / Ceres, or perhaps Triptolemus, a demigod who spreads agriculture to humanity under the guidance of Demeter / Ceres, both embodying the living grain. People could pray to Neper for abundant harvests, nourishment and sustenance, strength in adversity, renewal and the cycle of life, and spiritual rebirth.

---

[297] Willcockx, S. (n.d.).

Nephthys: Goddess of Mourning and Lamentation

Left: 'Nephthys' in hieroglyphs

Nephthys is a goddess associated with death, mourning, night, protection, the house, service, lamentation, and the air. Her name means 'Lady of the House', where 'house' refers to the sky temple or divine enclosure rather than a domestic dwelling. She is also called the 'Invisible One' and sometimes the 'Useful' or 'Helpful' goddess[298]. A key figure in funerary practices, Nephthys mourns the dead alongside her sister Isis[299]. She guards and guides the deceased safely to the afterlife, using her magic and lamentation to nurture resurrection and rebirth.

In the Osiris myth, Nephthys seduces Osiris, sometimes through trickery, leading to the birth of Anubis. She aids Isis in locating Osiris's body after his murder by Set and mourns him through ritual lamentation. She further helps resurrect Osiris long enough for Horus[300] to be conceived. Across various Pyramid and Coffin Texts, Nephthys is invoked for her protective and mourning powers. Often paired with Isis[301], Nephthys sometimes merges with her in magical and funerary contexts. She shares significant roles with Anubis (her son in some traditions)[302] in embalming and protecting the dead. She also overlaps in protective functions with deities such as Serket and Bastet.

Visually, Nephthys typically appears as a woman wearing a headdress displaying the hieroglyphs for her name, a basket (neb) above a stylised house or temple (het). She may spread falcon wings in a protective gesture over coffins or tomb scenes. In funerary papyri, she appears alongside Isis, flanking the corpse or sarcophagus with arms raised in mourning. Occasionally, she takes the form of a kite, a bird of prey connected to mourning. Nephthys was worshipped in Heliopolis, where she is part of the Ennead[303], Abydos, closely linked to Osiris and funerary rituals, and Dendera, where she is honoured as part of the funerary pantheon. She regularly features in temples dedicated to Isis and Osiris, particularly in rituals related to death, rebirth, and protection.

The Old Kingdom: Nephthys appears in the Pyramid Texts[304] as a mourner of Osiris, helping to restore him to life. She protects the pharaoh's body and soul in the afterlife and plays an important role in funerary religion and beliefs about life after death.

---

[298] Wilson, P. (1997). A Ptolemaic Lexikon: A lexicographical study of the texts in the Temple of Edfu. OLA. Vol. 78.
[299] Shahawy, Abeer El (2005). The funerary art of Ancient Egypt: a bridge to the realm of the hereafter. Farid Atiya Press. p. 73. ISBN 978-977-17-2353-0. Retrieved 2024-11-26.
[300] Lévai, Jessica (2007). Aspects of the Goddess Nephthys, Especially During the Graeco-Roman Period in Egypt. UMI.
[301] Shahawy, Abeer El (2005).
[302] Lévai, Jessica (2007).
[303] Porter, B.; Moss, R. (eds.). Theban Temples. Topographical Bibliography of Ancient Egyptian Hieroglyphic Texts, Reliefs, and Paintings. Vol. II (Second ed.). Oxford, UK.
[304] Faulkner, R.O., ed. (1969). Ancient Egyptian Pyramid Texts. Oxford, UK: Oxford University Press.

Nephthys, Wikipedia Creative Commons, Public Domain

The First Intermediate Period: Nephthys's worship grows slowly alongside local cults of Osiris, the rising god of the afterlife. As Osiris's story spreads to local areas, Nephthys, connected to his death and return, becomes more important. She is often called on in tomb writings to protect and guide ordinary people in the afterlife, not just pharaohs.

The Middle Kingdom: Nephthys becomes well known and appears with Isis in tomb art, guarding coffins and mourning. In the Coffin Texts she helps protect and raise the dead. She also features in Lamentations, where her grief for Osiris guides ritual mourning and shows her key role in beliefs about death and rebirth.

The Second Intermediate Period: The worship of Nephthys grows stronger in places like Thebes and Abydos. She is honoured as both a mourner of Osiris and a guardian of the dead, often called on in rituals. Her role as protector becomes clearer in guarding against chaos in the afterlife.

The New Kingdom: Nephthys becomes more prominent in texts and temple art. She features in the Book of the Dead, helping with the resurrection and protecting the deceased alongside Isis. Her image often appears in tombs, spreading her wings over sarcophagi. Her worship is included in major temple rituals for Osiris, Isis, and Amun.

The Third Intermediate Period: Nephthys sees a revival and becomes popular among ordinary people. She is often called on in magic spells for protection, healing, and safe passage to the afterlife. Her link with Anubis grows stronger, as both protect the dead. Nephthys appears in amulets and texts as a guardian goddess who wards off evil and keeps souls safe.

The Late Period: Nephthys's role and depiction become more standardised, closely tied to the mystical ceremonies of Osiris and funerary practices, and worship of her expands in smaller local groups.

The Ptolemaic Period: Nephthys is merged with similar Greek gods, creating new combined worship. She stays important in Egyptian religion, shown in temple carvings at places like Dendera and Edfu. Nephthys continues to play a key role in religious ceremonies despite changing times.

The Roman Period: Worship of Nephthys continues, especially in funerary rites for Osiris, a god of the afterlife. In Roman Egypt, these rites still include Nephthys as a protector guiding the dead. Despite Roman changes, traditions around Osiris and Nephthys last in temples and local rituals.

The Byzantine Period: The cult of Nephthys slowly fades and vanishes as temples close and old practices stop. However, her themes of mourning and resurrection influence early Christian art, helping connect ancient Egyptian beliefs with new Christian symbols.

As a goddess of mourning and protection of the dead, Nephthys is comparable to the Greek / Roman goddess Hekate / Trivia or Persephone / Proserpina, as both goddesses dwell between life and death, guiding souls, and presiding over transitions. Nephthys could be prayed to for comfort in grief, protection of the dead, safe passage through darkness, and peace in the home.

Nepit: Goddess of Grain

Left: 'Nepit' in hieroglyphs

Nepit is a goddess of grain (particularly cereal crops like wheat and barley), and fertility and agricultural abundance[305]. Her name translates simply as 'grain' and she serves as the female counterpart to the god Neper[306]. She is sometimes referred to as the 'goddess of grain' or the 'female form of Neper'[307]. Closely connected to the agricultural cycle, Nepit embodies the nourishment and prosperity that grain provides. She plays a vital role in ensuring crop fertility and the availability of food, especially in farming communities.

Nepit does not feature in any major mythological narratives. Most references to her are found in religious or agricultural texts, where she appears alongside Neper in discussions of grain, fertility, and seasonal renewal. In some contexts Nepit and Neper are linked to broader themes of death and rebirth, occasionally merging with aspects of Osiris, whose mythology reflects similar cycles through the symbolism of the harvest. Nepit also shares attributes with goddesses Isis and Hathor, both of whom are also connected to agriculture and motherhood[308]. Nepit is portrayed as a woman holding sheaves of grain or marked with hieroglyphic signs representing cereals. There are no known temples built specifically for her, nor distinct cult centres separate from those of Neper. Her worship appears to have been local and informal, focused in rural areas, small shrines, and domestic practices rather than large state-sponsored rituals.

The Pre-Dynastic and Early Dynastic Periods: There is no direct evidence naming Nepit, but early crop and fertility rituals are likely to have involved symbolic or unnamed figures or proto-deities from folk traditions, with seasonal rites honouring the land's fertility. Grain and fertility are central to Egyptian life, and food-offering rituals involving grain such as bread or beer are common in tombs and shrines[309]. An early form of the goddess Nepit may well have been part of these practices.

The Old Kingdom: Nepit begins to appear in written sources as a symbolic female form of grain, often alongside Neper. Together, they represent the agricultural cycle, Nepit as the nurturing force, Neper as the generative force. Egyptians give divine form to essential natural elements like crops. Nepit does not play a major role in temple religion but is honoured informally in rural areas through seasonal, practical rituals linked to farming and harvests[310].

---

[305] Nepit. Retrieved October 5, 2025, from https://worldmythos.com/nepit/
[306] Pinch, Geraldine. Egyptian Mythology p.171., Oxford University Press, USA (April 8, 2004) ISBN 0-19-517024-5.
[307] Talestone (n.d.). Nepit: Goddess of Grain and Fertility. Talestone - Wonders of the Past. Retrieved October 5, 2025, from https://talestone.com/gods/nepit
[308] Nepit. Retrieved October 5, 2025, from https://worldmythos.com/nepit/
[309] Talestone (n.d.).
[310] Nepit. Retrieved October 5, 2025, from https://worldmythos.com/nepit/

The First Intermediate Period: As state-sponsored temple religion declines, local practices tied to farming and daily survival continue. Nepit is still honoured at the household or community level, especially in rural areas. She appears in agricultural and funerary texts, with smaller rituals and prayers keeping her worship alive despite the loss of grand temples.

The Middle Kingdom: Nepit becomes more clearly defined as a goddess of both grain and the afterlife[311]. As a feminine counterpart to Neper, she is linked to fertility and spiritual nourishment. She may be invoked in funerary texts to provide food for the dead and support their rebirth. Grain, symbolising life through its growth cycle, strengthens her role in these beliefs.

The Second Intermediate Period: Nepit is rarely shown in art or inscriptions from this period, but grain remains central to religion and daily life. As its personification, she continues to be honoured in local rituals and household worship, even if not formally recorded.

The New Kingdom: Nepit fits into the wider religious themes connecting food to resurrection. In funerary texts, grain often represents the rebirth of the dead, and Nepit may be referenced in offerings or hymns tied to this idea.

The Third Intermediate Period: Worship of Nepit becomes more local and community based. She remains connected to farming, grain, and seasonal fertility, especially in rural areas. Though there are no major temples or organised cults, her symbolic role in growth and sustenance is still meaningful in agricultural life.

The Late Period: Nepit continues to appear in agricultural texts and magical spells. She guards crops vital to survival and is linked to rebirth, reflecting beliefs that grain, like the dead, can rise again. She is important not just to farmers but also in funerary rituals. She remains spiritually relevant to fertility and protection.

The Ptolemaic Period: Nepit's role is merged with Greek deities like Demeter or Persephone, who are also linked to grain and fertility. While she has no separate cult, her functions live on in blended rituals focused on harvest and abundance, especially in rural areas where older traditions continue.

The Roman Period: Nepit's presence continues in everyday farming customs and seasonal rituals. Although no longer worshipped in grand temples or formal cults, her role shifts to folk practices tied to the practical rhythms of rural life. Nepit's importance becomes more symbolic and connected to crop success and food supply rather than official religion or myths.

The Byzantine Period: Pagan practices are suppressed or fade away. However, symbols tied to Nepit such as grain, fertility, and rebirth, persist by being absorbed into Christian traditions. These themes reappear in Christian art, hymns, and festivals like Easter and harvest celebrations, allowing ancient Egyptian ideas to survive in a new religious form and connect past and present beliefs.

As a god of grain, Nepit is comparable to the Greek / Roman goddess Demeter / Ceres, as both embody the fertile earth and the life-giving grain that sustains humanity. People could pray to Neper for abundant harvests, nourishment and sustenance, strength in adversity, renewal and the cycle of life, and spiritual rebirth.

---

[311] Talestone (n.d.). Nepit: Goddess of Grain and Fertility. Talestone - Wonders of the Past. Retrieved October 5, 2025, from https://talestone.com/gods/nepit

Nu: God of the Primordial Waters

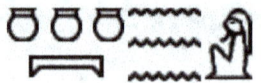

Left: 'Nu' in hieroglyphs

Nu is a god of the primeval waters, chaos, abyss, and the unformed state of the universe. His name means 'watery one' or 'inert one'. He is also referred to as the 'Father of the Gods' and 'Primordial Ocean'. Nu embodies the boundless, formless waters that existed before creation. He represents the source from which all matter and life emerge[312]. Nu sustains the cosmos by providing the chaotic basis necessary for creation. He is invoked in spells and religious texts as the background essence from which order is drawn.

Nu features in various creation myths, particularly the Heliopolitan tradition. In this account, he is the origin from which the creator god Atum arises[313]. During the mythological story of Ra's ageing, Nu is said to lift the sun god into the sky, offering renewal and restoration[314].

Nu is sometimes associated with other creator or water deities, such as Atum, Ptah, and Heka, though he retains his own identity as a distinctly primordial figure. Nu also forms a male-female pair with Naunet, his feminine counterpart[315], as part of the Ogdoad.

Nu is typically depicted as a bearded man with water rippling around him or carrying a barque (boat) upon the primordial waters. He is also shown with blue or green skin to symbolise his watery nature, or with upraised arms lifting the solar barque.

The Pre-Dynastic and Early Dynastic Periods: There is no direct evidence of Nu during this period, and no known temples or images associated with him. The concept of a primordial watery chaos exists in early myth-making traditions. Early cosmological ideas are beginning to form, laying the groundwork for later religious developments. Nu's identity as the personification of the primeval waters is present in emerging priestly cosmologies, particularly in Heliopolis.

The Old Kingdom: Nu appears in the Pyramid Texts described as the watery abyss from which the creator god Atum emerges. He is invoked in spells concerning creation, rebirth, and the sun god Ra's journey. His religious role becomes firmly established.

The First Intermediate Period: Religious decentralisation occurs, but Nu remains present in funerary and cosmological references. His importance persists in creation stories.

---

[312] Silverman, David P. (2003). Ancient Egypt. Oxford University Press. p. 120. ISBN 0-19-521952-X.
[313] McBride, Daniel R. (2003). The Oxford Essential Guide to Egyptian Mythology. Berkley. ISBN 0-425-19096-X.
[314] Wilkinson, Richard H. (2003). The Complete Gods and Goddesses of Ancient Egypt. Thames & Hudson. pp. 206–207. ISBN 0-500-05120-8.
[315] Budge, E. A. Wallis (1920). An Egyptian Hieroglyphic Dictionary. J. Murray. p. 350.

Nu, Wikipedia Creative Commons, Public Domain

The Middle Kingdom: Coffin Texts include many references to Nu. He is invoked as a cosmic force assisting the deceased in transformation and rebirth. His mythological significance deepens. His counterpart Naunet is also mentioned, indicating the Ogdoad religion's growth.

The Second Intermediate Period: The Ogdoad cosmology, in which Nu and Naunet are key members, becomes more regionally important, especially in Hermopolis.

The New Kingdom: Nu is featured in The Book of the Dead, Amduat, and other funerary texts. He lifts Ra's barque into the sky each morning. He appears in temple inscriptions and tomb scenes. He still has no dedicated cult, but the Ogdoad gains ritual importance in Hermopolis. Religious roles expand as priests and scribes incorporate more cosmological layers into their writings.

The Third Intermediate Period: As priesthoods gain influence, older theological systems, including those involving Nu, are preserved and adapted. Hermopolis continues to be a centre for Ogdoad worship.

The Late Period: There is renewed interest in traditional religion and cosmology. The god Nu appears in more sophisticated and syncretic theological texts. He has continued symbolic significance, especially in the temple rituals involving creation myths. The aspect of Nu that represents primordial chaos becomes dominant[316].

The Ptolemaic Period: Greek influence blends with Egyptian religion. Nu is sometimes equated with abstract Greek philosophical ideas of chaos or the boundless. He is still not personally worshipped, but is retained in religious literature and temple inscriptions.

The Roman Period: Egyptian religion continues under Roman rule, but then gradually declines. Nu survives in esoteric temple inscriptions and late cosmological texts. His name and concept appear in Hermetic writings, reflecting Hellenistic reinterpretations of Egyptian cosmology.

The Byzantine Period: Christianity spreads; temples close and pagan worship is suppressed. Nu, along with the rest of the Egyptian pantheon, fades from active religious practice. He survives only in texts, inscriptions, and later academic or mythological references.

As the personification of the primordial waters of chaos that existed before the creation of the world, Nu is comparable to the Greek primordial god Chaos, as both represent the undifferentiated void from which the cosmos is formed. Because Nu is so vast and abstract, he is not prayed to in the same way as other gods. However, he is a subject of reverence in hymns, text, and invocations. He could be invoked in themes of renewal and rebirth, protection and stability, mystical knowledge, creative power, and purification and healing.

---

[316] McBride, Daniel R. (2003). The Oxford Essential Guide to Egyptian Mythology. Berkley. ISBN 0-425-19096-X.

Nut: The Sky Goddess

Left: 'Nut' in hieroglyphs

Nut is a goddess of the sky, the stars, the cosmos, mothers, astrology, astronomy, and the cyclical passage of time[317]. Her name means 'sky' in ancient Egyptian. She is also known as the 'Sky Mother' and 'She Who Holds a Thousand Souls'. She is considered to be one of the oldest deities in the Egyptian pantheon[318]. She is the granddaughter of Atum (the creator god who produces the first divine pair), the daughter of Shu (god of air) and Tefnut (goddess of moisture), the sister and wife of Geb (god of the earth), the mother of Osiris, Isis, Set, Nephthys, and sometimes Horus the Elder[319], and the grandmother of Horus the Younger (son of Isis and Osiris)[320].

Nut spans the heavens, forming the sky itself. Each evening, she swallows the sun god Ra, and each morning, she gives birth to him anew, marking the rhythm of day and night. She shields the earth with her body, separating it from the heavens, and is considered a guardian of the dead, offering protection to souls journeying through the afterlife.

Nut is usually depicted as a woman stretching across the sky with her body arched over the earth[321], with her fingertips and toes touching the ground. Her skin is dark blue or black, covered in golden stars, symbolising the night sky. In tomb art, she may also appear standing with outstretched arms or as a celestial cow, embodying the vault of the heavens, or as a woman with the symbol of a situla or water pot ('*nw*') above her head, which is thought to symbolise the uterus. Some scholars suggest that the Egyptians saw the Milky Way as a celestial depiction of Nut[322]. Her imagery is especially prominent in tombs from the New Kingdom onwards, including the Valley of the Kings and Queens (Thebes). She is closely associated with Heliopolis, due to her role in solar mythology, and with Hermopolis through her ties to cosmic creation.

The Pre-Dynastic and Early Dynastic Periods: Early representations of the sky and natural cycles suggest that the idea of a sky goddess is developing during this period. Nut's identity later begins to take shape in priestly cosmologies. References to the heavens and celestial order allude to a divine feminine presence, though Nut is not yet central in surviving texts from this period.

---

[317] Pinch, Geraldine (2002). Handbook of Egyptian Mythology. Handbooks of World Mythology. ABC-CLIO. pp. 173–174. ISBN 1-57607-763-2.
[318] The Oxford Encyclopedia of Ancient Egypt, by Leonard H. Lesko, 2001.
[319] Griffiths, J. Gwyn, ed. (1970). Plutarch's De Iside et Osiride. University of Wales Press, pp.135-137
[320] Hart, George (200t). The Routledge Dictionary of Egyptian Gods and Goddesses. Routledge. p. 110
[321] Cavendish, Richard (1998). Mythology, An Illustrated Encyclopaedia of the Principal Myths and Religions of the World. Tiger Books International. ISBN 1-84056-070-3.
[322] Graur, Or (2024). "The Ancient Egyptian Personification of the Milky Way as the Sky-Goddess Nut: An Astronomical and Cross-Cultural Analysis". Journal of Astronomical History and Heritage. 27: 28–45. arXiv:2404.01458. doi:10.3724/SP.J.1440-2807.2024.01.02.

The Old Kingdom: Nut appears in the Pyramid Texts, invoked as a protector of the dead, often depicted on sarcophagi and burial chamber ceilings. She plays a role in the afterlife, embracing and nurturing the deceased king. Her imagery and functions are already well-defined by this point.

Nut, being held up by Shu (the air), separating her from Geb (the earth), Wikipedia Creative Commons, Public Domain

The First Intermediate Period: Religious decentralisation reduces royal art and inscriptions, but Nut remains present in local tomb art. Her role as a celestial mother and protector continues, especially in private burials.

The Middle Kingdom: Nut appears in the Coffin Texts, where she continues to receive and guide souls into the afterlife. Her association with rebirth and cosmic order is reinforced. Her presence expands beyond royal tombs into elite and non-royal funerary practice.

The Second Intermediate Period: Limited evidence from monuments survives, but traditional religious beliefs persist. Nut's imagery and religious role are preserved in tombs and coffin decorations, especially in Thebes and surrounding regions.

The New Kingdom: Nut reaches her most prominent visual and textual presence. She is painted on the ceilings of royal tombs (e.g. in the Valley of the Kings and Queens, Thebes), arching across the sky and swallowing the sun. The Book of Nut, a cosmological text detailing the movements of the sun and stars through her body, appears in tombs such as that of Ramesses IV[323]. Nut features heavily in the Book of the Dead and other funerary texts. Her cosmic function is deeply embedded in royal theology.

The Third Intermediate Period: Nut's importance is maintained in art and texts. She remains a key figure in tomb decorations, particularly for elite burials. Her protective, maternal aspects are stressed in increasingly personal funerary traditions.

The Late Period: A resurgence of traditional religious forms enhances the use of traditional iconography. Nut continues to be depicted on coffin lids, ceilings, and funerary papyri. Her role is stable and traditional, with less innovation but widespread repetition of her key attributes.

The Ptolemaic Period: Under Greek rule, Egyptian cosmology is preserved and often reinterpreted. Though not syncretised with Greek deities in a major way, she remains respected as a symbol of the cosmos and protector of the dead.

The Roman Period and Byzantine Periods: Temples and tombs still include references to Nut, though traditional Egyptian religion is slowly declining. Nut's iconography and mythology persist in funerary contexts, particularly in late tombs and mummy cartonnage. With the spread of Christianity and the closure of Egyptian temples, the active worship of Nut comes to an end. Her name and imagery survives in texts and art but no longer form part of living religious practice.

As a sky goddess and a cosmic mother, Nut is comparable with the Greek goddess Urania (a female form of the god Uranus). Where Uranus is the Greek sky god, Nut can be seen as his feminine counterpart, the living heavens. Nut could be prayed to for protection and comfort, rebirth and renewal, afterlife and resurrection, and cosmic order and harmony.

---

[323] Alexandra von Lieven: Grundriss des Laufes der Sterne. Das sogenannte Nutbuch. The Carsten Niebuhr Institute of Ancient Eastern Studies, Kopenhagen 2007

Onuris: God of War

Left: Two Variations of 'Onuris' in hieroglyphs

Onuris is a god of war and hunting, protection in battle, and sometimes defender of the sun god Ra. His name means 'He Who Leads Back the Distant One'[324], and also sometimes 'The Sky Bearer'.

He is also known as 'Lord of Lances', 'Slayer of Enemies', and sometimes appears as Onuris-Shu when associated with the air god Shu. In different traditions he is either the grandson or the son of Ra, and the brother of Shu or other solar deities.

He defends Ra and Egypt from chaos, acting as patron of the army and royal warriors. In festivals mock battles are held in his honour to commemorate his martial attributes.

Onuris features in the 'Faraway Goddess' or 'Distant Goddess' myth. The goddess Menhit flees to Nubia and transforms into a lioness. Onuris is sent to bring her back, which restores divine balance. Onuris also appears in stories about the Eye of Ra (a divine feminine aspect of Ra), which wanders and must be returned.

Onuris is identified with Shu in later periods, forming Onuris-Shu, due to shared iconography (especially the feathered crown) and overlapping functions (holding up the sky, and restoring order).

Onuris is depicted as a bearded man wearing a robe or kilt[325], often with a headdress of two or four tall feathers[326]. He carries a spear or lance and sometimes a rope or lasso (especially in scenes of capturing the distant goddess). Occasionally he has a lion's head, emphasising ferocity and strength. In statues he may wear thick curly hair under his feathered crown.

His main centres of worship are Thinis (in Upper Egypt), Abydos, and later in the Delta region at Sebennytos. Temples dedicated to him and his cult festivals are particularly noted in those locations.

The Pre-Dynastic and Early Dynastic Periods: There is no clear evidence of Onuris at this stage. Concepts of regional warrior or hunting deities may foreshadow later attributes associated with him. Possible early cult activity begins in Thinis (Upper Egypt), although it is not well documented.

The Old Kingdom: Onuris is not yet prominent in state religion or texts. However, Thinite religious traditions, where he is eventually centred, preserve his early identity as a warrior god and hunter. People could pray to Onuris for

---

[324] The Way to Eternity: Egyptian Myth, F. Fleming & A. Lothian, p. 56
[325] Turner and Coulter, Dictionary of ancient deities, 2001
[326] Wilkinson, Richard H. (2003). The Complete Gods and Goddesses of Ancient Egypt. Thames & Hudson. p. 118

The First Intermediate Period: Regional deities gain more local prominence due to the weakening of central authority. Onuris may gain increased importance in Thinis and surrounding areas.

Onuris, Wikipedia Creative Commons, Public Domain

The Middle Kingdom: Onuris is recognised as a protector deity and a warrior figure. His mythological role in retrieving the Distant Goddess begins to be more formally integrated into temple and mythological traditions.

The Second Intermediate Period: Political fragmentation may limit widespread worship, but regional cults like that of Onuris continue. His link to Upper Egyptian military identity becomes more established.

The New Kingdom: Onuris rises in importance due to the emphasis on military success and royal protection. He is venerated in temples, invoked in battle contexts, and occasionally depicted with lion-headed features. His connection to the goddess Menhit, whom he brings back from Nubia, is fully integrated into theological narratives. Greeks in Egypt later equate him with Ares (Roman: Mars), foreshadowing syncretism in the Ptolemaic period.

The Third Intermediate Period: There is continued worship of Onuris in Thinis and surrounding towns. His functions as protector and warrior deity are retained, though less central in state cults.

The Late Period: A revival of traditional religion includes greater attention to deities with deep local roots. Onuris enjoys renewed religious and artistic presence. His identification with Shu (as Onuris-Shu) becomes more common in texts and reliefs.

The Ptolemaic Period: Onuris is actively worshipped, particularly in Thinis, Abydos, and parts of the Delta, such as Sebennytos. Greek rulers and priests identify him with Ares (Roman: Mars), increasing his appeal among Hellenised Egyptians. His iconography, warrior with tall feathers, spear, and rope, continues in temple art.

The Roman Period: Temples and inscriptions still honour Onuris, often alongside other martial or solar deities. His warlike and protective aspects remain relevant in temple cults and religious texts.

The Byzantine Period: With the Christianisation of Egypt and suppression of traditional temple worship, Onuris' cult declines and eventually disappears. His name and myths survive only in inscriptions and historical accounts.

Onuris is equated with the Greek / Roman god Ares / Mars, a god of war and bravery on the battlefield, but also seen as a rampant destructive force. In the legend of Olympian gods fleeing from Typhon and taking animal form in Egypt, Ares is said to have taken the form of a fish as Lepidotus or Onuris[327]. People could pray to Onuris for victory and courage in battle, protection and defence, justice and restoration of peace and order, and courage, strength and determination, invoking him as a divine champion who conquers chaos and restores harmony to the world.

---

[327] Antoninus Liberalis, Metamorphoses 28 (trans. Celoria) (Greek mythographer 2nd century AD)

Osiris: God of the Afterlife and Resurrection

Left: 'Osiris' in hieroglyphs

Osiris is a god of the afterlife, resurrection, fertility, the dead, vegetation, agriculture, and the cycle of life and death[328]. His name is often interpreted to mean 'Mighty' or 'The Powerful One'. He is also referred to as 'Lord of the Underworld' and sometimes 'King of the Living'. He is the grandson of Ra, the son of Geb[329] and Nut, the brother of Isis, Set, Nephthys, and sometimes Horus the Elder (depending on the myth), the husband of Isis, and the father of Horus the Younger (also known simply as Horus). Horus is sometimes said to have sons known as the Four Sons of Horus, who are thus occasionally considered Osiris's grandsons in an extended family tree.

Osiris presides over the realm of the dead, ruling the Duat (the Egyptian underworld). He judges the souls of the deceased in the Hall of Ma'at, where hearts are weighed against the Feather of Ma'at. As a divine king, he ensures order, regeneration, and the continuation of life beyond death. His influence extends to the annual flooding of the Nile and the fertility of the land, symbolising rebirth and agricultural renewal.

There are several key myths involving Osiris. In the most famous, his brother Set murders him by sealing him in a coffin and casting it into the Nile. Isis, his wife and sister, retrieves his body, but Set dismembers it and scatters the pieces. Isis and Nephthys find and reassemble his body, and Isis briefly resurrects him to conceive their son, Horus. Osiris then becomes lord of the underworld. This myth forms the foundation of ancient Egyptian beliefs about death, resurrection, and divine kingship. Osiris is at times syncretised with other deities. He is closely identified with Ptah-Sokar-Osiris, a composite funerary god representing creation, death, and rebirth. He also shares traits with Heryshaf, a creator god, and later becomes associated with Serapis, a Greco-Egyptian deity intended to merge Hellenistic and Egyptian religious elements.

He is typically depicted as a mummified man with green or black skin, colours symbolising rebirth and the fertile Nile silt. He wears the Atef crown, and bears the crook and flail crossed over his chest[330]. He often has a straight false beard and is shown in a tightly wrapped linen shroud, sometimes standing or enthroned. The principal cult centre of Osiris is Abydos[331], considered to be his mythical burial place and a major pilgrimage site. Other important centres include Busiris and Philae Island, where his worship continues into the Greco-Roman period. His festivals, especially the Osiris Mysteries at Abydos, play a major role in public religious life.

---

[328] The Oxford Guide: Essential Guide to Egyptian Mythology, Edited by Donald B. Redford, pp. 302–307, Berkley, 2003, ISBN 0-425-19096-X

[329] Wilkinson, Richard H. (2003). The Complete Gods and Goddesses of Ancient Egypt. London: Thames & Hudson. p. 105. ISBN 978-0-500-05120-7.

[330] Strudwick, Helen (2006). The Encyclopedia of Ancient Egypt. New York: Sterling Publishing Co., Inc. pp. 118–119. ISBN 978-1-4351-4654-9.

[331] "The passion plays of osiris". ancientworlds.net. Archived from the original on 2007-06-26.

Osiris, Wikipedia Creative Commons, Public Domain

The Old Kingdom: Osiris appears in the Pyramid Texts of the 5th and 6th Dynasties (c. 2400 BCE)[332]. Osiris is presented as a dead and resurrected king, and the deceased pharaoh is identified with him in the afterlife.

The First Intermediate Period: Osiris worship begins to expand beyond royalty, becoming more accessible to non-royal individuals who seek eternal life by identifying with Osiris in death.

The Middle Kingdom: Osiris becomes the most important god of the dead for all Egyptians, not just kings. The Coffin Texts reflect this shift, with common people invoking Osiris to secure a blessed afterlife. The cult centre at Abydos grows in religious significance, becoming a major site of pilgrimage and ritual.

The Second Intermediate Period: The worship of Osiris continues steadily despite foreign rule by the Hyksos in parts of Egypt. His myth remains culturally resilient and central to Egyptian religious identity.

The New Kingdom: Osiris reaches the height of his prominence in funerary religion. The Book of the Dead (and other funerary texts) standardise depictions of Osiris and the judgment of the dead. Osiris Mysteries are celebrated annually at Abydos, including dramatic re-enactments of his death and resurrection.

The Third Intermediate Period: Regional religious centres continue the strong worship of Osiris, especially at Abydos and Busiris. He remains the dominant funerary deity, often syncretised with local gods or funerary figures like Sokar and Ptah.

The Late Period: Osiris worship continues with renewed intensity, especially under native Egyptian rule. Temples are renovated or expanded in his honour. The Osiris cult is formalised in complex rituals, and priesthoods flourish, especially at Abydos and Philae Island.

The Ptolemaic Period: Under Greek rule, Osiris is syncretised with Greek gods, particularly Dionysus (Bacchus) and Hades (Pluto). The composite god Serapis emerges, blending Osiris with Apis and Hellenistic elements, becoming a major deity in Alexandria.

The Roman Period: Osiris continues to be venerated in traditional temples across Egypt, particularly in southern regions like Philae Island. Osirian beliefs influence Roman religion and contribute to broader Mediterranean mystery cults. The cult of Isis and Osiris spreads throughout the Roman Empire.

The Byzantine Period: The last hieroglyphic inscription (at Philae Island, 394 CE) references traditional Egyptian gods, including Osiris. Worship of Osiris gradually disappears under Christian influence[333], but his legacy survives in religious syncretism and cultural memory.

As a god of the afterlife and resurrection, Osiris is comparable to the Greek / Roman god Hades / Pluto, who rules the underworld and governs the dead. Osiris could be prayed to for eternal life, safe passage after death, fertile crops, justice, healing, and spiritual renewal.

---

[332] Griffiths, John Gwyn (1980). The Origins of Osiris and His Cult. Brill. p. 44
[333] ""History of the Later Roman Empire from the Death of Theodosius I. to the Death of Justinian", The Suppression of Paganism – ch22, p. 371, John Bagnell Bury, Courier Dover Publications, 1958, ISBN 0-486-20399-9

Pakhet: Goddess of Hunting, War, and Protection

Left: 'Pakhet' in hieroglyphs

Pakhet is a lioness-headed goddess of hunting, war, and protection. Her name means 'She Who Scratches' or 'The Tearer'. She is also referred to as 'The Night Huntress'[334].

She is the granddaughter of Ra (if following the lineage through Tefnut or Sekhmet), the daughter of Sekhmet (or possibly Bastet or Tefnut, all lioness goddesses with whom she was linked), the sister of Maahes or Nefertem (depending on the maternal deity), the wife of Horus or another solar deity in some local traditions.

She prowls the desert and rocky regions, particularly active during the night, stalking prey and safeguarding sacred places. She is a solitary deity who acts with precision and force, embodying the stealth and swiftness of a wild cat. Her domain includes guarding against harmful spirits and defending the vulnerable.

Few myths directly feature Pakhet, and she does not appear prominently in narrative cycles like other deities. However, her role in religious life suggests a significant spiritual presence in borderland regions where the desert meets civilisation. Pakhet becomes syncretised with other lioness goddesses such as Sekhmet and Bastet. While Sekhmet is often seen as a force of plague and wrath, and Bastet as a gentler, domestic protector, Pakhet represents a blend, fierce yet controlled, acting alone but effectively.

She is depicted as a woman with the head of a lioness, sometimes shown poised in mid-pounce or with claws ready to strike. Her expression is intense, focused, and alert, symbolising vigilance and strength. She carries no elaborate regalia, embodying raw, elemental power.

Her primary centre of worship is at a temple built into the cliffs of Beni Hasan, known to the Greeks as the Speos Artemidos, or 'Cave of Artemis'[335]. The location is isolated and dramatic, mirroring her independent nature.

The Old Kingdom: Pakhet may exist as a regional deity, perhaps related to or absorbed into other lioness deities like Sekhmet or Bastet during this period.

---

[334] Sutherland, A. (2019, March 4). Pakhet 'Night Huntress': Egyptian War-Like Lioness Goddess Associated With Artemis. Retrieved October 8, 2025, from https://www.ancientpages.com/2019/03/04/pakhet-night-huntress-egyptian-war-like-lioness-goddess-associated-with-artemis/

[335] Leser (Iufaa), K. H., Dr (2009, December 12). Speos Artemidos / Beni Hassan. Retrieved October 8, 2025, from https://www.maat-ka-ra.de/english/bauwerke/speos_artemidos/speos_artemidos.htm

The First Intermediate Period: Political fragmentation leads to increased regional religious activity. Local deities gain prominence during this time. Pakhet may begin to emerge as a distinctive deity in Middle Egypt, especially near the Al Minya region.

Pakhet, Wikipedia Creative Commons, Public Domain

The Middle Kingdom: Pakhet becomes more visible during this period. Her association with lioness goddesses and desert hunting aligns with the Middle Kingdom's focus on controlling the deserts and trade routes. She is considered a fusion of Bastet and Sekhmet ('She Who Scratches').

The Second Intermediate Period: Regional deities retain importance. There is no direct evidence of shifts in Pakhet's cult during this period of Hyksos rule.

The New Kingdom: Pakhet's worship flourishes, particularly during the 18th Dynasty. The Temple of Pakhet at Speos Artemidos, near Beni Hasan is built by Hatshepsut[336] and later restored by Seti I. Hatshepsut associates Pakhet with divine femininity, strength, and protection. Her role expands to the protector of borders, goddess of war, desert hunter, and sometimes funerary deity.

The Third Intermediate Period: With a decline in State Support, like many deities outside Thebes or the Delta, Pakhet's official worship diminishes. Her temple at Speos Artemidos may remain active, but little new construction occurs.

The Late Period: Her cult persists in Middle Egypt, especially among local communities and priests.

The Ptolemaic Period: Pakhet is often worshipped syncretically as a form of Artemis (Roman: Diana) or Artemis-Sekhmet. The temple Speos Artemidos retains ritual importance, though it is seen through a Greek interpretation. Her cave temple is visited as a sacred pilgrimage site.

The Roman Period: As Christianity spreads and pagan temples close, worship of Pakhet fades. The memory of Pakhet survives in the form of temple ruins and occasional inscriptions.

The Byzantine Period: Worship of Pakhet effectively ends as an organised, state-supported religion. Her temple at Speos Artemidos is abandoned, or possibly reused for Christian purposes. Religious texts and rituals are suppressed; and priesthoods are dissolved. She lives on in residual folk beliefs in rural areas.

As a warrior and protector, Pahket is equated with the Greek / Roman goddess Athena / Minerva. As a huntress, she is equated with Artemis / Diana. As a goddess who punishes the enemies of Egypt or the pharaoh, she is comparable to Nemesis / Invidia. She could also be compared to the war goddess Enyo / Bellona. People could pray to Pahket for protection and defence, hunting and skill, justice and vengeance, courage and strength, and cosmic protection.

---

[336] Leser (Iufaa), K. H., Dr (2009, December 12). Speos Artemidos / Beni Hassan. Retrieved October 8, 2025, from https://www.maat-ka-ra.de/english/bauwerke/speos_artemidos/speos_artemidos.htm

Ptah: God of Craft, Architecture, and Metalwork

Ptah, Wikipedia Creative Commons, Public Domain

 Left: 'Ptah' in hieroglyphs

Ptah is a god of craftsmen, architects, creation, metalworking, and artisanship. His name means 'the Opener' or 'He Who Opens', referring to his creative function. He is also known as the 'Lord of Truth', 'Master Architect', and 'Creator of the Gods'[337]. He is the husband of Sekhmet (the lion-headed goddess of war and healing), and in some versions, his wife is also Bastet, or he is connected with both through differing local cults. He is the father of Nefertum (a lotus god associated with beauty, healing, and the rising sun). Sometimes he is also considered to be the father of Imhotep, the deified architect and healer.

Ptah brings the world into existence through thought and speech. By conceiving ideas in the heart and giving them form with the tongue, he embodies intellectual creation. He is revered as a divine artisan who shapes reality, supports the work of craftsmen, and ensures harmony in constructed forms and sacred architecture. There are few narrative myths specifically focused on Ptah, but he plays a central role in the Memphite Theology, a philosophical text inscribed on the Shabaka Stone. This theology presents Ptah as the prime mover, who creates the gods themselves through mind and voice, offering one of the earliest expressions of creation by divine reason or speech[338]. Ptah is frequently identified with other creator deities. He is linked with Sokar, a god of the necropolis, and with Osiris, forming the composite deity Ptah-Sokar-Osiris[339], who represents creation, death, and rebirth.

Ptah is depicted as a mummified man, with green skin symbolising regeneration. He wears a close-fitting blue cap and false beard, holding a staff that combines the ankh, djed, and was-sceptre symbols. His figure often stands on a plinth signifying *ma'at*. His principal cult centre is Memphis, where he is venerated as patron of artisans and protector of the city. His temple, *Hut-ka-Ptah* ('Mansion of the Ka of Ptah') is the basis for the Greek '*Aigyptos*', the Latin '*Aegyptus*', and the English 'Egypt'[340]. The Memphite priesthood holds him as supreme among gods, with influence that extends across temple workshops and royal building projects.

The Pre-Dynastic Period: Ptah emerges as a local deity in Memphis, although no direct records of him exist from this early period. His worship may have developed from indigenous Memphite beliefs tied to creation and craftsmanship.

---

[337] Allen, James P. (1988). Genesis in Egypt: The Philosophy of Ancient Egyptian Creation Accounts. Yale Egyptological Study. pp. 38–41
[338] Mertz, B. G. (2025, September 10). Memphis. Retrieved October 8, 2025, from https://www.britannica.com/place/Memphis-ancient-city-Egypt
[339] The Metropolitan Museum of Art (n.d.). Ptah-Sokar-Osiris Figure of the Temple Musician Ihyt. The Met. Retrieved October 8, 2025, from https://www.metmuseum.org/art/collection/search/553823
[340] Wiktionary (2025, October 2). Egypt. https://en.wiktionary.org/wiki/Egypt

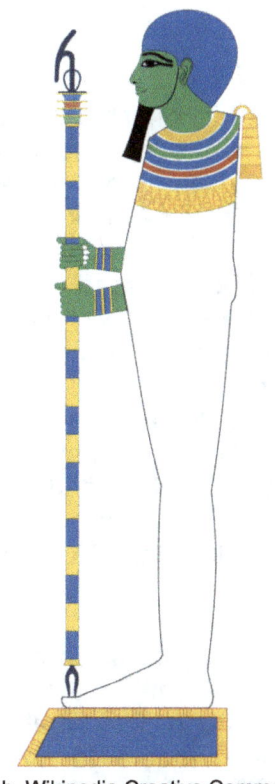

Ptah, Wikipedia Creative Commons, Public Domain

The Early Dynastic Period: Ptah becomes the patron god of Memphis, the new political capital under the unification of Upper and Lower Egypt. Ptah's temple at Memphis is founded during this era, establishing him as a significant deity early on.

The Old Kingdom: Ptah rises to state-level prominence as Memphis thrives as the political centre. He is part of the Memphite Triad: Ptah (the creator god), Sekhmet (his consort, goddess of war and healing), and Nefertem (their son, god of beauty and healing). Ptah is portrayed as a creator deity who brings the world into being through thought and speech. He gains strong association with craftsmen, builders, and artisans, especially those working on pyramids and temples.

The First Intermediate Period: Political fragmentation leads to decreased central authority, but Ptah's worship persists locally in Memphis and among craftsmen.

The Middle Kingdom: The revival of central authority restores Memphis' importance. Ptah's role as universal creator becomes more defined and integrated into state ideology. His worship spreads beyond Memphis, gaining favour in other parts of Egypt.

The Second Intermediate Period: Hyksos rule in the north diminishes centralised worship, but Ptah remains relevant among native Egyptians.

The New Kingdom and Third Intermediate Periods: Ptah enjoys immense popularity, especially in Thebes. Worship of Ptah spreads to Nubia, Syria-Palestine, and elsewhere through temples and stelae (inscribed stone or wooden slabs). Ptah continues to be worshipped, particularly in Memphis and Lower Egypt. His role evolves to include syncretism with other gods, such as: Ptah-Sokar-Osiris, a fusion deity combining Ptah (creation), Sokar (death), and Osiris (afterlife), commonly featured in funerary practices.

The Late Period: There is a revival of traditional religious practices under native dynasties. Ptah's temple complex is renovated. Worship of Ptah as a funerary and creator god continues to grow. Craftsmen still invoke Ptah as a patron.

The Ptolemaic Period: Greek rulers embrace Egyptian religion. Ptah remains an important deity. Temples are renovated and built in Memphis and other cities, blending Greek and Egyptian elements.

The Roman Period: Ptah's worship is diminished in prominence. The cult of Ptah becomes more associated with funerary contexts, especially through the Ptah-Sokar-Osiris triad. Temples remain at Memphis.

The Byzantine Period: With the rise of Christianity, pagan temples are closed, and the worship of traditional gods like Ptah ceases. By the 6th century CE, temples are abandoned or repurposed.

As a creator and patron of artisans, Ptah is comparable to the Greek / Roman god Hephaestus / Vulcanus. As a symbol of cosmic stability, he is comparable to Cronus / Saturn. As a god of intellectual creation and wisdom, he is comparable to Hermes / Mercury. People could pray to Ptah for skill in craftsmanship, inspiration, the successful realisation of plans, protection and stability, healing, and wisdom.

Ra: The Sun God

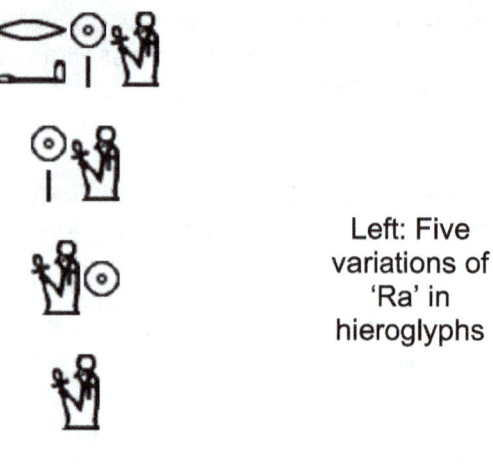

Left: Five variations of 'Ra' in hieroglyphs

Ra is a god of the sun, order, kingship, the sky, and creation. His name means 'sun' in ancient Egyptian, symbolising the life-giving force of daylight. He is also known as Ra-Horakhty ('Ra, who is Horus of the Two Horizons'), and sometimes as Atum-Ra when merged with the creator god Atum. He is the son of Nu, as he is said to have emerged from the waters of chaos at the dawn of creation[341]. He is sometimes associated with Hathor or Ma'at as a ruling partner. He is the father of Shu (air) and Tefnut (moisture) in some creation myths, particularly when merged with Atum as Atum-Ra. He is the grandfather of Geb (earth) and Nut (sky), through Shu and Tefnut.

Ra travels across the sky in his solar barque each day, bringing light and warmth to the world. At night, he journeys through the Duat, the underworld, navigating its dangers to emerge reborn each morning[342]. His daily cycle represents life, death, and renewal, divine authority and cosmic balance.

Numerous stories in Egyptian mythology feature Ra, including the tale where he creates humanity from his tears[343]. In another myth, the goddess Isis tricks Ra into revealing his secret name, gaining power over him. There is also the narrative of his nightly voyage through the underworld, where he confronts challenges to ensure that the sun rises again the next day.

Ra is closely linked with other major deities. He merges with Amun to form Amun-Ra, a supreme creator god during the New Kingdom. He is also combined with Horus as Ra-Horakhty, representing the rising sun and divine kingship.

Ra is commonly depicted as a man with the head of a falcon, crowned with a solar disk encircled by a uraeus. Sometimes, he appears as a full falcon or as a scarab beetle when associated with the morning sun[344]. His solar barque, Mandjet, often accompanies him in art.

---

[341] Shorter, Alan (2009). The Egyptian Gods. Borgo Press. ISBN 978-1434455147.
[342] Hart, George (1986). A Dictionary of Egyptian Gods and Goddesses. London: Routledge & Kegan Paul Inc. ISBN 978-0-415-05909-1.
[343] Shorter, Alan (2009).
[344] Pinch, Geraldine (2004). Egyptian Mythology: A Guide to the Gods, Goddesses, and Traditions of Ancient Egypt. Oxford University Press. ISBN 978-0-19-517024-5.

The primary centre of Ra's worship is Heliopolis. This city houses major temples and is a prominent religious hub. Worship of Ra also extends to other important sites like Thebes and Abu Simbel, especially when merged with other deities.

Ra, Wikipedia Creative Commons, Public Domain

The Early Dynastic Period and Old Kingdom: Ra emerges as a central deity in the solar cult centred at Heliopolis. During the Fourth Dynasty (c. 2600 BCE), pharaohs, especially those of the Pyramid Age, begin identifying themselves as 'sons of Ra'. He rises to prominence as the supreme sun god during the Fifth Dynasty and solar temples are constructed near pyramids. The Pyramid Texts frequently reference Ra as the king of the gods and ruler of the heavens.

The First Intermediate Period: Political fragmentation reduces state-sponsored worship, but local and personal devotion to Ra continues.

The Middle Kingdom: Ra remains a key figure, but syncretism begins. Amun-Ra becomes prominent as the Theban god Amun merges with Ra.

The New Kingdom: At the height of Ra's influence, Amun-Ra becomes the king of the gods and is worshipped throughout Egypt. Pharaohs build grand temples in honour of Amun-Ra, such as Karnak (Thebes). Ra-Horakhty (a fusion of Ra with Horus) emerges, symbolising the rising sun and royal power. The Book of the Dead and other funerary texts depict Ra's nightly journey through the Duat (underworld). During the reign of Akhenaten (c. 1353-1336 BCE), Ra's worship shifts during the Amarna Period when Akhenaten promotes the Aten, a solar disk aspect of Ra, as the sole deity. This monotheistic turn (Atenism) is short-lived and reversed after Akhenaten's death by his son Tutankaten (Tutenkhamun).

The Third Intermediate Period: Worship of Ra in his various forms continues, but political instability leads to increased regional variation. Local gods begin to eclipse Ra in some areas, though Amun-Ra remains influential.

The Late Period: Ra regains importance as Egypt seeks to revive its ancient traditions during periods of foreign rule. Syncretic deities like Ra-Horakhty and Amun-Ra remain central in religious texts and temple worship.

The Ptolemaic Period: Ra remains a central figure in Egyptian religion but undergoes reinterpretation as Greek and Egyptian beliefs blend. He is increasingly identified with the Greek sun god Helios (Roman: Sol) and contributes to the creation of syncretic deities like Serapis, who combines aspects of Ra, Osiris, and Apis. His image and mythology adapt to a new religious landscape shaped by both cultures.

The Roman and Byzantine Periods: Worship of Ra continues under Roman rule but begins to decline with the spread of Christianity. By the 4th–5th century CE, Ra's temples are closed. Christianity, especially Coptic Christianity, replaces Egypt's traditional religion. Ra becomes a figure of the mythological past, preserved in texts and temple ruins, but not part of living religious practice.

As a sun god, Ra is equated with the Greek / Roman god Helios / Sol. People could pray to Ra for life and vitality, protection and order, renewal and birth, guidance and illumination, and cosmic harmony.

Renenutet: Goddess of Grain and Nourishment

Left: 'Renenutet' in hieroglyphs

Renenutet is a goddess of grapes, grain[345], nourishment, harvest, fertility, abundance, and protective nursing[346]. Her name variously translates as 'She Who Rears', 'The Nourisher', or similar meanings relating to nourishment or protection. She is also known as Thermouthis or Hermouthis in Greek sources.

In some traditions she is the granddaughter of Ra, and the daughter of Geb and Nut. She is possibly the mother or sister of a serpent goddess called Nehebkau. In other traditions she is the wife of Geb, or the wife of Sobek, particularly in the Faiyum region[347]. She is the mother of Neper[348], and sometimes the mother or foster-mother of Horus. She is also associated or paired with Shai, a god of fate and destiny, particularly when deciding one's fate, especially newborn children.

She governs the success of the harvest, oversees food storage, and ensures the fertility of the land. As a divine nurse, she safeguards children and the pharaoh, especially during infancy, by endowing them with a protective destiny. Farmers regard her as a direct influence on their grain yields, crediting her with the prosperity of their crops.

There are no extensive myths exclusively centred on Renenutet, but she features in agricultural hymns and temple inscriptions. Her presence is invoked at harvest festivals, and she is sometimes mentioned in texts related to childbirth and nurturing. Her protective role extends into the afterlife, where she is occasionally linked to the sustenance of souls.

Renenutet is frequently identified with Wadjet, the cobra goddess of Lower Egypt, especially when depicted in protective forms. She is also associated with Isis and Hathor in her nurturing aspect.

She is typically portrayed as a cobra or a woman with the head of a cobra, sometimes nursing a child. On occasion, she appears as a full woman crowned with a uraeus or holding symbols of fertility and plenty, such as sheaves of grain. Her serpent form represents her protective nature and divine authority. Her main cult centre is at Terenuthis in the Nile Delta, but she is also venerated at Medinet Madi in the Faiyum region, where a temple dedicated to her and the crocodile god Sobek stands.

---

[345] Marini, Paolo. "Renenutet: worship and popular piety at Thebes in the New Kingdom". Journal of Intercultural and Interdisciplinary Archaeology.
[346] Pinch, Geraldine (2003). Egyptian mythology: a guide to the gods, goddesses, and traditions of ancient Egypt. New York: Oxford University Press. ISBN 0195170245.
[347] Francoise Dunand and Christiane Zivie-Coche (trans. David Lorton). (2004). Gods and Men in Egypt: 3000 BCE to 395 CE. Ithaca: Cornell University Press. [hereafter: Gods and Men].
[348] Francoise Dunand and Christiane Zivie-Coche (trans. David Lorton). (2004).

The Old Kingdom: Renenutet is mentioned in Pyramid Texts, especially in association with nurturing the king in the afterlife. She appears as a protective maternal figure and provider of sustenance. She is still a local or lesser deity during this period, with agricultural and protective associations.

The First Intermediate Period: There is limited evidence of major cult activity during this period due to political instability and decentralised religion, but she is worshipped locally, at rural level, especially in agricultural communities.

Renenutet, Wikipedia Creative Commons, Public Domain

The Middle Kingdom: Renenutet rises in prominence and her agricultural role is formalised. Worship tied to fertility, grain, and harvest; she becomes known as a goddess of the storehouse. She is linked with Thermouthis (a Greek name later associated with her) and Sobek (a crocodile god), forming part of regional triads. Her main cult centre begins to take shape at Terenuthis (modern Kom el-Rahman) in the Faiyum region.

The Second Intermediate Period: Regional variations and syncretism increase. Worship continues without major changes; the Faiyum region remains important.

The New Kingdom: This is the peak of Renenutet's national recognition. She is associated with the royal 'ka' (life force) and with nurturing the pharaoh. She becomes linked with the goddess Wadjet, another cobra deity and protector of kings. She is integrated into temple rituals and connected with other deities like Isis, Hathor, and Geb. Her role in the annual harvest festival becomes more prominent. Her worship continues at Faiyum, and at cult temples dedicated to the harvest and fertility gods.

The Third Intermediate Period: There is a decline in centralised temple worship across Egypt. Renenutet's worship continues locally, especially in agricultural regions. She remains an important household deity for fertility and food storage.

The Late Period: There is a revival of traditional religious practices, including renewed attention to older deities. Renenutet's association with grain supply and protection continues, along with personal piety. Her iconography and links to Roman and Greek snake goddesses begin to evolve.

The Ptolemaic Period: Renenutet is syncretised with the Greek goddess Demeter (Roman: Ceres), due to shared fertility and agricultural functions. She is known by the name Thermouthis in Greek, and depicted as a serpent or woman with a cornucopia (a 'horn of plenty' representing abundance). Worship of Renenutet continues at Terenuthis (Tarrana). She plays a role in Greco-Egyptian magical texts, amulets, and domestic religion.

The Roman and Byzantine Periods: Renenutet (as Thermouthis) remains a popular local deity in the Faiyum and beyond. Her worship appears in Greek magical papyri and local cult practices. There is a gradual decline of traditional Egyptian religion due to Christianisation of Egypt by the 4th century CE.

As a goddess of the harvest and abundance, she is equated with the Greek / Roman goddess Demeter / Ceres. People could pray to Renenutet for agricultural success, protection, fertility and family, prosperity and sustenance, and order and stability.

Satis: Fertility Goddess of the Nile

Left: 'Satis' in hieroglyphs

Satis is a goddess of the Nile's annual flooding, fertility, hunting, and the protection of Egypt's southern frontier. Her name means 'She Who Shoots' or 'She Who Pours'[349], referring to her association with archery, and her role in delivering the Nile's floodwaters. She is the wife of Khnum, the ram-headed creator god who fashions humans on his potter's wheel and controls the Nile's flow, and the mother of Anuket, another fertility goddess of the Nile. Satis, Khnum, and Anuket are collectively worshipped as the Elephantine Triad. Satis ushers in the annual flood, brings life-giving waters to the land, and ensures agricultural renewal. As a guardian of Egypt's southern border, she watches over Aswan and the First Cataract of the Nile. She also protects the pharaoh and sacred spaces.

Satis features in regional religious texts and temple inscriptions. Her presence is noted in rituals related to the Nile's rising, and she appears in offering scenes alongside other southern deities. She is revered particularly during ceremonies that invoke the inundation and renewal of the land. Satis shares attributes with Isis in her life-giving functions, and is sometimes linked to Neith through their mutual roles as hunters and protectors. The Greeks equate her with Artemis (Roman: Diana) due to her association with archery. She is usually depicted as a tall woman wearing the Hedjet (white crown of Upper Egypt) adorned with antelope horns. She often carries a bow and arrows, symbolising precision and might. Occasionally, she is shown pouring water, emphasising her power over the Nile's flood. Her principal cult centre is at Elephantine Island. Temples dedicated to her also exist at Sehel Island and other sites in southern Egypt and Nubia.

The Pre-Dynastic Period: Satis emerges as a local deity in Nubia and Upper Egypt, especially at Elephantine Island. She may have originated as a Nubian goddess of fertility or war, later incorporated into the Egyptian pantheon. She is revered by local Nilotic and Nubian communities connected to the Nile's life-giving flood.

The Early Dynastic Period: Satis is incorporated into the Egyptian state religion as the unification of Upper and Lower Egypt occurs. She begins to appear in royal inscriptions and offering texts. She is recognised as a guardian of the southern frontier, especially at Elephantine Island, a key strategic location.

The Old Kingdom: The worship of Satis becomes state-sanctioned, especially in Upper Egypt. Her role as a Nile goddess becomes formalised. She appears in the Pyramid Texts as one of the deities

---

[349] Hill, J (2016), "Satet", Ancient Egypt Online.

associated with purification and sustenance. Alongside Khnum (creator god of the cataract region) and Anuket (her daughter or counterpart), she becomes part of the Elephantine Triad.

The First Intermediate Period: Political instability leads to reduced centralised religious activity. Local cults (like that of Satis at Elephantine Island) remain strong, especially since the Nile and fertility are crucial to survival.

Satis, Wikipedia Creative Commons, Public Domain

The Middle Kingdom: Satis undergoes a revival, and her temple at Elephantine Island is expanded under Senusret I and other rulers. Her role as goddess of the inundation is emphasised. She becomes further linked to royal ideology. The inundation she brings is seen as a gift to the pharaoh. The Elephantine Triad of Satis, Anuket, and Khnum gains increased religious prominence.

The Second Intermediate Period: Satis's cult persists locally in the Upper Egyptian and Nubian regions. Hyksos control over parts of Egypt has little effect on Elephantine Island, which remains culturally southern and traditional.

The New Kingdom: The worship of Satis reaches a high point. There are major temple constructions and expansions at Elephantine Island under Thutmose III, Amenhotep III, and Ramesses II. She is frequently depicted in temple reliefs, offering water and blessings to the pharaoh. Her worship spreads along the Nile into Lower Nubia as Egyptian influence extends south. She is seen as a protective war goddess, guarding the southern frontier of Egypt.

The Third Intermediate Period: Local worship continues, especially in Upper Egypt and Nubia. Elephantine Island remains a religious and military outpost, so her protective and inundation roles continue. Libyan and Nubian rulers honour her as part of their adoption of Egyptian traditions.

The Late Period: There is a revival of traditional Egyptian cults, including that of Satis. She remains prominent at Elephantine Island, where her temple continues to function. Some syncretism begins with foreign deities, especially in Lower Egypt, but Satis retains her strong identity in the south.

The Ptolemaic Period: Satis is still actively worshipped at Elephantine Island. The Greek rulers support local cults to legitimise their rule, Satis is seen as a Nubian-Hellenistic guardian goddess. Her temple is renovated, and rituals continue.

The Roman and Byzantine Periods: Her worship continues in southern temples, though increasingly mixed with Roman iconography and religious practices. Eventually, the rise of Christianity leads to the decline and closure of Egyptian temples. Her temple at Elephantine Island is among the last to fall into disuse.

As a goddess of the river and floods, Satis is comparable to the Greek Naiads (water spirits) and Potamoi (river deities). As a goddess of fertility and abundance, she is equated with Demeter / Ceres. As a goddess of protection and hunting she is similar to Artemis / Diana. People could pray to Satis for fertile floods, agricultural abundance, protection of the pharaoh and people, safe travel, family fertility, and prosperity.

Sekhmet: Goddess of War and Medicine

Left: 'Sekhmet' in hieroglyphs

Sekhmet is a goddess of war, destruction, healing, plagues, and protection. Her name means 'The Powerful One'. She is the granddaughter of Nut and Geb, the daughter of Ra (as the Eye of Ra), the sister of Bastet[350], Hathor, and Tefnut, the wife of Ptah (in Memphite religion), and the mother of Nefertum and possibly Maahes. She unleashes divine wrath against enemies of the gods, leading battles and punishing transgressors with fire and disease. At the same time, she governs medicine and healing, holding sway over both illness and its cure[351]. As a fierce guardian, she defends *ma'at*, and ensures justice is upheld through force if necessary.

A central myth tells of Sekhmet's near-destruction of humanity. Sent by Ra to punish mankind's rebellion, she becomes consumed by bloodlust. To stop her, Ra tricks her into drinking dyed beer that resembles blood. Drunk and pacified, she ceases her slaughter, transforming from wrathful force to a more benevolent presence[352][353].

Sekhmet is closely linked to Hathor and Bastet, often seen as two sides of the same divine feminine power, ferocity and gentleness. She is considered the counterpart of Ptah, and together with their son Nefertum, they form the Memphite Triad. Her healing aspects also bring her into alignment with Isis in some local traditions. She is depicted as a lion-headed woman, symbolising ferocity and solar power, often crowned with the sun disk and uraeus (cobra). Her primary cult centre is in Memphis, where she is venerated as the consort of Ptah. At Karnak (Thebes), hundreds of her statues are erected in ritual processions. She is especially honoured during ceremonies seeking protection, healing, and purification.

The Old Kingdom: The earliest mentions of Sekhmet appear in Pyramid Texts[354]. She is associated with royal power, and protecting the pharaoh in the afterlife. She is known as a violent aspect of the sun god Ra, sent to punish humanity in the myth of the Destruction of Mankind. She begins to emerge as a significant national deity. She begins her role as protector of *ma'at* and punisher of those who defy it.

---

[350] Wilkinson, Richard H. (2003). The Complete Gods and Goddesses of Ancient Egypt. Thames & Hudson. pp. 178, 181.
[351] Wilkinson, Richard H. (2003). p. 181.
[352] Lichtheim, Miriam (2006) [1976]. Ancient Egyptian Literature, Volume Two: The New Kingdom. University of California Press. pp. 197–199.
[353] Pope, Marvin H. (1977). Song of Songs. The Anchor Bible. Vol. 7C. New York City, United States: Doubleday. ISBN 978-0-385-00569-2.
[354] Lange-Athinodorou, Eva (29 February 2016). "The Lioness Goddess in the Old Kingdom Nile Delta: A Study in Local Cult Topography". Sapientia Felicitas Festschrift für Günter Vittmann. Les Cahiers Égypte Nilotique et Méditérranéenne. pp. 303–304.

The First Intermediate Period: Political fragmentation decentralises religion, but Sekhmet's protective and destructive powers remain. She continues to be worshipped in connection with local royal cults and temples.

The Middle Kingdom: Sekhmet experiences a rise in popularity, especially among royal and priestly classes. She starts to appear more frequently in temple inscriptions and royal texts. Her dual nature (destroyer and healer) becomes more developed. She is invoked in magical healing spells and protective rituals.

The Second Intermediate Period: Her worship persists, particularly in Upper Egypt. Her destructive power is emphasised during times of instability and invasion (e.g., during the Hyksos period).

Sekhmet, Wikipedia Creative Commons, Public Domain

The New Kingdom: This is the golden age of Sekhmet's worship[355]. She is one of the most prominent goddesses during this period. She is closely associated with the Theban triad: Mut (as consort), Amun (as consort of Mut), and Khonsu (their son). In Thebes, Sekhmet is sometimes considered an aspect of Mut, leading to massive temple construction and ritual activity. Amenhotep III builds hundreds of Sekhmet statues, an estimated 600 to 730, for his mortuary temple at Kom el-Hetan (Luxor, Thebes)[356]. Sekhmet is invoked in rituals of healing, plague prevention, and protection in battle.

The Third Intermediate Period: Sekhmet becomes more closely integrated into domestic religious practice and magical healing texts. She is invoked in funerary spells, particularly for protection in the afterlife.

The Late Period: Religious revival and renewed attention to older deities benefits Sekhmet's cult. Her role as a protector against disease and demons makes her vital in both elite and common households. She often appears alongside Bastet and Mut.

The Ptolemaic Period: Worship remains strong at Memphis (as consort of Ptah, with son Nefertem) and at Thebes (as an aspect of Mut).

The Roman and Byzantine Periods: Sekhmet continues to be worshipped, particularly in Thebes and Memphis. Her healing and protective roles are emphasised in magical texts and private devotion. With the rise of Christianity and suppression of traditional religion by the 4th century, public worship declines. Despite Christian suppression, belief in Sekhmet persists, especially in rural Egypt. While her official worship is banned and temples closed or repurposed, her image and attributes as a healer and protector survive in folk practices. Elements of Sekhmet's identity are absorbed into Christian traditions, with her qualities reflected in saints like Saint George or Saint Menas. Amulets and lion-headed figures continued to circulate, showing how older beliefs endured beneath the surface of Christian orthodoxy.

As a goddess of war and vengeance and protector of the pharaoh, Sekhmet is equated to the Greek / Roman goddess Athena / Minerva or Enyo / Bellona. As a goddess of disease and healing she is equated to Hygieia / Salus. People could pray to Sekhmet for protection and victory, justice, healing and disease prevention, divine power and authority, and courage and strength.

---

[355] Lange-Athinodorou, Eva (29 February 2016). pp. 304–305.
[356] Ciaccia, Olivia (6 April 2022). "Seeking Sekhmet: The veneration of Sekhmet Statues in contemporary museums". Pomegranate. 23 (1–2). doi:10.1558/pome.18653. ISSN 1743-1735.

Serket: The Scorpion Goddess of Healing

Left: Two variations of 'Serket' in hieroglyphs

Serket is an ancient Egyptian goddess associated with scorpions, magic, healing, protection, and the afterlife. Her name translates as 'She Who Causes the Throat to Breathe' or 'The One Who Tightens the Throat'. She is described as the daughter or granddaughter of Geb and Nut, the daughter or sister of Neith, and the sister of Isis and Nephthys. She is sometimes considered the wife of Ptah and associated with Horus or Osiris.

Serket serves as a protector against venomous creatures, guarding both the living and the dead from poisonous bites and stings[357]. She uses her magical powers to heal and protect, especially in funerary contexts, safeguarding the deceased during their journey through the underworld.

Serket appears in funerary texts such as the Book of the Dead, where she protects the canopic jar containing the intestines of the deceased. She is invoked in spells for protection from venomous animals and plays a critical role in the preservation and safe passage of souls. Due to shared traits of protection and healing, Serket is often identified with Isis, and sometimes with Neith, Nephthys, or the cobra goddess Wadjet. In Greek tradition, she is linked to Hecate (Roman: Trivia).

She is usually depicted as a woman with a scorpion on her head, symbolising her dominion over venomous creatures. Occasionally, she appears fully in scorpion form or as a woman with a scorpion's tail. Her main centres of worship are near Heliopolis and Saqqara[358], where she serves as a guardian of the dead. Shrines to her are often found near burial sites.

The Pre-Dynastic Period: Serket originates as a local protective deity in regions of Upper Egypt or the western desert, where scorpions are common. Worship centres on protection from scorpion stings, especially for children, mothers, and the vulnerable.

The Early Dynastic Period: Serket is absorbed into the emerging pantheon as religious systems are formalised. Her association with healing and protection begins to link her with royal ideology. She becomes one of the guardians of the pharaoh.

The Old Kingdom: Serket is mentioned in the Pyramid Texts, identified as a protector of the deceased king and a guide in the afterlife. She begins her key role as a protector of the Four Sons of Horus, specifically protecting Qebehsenuef, the canopic god associated with the intestines.

---

[357] "Pharaonic Gods". 2008-05-13. Archived from the original on 13 May 2008. Retrieved 2025-03-14.
[358] Wilkinson, Richard H. (2003). The Complete Gods And Goddesses Of Ancient Egypt. Thames & Hudson. ISBN 0-500-05120-8.

Serket, Wikipedia Creative Commons, Public Domain

The First Intermediate Period: Local cult worship continues, particularly in desert-edge communities and oases where scorpions pose a real threat. Magical spells against scorpion stings invoking Serket are transmitted orally.

The Middle Kingdom: Her role in protective and funerary magic expands. Serket is now more widely depicted in tombs, especially in royal and elite contexts. Coffin Texts invoke Serket for healing and warding off venomous creatures. Her association with other funerary goddesses, Isis, Nephthys, and Neith, grows stronger.

The Second Intermediate Period: Worship is maintained in local and domestic settings, especially as a protector against harm and magic. There is some continued integration with funerary practices in Theban tombs.

The New Kingdom: Serket is frequently depicted in royal tombs, such as those in the Valley of the Kings and Queens (Thebes), standing guard over the pharaoh's organs and sarcophagus. Her image is placed on canopic chests, coffins, and amulets. She is connected closely with Isis, Nephthys, and Neith as the four goddesses protecting the deceased. She is associated with the solar barque, protecting Ra during his night journey through the underworld. She is also invoked in healing spells and protective household amulets.

The Third Intermediate Period: Worship continues in funerary and magical contexts. Her image remains popular on protective amulets, coffins, and magical papyri. She is seen more as a protective household deity as well as a funerary goddess.

The Late Period: With the revival of ancient traditions, Serket's cult sees renewed attention. She continues as a guardian of canopic jars and a healer of poisons and disease. In magical papyri, she is invoked in exorcisms, scorpion-sting cures, and protective charms.

The Ptolemaic Period: She is still invoked in Greco-Egyptian magical texts. She is be equated or syncretised with Greek healing goddesses like Hygeia (Salus) or Artemis (Diana) (protector of childbirth and animals). She appears in Demotic and Greek texts as a potent magical figure against venom and evil spirits. Her healing role becomes a bridge between Egyptian religion and Hellenistic magic.

The Roman and Byzantine Periods: She continues to appear in late magical papyri, especially in spells related to stings, bites, curses, and possession. Some domestic cult worship may persist among Egyptian healers and magicians. As Christianity spreads, traditional temples close, and Serket's formal worship declines. Serket's legacy persists indirectly through folk beliefs and magical traditions, especially in rural areas where older practices endure beneath the surface of Christian dominance. References to Serket are still found in magical papyri and amulets used by local healers and magicians, often blending Christian and ancient Egyptian elements.

As a goddess of protection from venom and danger, Serket is equated with the Greek / Roman goddess Hygieia / Salus. As a guardian of the dead she is equivalent to Hekate (Trivia). People could pray to Serket for protection from venom, poisons, and dangerous animals, guardianship of the dead, healing and medical aid, divine protection and life preservation, and spiritual and magical protection.

Set: God of Chaos, Storms, and Violence

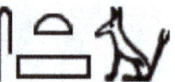

Left: 'Set' in hieroglyphs

Set is a god of chaos, deserts, storms, violence[359], foreigners[360], and, paradoxically, protection. His name means 'Instigator of Confusion' or 'Pillar of Stability', depending on the period and interpretation. He is the grandson of Shu and Tefnut, the son of Geb and Nut, the brother of Osiris, Isis, the brother and husband of Nephthys, and the father of Anubis in some traditions[361]. He governs the wild, arid lands beyond civilisation and embodies the disruptive forces of nature and conflict. As a god of storms and disorder, he brings tempests and drought, yet also protects Ra's solar barque from the serpent Apep during its nightly journey through the underworld. In certain periods, he is seen as a powerful defender of cosmic order against true chaos.

Set features prominently in one of Egypt's most famous myths, the Osirian cycle. He murders his brother Osiris out of jealousy, dismembers his body, and seizes the throne. Isis, Osiris's wife, retrieves the body and resurrects Osiris long enough to conceive their son Horus. A prolonged conflict follows between Set and Horus, ending with Horus ultimately prevailing and Set being banished or integrated into Ra's retinue, depending on the version[362]. Set is often identified with foreign or marginal deities, especially during the New Kingdom when he becomes associated with gods from Syria and the Levant. His dual nature also leads to comparisons with Apophis, though unlike Apophis, Set is not always an enemy of order and can be a necessary, if unpredictable, force.

Set is depicted with a distinctive creature's head, sometimes called the Set animal, with a curved snout, square ears, and forked tail, unlike any known animal. He may also appear as a man with this animal's head, wielding a was-sceptre or ankh, symbolising power and vitality. Set's primary cult centres include Naqada and Avaris, and later Pi-Ramesses, where he is worshipped as a patron deity by several Ramesside pharaohs. He also has temples in Sepermeru and is venerated in desert regions associated with foreign trade and military activity. His worship reflects both fear and reverence for his unpredictable power.

The Pre-Dynastic Period: Set is a local god of the desert, storms, and wild animals, especially in Upper Egypt. He is worshipped in Naqada or Ombos which later becomes a cult centre.

---

[359] Herman Te Velde (2001). "Seth". Oxford Encyclopedia of Ancient Egypt. Vol. 3.
[360] te Velde, Herman (1967). Seth, God of Confusion: A study of his role in Egyptian mythology and religion. Probleme der Ägyptologie. Vol. 6. Translated by van Baaren-Pape, G.E. (2nd ed.). Leiden, NL: E.J. Brill. ISBN 978-90-04-05402-8.
[361] E.A. Wallis Budge, "Nephthys", in "The Gods of the Egyptians or Studies in Egyptian Mythology: Volume 2", London: Methuen & Co, 1904, p.254.
[362] Strudwick, Helen (2006). The Encyclopedia of Ancient Egypt. New York: Sterling Publishing Co., Inc. pp. 124–125. ISBN 978-1-4351-4654-9.

Set, Wikipedia Creative Commons, Public Domain

The Early Dynastic Period: Set is a prominent deity, a god of war and storms, sometimes appearing alongside Horus as a balancing force, and as a protector of the pharaoh.

The Old Kingdom: Set appears in the Pyramid Texts as both a helper of the pharaoh and a killer of Osiris. The duality of Set becomes evident when he helps Ra battle Apep at night but also betrays Osiris. Worship centres at Ombos and other Upper Egyptian regions.

The First Intermediate Period: Local rulers promote Set in certain regions. Political instability mirrors Set's chaotic nature, possibly enhancing his symbolic relevance.

The Middle Kingdom: Set is now more firmly established as Osiris's rival, and his negative aspects gain emphasis. Still venerated for his protective role against Apep, he remains a complex deity, not yet fully demonised, and a necessary force within the cosmic balance.

The Second Intermediate Period: The Hyksos, a group of West Asian rulers, adopt Set as their main god, identifying him with their own storm god (e.g., Baal or Hadad). In Avaris, Set is elevated to supreme status, and worshipped as Sutekh. This association with foreigners marks a turning point in his perception by native Egyptians.

The New Kingdom: Set is still feared for his chaotic nature, but respected and honoured. He appears in temples such as Karnak (Thebes), Avaris, and Pi-Ramesses. He is invoked in protection spells and military contexts. Despite his role in the Osiris myth, Set is not yet viewed as entirely evil.

The Third Intermediate Period: After the fall of the Ramesside dynasty and the loss of empire, Set's image declines sharply. He is increasingly associated with foreign enemies, chaos, and disorder. In many religious texts, he becomes a symbol of evil, and his myths are rewritten to highlight his betrayal and failure.

The Late Period: Set is now fully demonised, regarded as a god of chaos, evil, foreigners, and deserts. His name is often omitted or replaced in religious inscriptions. He is linked to Apep, the serpent of chaos, even though he was once Apep's enemy.

The Ptolemaic Period: In magical papyri, Set appears as a demonic or chaotic figure, sometimes invoked in curse spells or aggressive magic.

The Roman Period: Popular religion and magic still make references to Set as a force to be banished or repelled. He is occasionally used as a powerful magical force, invoked to defeat other evil beings.

The Byzantine Period: Set becomes equated with Satan or diabolic forces in Christianised interpretations of Egyptian mythology. His memory survives only in demonised folklore, magical texts, and the moral allegories of Christian writers.

As a god of chaos, storms, fury, and destructive forces, Set has similarities with Greek / Roman monster Typhon / Typhoeus. He also has similarities with Ares / Mars as a personification of chaotic strength and destructive force. Set could be prayed to for protection against enemies, defence against chaos, survival in harsh environments, and a harnessing of destructive power for protection and justice.

Shu: God of the Air

Left: 'Shu' in hieroglyphs

Shu is a god of air, light, wind, atmosphere, and space between earth and sky. His name means 'He Who Rises Up', referring to his role in holding apart the sky goddess Nut from the earth god Geb. He is sometimes referred to as 'The Uplifter' or 'The Separator'. He is the son of Atum (or Ra-Atum), the brother and husband of Tefnut, the father of Geb and Nut, and the grandfather of Osiris, Isis, Set, and Nephthys[363].

He personifies the air[364] and acts as the vital force that allows life to exist between sky and earth[365]. Shu supports the heavens, enabling the sun to travel across the sky. He also represents sunlight and dryness, counterbalancing his twin sister Tefnut, who embodies moisture. His role is fundamental to the structure of the cosmos, maintaining the separation that allows creation to function.

Shu appears in the Heliopolitan creation myth, where he is born from Atum along with Tefnut. After becoming lost in the primeval waters, Shu and Tefnut are joyfully reunited with Atum, marking the beginning of ordered creation. Later, he intervenes when Nut and Geb are found in eternal embrace, at Ra's command, Shu lifts Nut into the sky, establishing the world's structure by creating the air-filled space between heaven and earth. As part of the Ennead[366], he plays a key role in the divine lineage but remains distinct in function. His attributes are occasionally absorbed into broader solar theology, linking him loosely to Ra. He is venerated within temple complexes dedicated to Atum and Ra, especially involving creation and cosmic order. Shu is typically depicted as a man wearing a feather on his head, symbolising air and lightness. He is often shown with outstretched arms, physically lifting the sky above the earth, sometimes with Nut arched over him. In artistic renderings, his body is sometimes painted yellow or gold.

The Pre-Dynastic Period: Shu exists in early cosmologies and creation myths, especially in Heliopolis. Core ideas about primordial forces like air and light are forming.

The Early Dynastic Period: Shu becomes part of state religion in the Ennead. As a god of air, he represents the force that separates Nut (sky) from Geb (earth), enabling space, time, and life.

---

[363] Owusu, Heike (2008). Egyptian Symbols. Sterling Publishing Co. Inc. p. 99. ISBN 9781402746239. Retrieved 6 October 2014.
[364] Owusu, Heike (2008).
[365] Dunan, Francoise (2004). Gods and Men in Egypt. Ithaca and London: Cornell University Press. p. 41. ISBN 978-0801488535. Retrieved 23 May 2017.
[366] van Dijk, Jacobus. "Myth and mythmaking in ancient Egypt" (PDF). Simon & Schuster. Archived (PDF) from the original on 2011-03-13. Retrieved 23 May 2017.

The Old Kingdom: Shu is firmly established in royal religion. He appears in Pyramid Texts, where he is invoked to help the deceased king ascend to the sky. He functions as a cosmic stabiliser, enabling *ma'at*[367] by keeping heaven and earth apart.

Shu, Wikipedia Creative Commons, Public Domain

The First Intermediate Period: No evidence of a decline in belief, but less state support means fewer formal invocations. Heliopolitan religion continues to influence local religious practice.

The Middle Kingdom: There is renewed state investment in religion, which revives the Ennead's importance. Shu appears more often in Coffin Texts and funerary art. His image as the separator of sky and earth is frequently used as an allegory for order vs. chaos.

The Second Intermediate Period: Political fragmentation leads to reduced emphasis on centralised religion. Shu continues to be invoked in local traditions and priestly teachings at Heliopolis.

The New Kingdom: Shu reaches greater prominence in temple iconography. He appears in Theban tombs, cosmological ceilings, and solar texts. He is regularly shown holding up Nut, especially in temples such as Karnak (Thebes) and Dendera. His role is emphasised in texts like the Book of the Dead, which emphasise cosmic order and rebirth.

The Third Intermediate Period: Shu remains a symbol of cosmic balance, especially in religious art and spells. There is no evidence of independent temples, but he is still venerated as part of the Ennead.

The Late Period: With the revival of traditional religion, Shu's status as part of the Ennead is reaffirmed. Heliopolitan cosmology is preserved in religious temples and texts. Shu continues to appear in temple reliefs, often shown separating Nut and Geb.

The Ptolemaic Period: Shu appears in temple inscriptions and scenes, particularly at Dendera, Edfu, and Philae Island. He is seen as part of the timeless Egyptian cosmic order. The Greeks associated Shu with Atlas, the primordial Titan who held up the celestial spheres, as they are both depicted holding up the sky[368].

The Roman Period: Shu continues to appear in temples, texts, and papyri. His role becomes increasingly symbolic, representing the concept of separation and breath in Egyptian thought. His image appears in temples like Philae Island and Esna.

The Byzantine Period: As Christianity becomes dominant and pagan temples are closed, Shu's worship ceases entirely. He survives in mythological texts and Coptic adaptations of Egyptian cosmology, but as a theological figure, not a living cult. Some echoes of Shu's concepts (air, breath, separation of heaven and earth) persist in Gnostic and esoteric traditions influenced by Egyptian thought.

As a god or personification of air and atmosphere, Shu is equated with the Greek / Roman gods Aether (the bright upper air) and Aeolus (governor of the winds). People could pray to Shu for health, the breath of life, peace, balance, clarity, strength, and protection from chaos.

---

[367] Lazaridis, Nikolaos (2008). "Ethics". UCLA Encyclopedia of Egyptology. Retrieved 22 May 2017.
[368] Remler, Pat (2010). Egyptian Mythology, A to Z. Infobase Publishing. p. 24. ISBN 9781438131801. Retrieved 6 October 2014.

Sobek: The Crocodile God of the Nile

Left: 'Sobek' in hieroglyphs

Sobek is a god of water, fertility, crocodiles, military prowess, and protection. His name means 'watcher' or 'he who causes to be fertile'. He is also known as the 'Lord of the Waters' and sometimes the 'Rager' due to his fearsome nature. He is the son of either Set or Neith, depending on the tradition[369]. He is paired with Renenutet as his divine companion[370]. Sobek governs over the Nile and marshlands, ensuring their fertility and safeguarding people from the dangers of crocodiles. He also embodies raw strength and serves as a protective deity. As a crocodile god, he controls the behaviour of these dangerous animals and is believed to appease them or turn them against Egypt's enemies.

Several myths feature Sobek, particularly in relation to the Nile's origins and his role in protecting the solar deity. In one tradition, Sobek is said to have created the Nile from his sweat while forming the world. In others, he aids the gods in battles against the forces of chaos. In later mythology Sobek is fused into the Osirian cycle, helping to recover Osiris's body and protect Horus in his infancy. Sobek is sometimes merged with other deities, most notably as Sobek-Ra, combining his might with the solar power of Ra. In some cases, he is associated with Set or Horus, though these identifications are less frequent.

Sobek is typically depicted as either a man with the head of a crocodile or a full crocodile adorned with a headdress featuring feathers, horns, or a solar disk. His imagery often emphasises strength and dominance, and he sometimes wears royal regalia to signify his protective function for the pharaoh. His main cult centres are Crocodilopolis (Faiyum) and Kom Ombo. In these regions, sacred crocodiles are kept in temples, often adorned with jewellery and mummified after death.

The Early Dynastic Period: Crocodile symbolism is present in Nile-centric art and amulets, possibly reflecting early reverence for the animal's power and danger.

The Old Kingdom: Sobek begins to appear as a local deity associated with the Faiyum region, particularly near Crocodilopolis. His connection with water, fertility, and the Nile becomes increasingly prominent. He appears in Pyramid Texts which praise the pharaoh as the living incarnation of the crocodile god[371].

---

[369] "Gods of Ancient Egypt: Sobek". www.ancientegyptonline.co.uk.
[370] Francoise Dunand and Christiane Zivie-Coche (trans. David Lorton). (2004). Gods and Men in Egypt: 3000 BCE to 395 CE. Ithaca: Cornell University Press. [hereafter: Gods and Men].
[371] Bresciani, Edda (2005). "Sobek, Lord of the Land of the Lake". Divine Creatures: Animal Mummies in Ancient Egypt. Cairo: The American University in Cairo Press. pp. 199–206. ISBN 9789774248580.

The First Intermediate Period: Regional cults gain strength amid political decentralisation. Sobek becomes a significant local deity in various parts of Egypt, including the Faiyum and Upper Egyptian towns like Kom Ombo.

Sobek, Wikipedia Creative Commons, Public Domain

The Middle Kingdom: Sobek gains national recognition, particularly under the 12th Dynasty rulers who patronise his cult at Crocodilopolis. Kings such as Amenemhat III align themselves with Sobek to reinforce their divine authority, even incorporating his name into royal titles (e.g., Sobekneferu). Fusion with Ra as Sobek-Ra enhances his cosmic significance. Cult centres expand, with temple-building in the Faiyum and beyond.

The Second Intermediate Period: Despite political instability, Sobek retains strong regional support. He continues to be invoked for protection and fertility.

The New Kingdom: Sobek enjoys sustained state-sponsored worship. Temples are built or expanded at Kom Ombo and Crocodilopolis. He is depicted in royal tombs and religious texts, often alongside solar deities or in composite forms (e.g., Sobek-Ra, Sobek-Horus)[372]. Crocodile cults, including mummification of sacred crocodiles, become more established.

The Third Intermediate Period: Though Egypt is politically fragmented, religious traditions remain resilient. Mummified crocodiles and dedicated cemeteries increase in number.

The Late Period: Sobek's imagery and attributes are further systematised. Temples at Kom Ombo and Medinet el-Faiyum receive enhancements. Syncretism with other gods becomes more elaborate, Sobek remains adaptable and widely venerated.

The Ptolemaic Period: This is a high point for Sobek in terms of temple construction and iconography, particularly at Kom Ombo, where he shares a dual temple with the falcon god Horus. Worship continues with full priesthoods, festivals, and extensive mummification of crocodiles. Greek identification of Sobek with Pan (Faunus), Asklepios (Aesculapius, Vejovis), or Helios (Sol) reflects Hellenistic attempts to integrate Egyptian deities into their worldview. Pilgrimage and healing cults associated with Sobek flourish.

The Roman Period: Worship persists strongly in rural areas; Kom Ombo remains active as a cult centre. Roman emperors continue to support temples, though Christianity's rise begins to eclipse older traditions. Sobek's crocodile symbolism remains potent, even as temple rituals wane.

The Byzantine Period: Sobek's worship ceases with the decline of traditional Egyptian religion in Late Antiquity. His legacy survives through archaeological remains, including vast crocodile cemeteries, temples, and inscriptions.

As a god of the river and fertility, Sobek has some similarities with the Greek / Roman god Poseidon / Neptune, as both rule over water, fertility, and its destructive and creative aspects. People could pray to Sobek for fertile Nile floods, abundance, protection, strength, courage, safe travel on the river, and renewal of life.

---

[372] Zecchi, Marco (2010). Sobek of Shedet : The Crocodile God in the Fayyum in the Dynastic Period. Umbria: Tau Editrice. p. 206. ISBN 9788862441155.

Tatenen: God of the Primordial Mound

Left: 'Tatenen' in hieroglyphs

Tatenen is a god of the primordial mound, creation, Earth's fertility, and underground minerals. His name means 'the risen land' or 'the emerging earth'[373]. He is sometimes called the 'Father of the Gods'[374] and 'Lord of Eternity'. Tatenen personifies the primeval mound that first emerged from the watery chaos of Nu at the dawn of time. As a self-created deity, he embodies the Earth's creative forces, bringing forth vegetation, minerals, and life[375]. His influence extends beneath the surface, where he ensures the continual renewal of natural resources and the cycle of life.

Although not prominent in mythological stories, Tatenen holds a foundational role in Egyptian cosmology. In some Theban and Memphite traditions, he merges with the god Ptah to form Ptah-Tatenen[376], a powerful creative force who brings the cosmos into existence through thought and speech. In this aspect, he is associated with both the intellectual and physical dimensions of creation, and shares thematic ties with other creator gods like Atum and Khnum. He is usually depicted as a man wearing a tall, flat-topped crown with two plumes and ram horns, often coloured green to symbolise fertility and renewal[377]. He may also carry symbols of power such as the was-sceptre and ankh, reflecting his role as an earth deity and life-giver. Tatenen was primarily worshipped in Memphis, where, as Ptah-Tatenen, he was honoured as a creator and protector, especially in relation to the royal family and the nation's wellbeing. His cult emphasised the Earth as both origin and provider.

The Early Dynastic Period: Early religious ideas about the primordial mound, the first land to emerge from the chaotic waters, are present and lay the foundation for Tatenen's later development.

The Old Kingdom: Tatenen appears in theological texts as a personification of the primordial earth. His name means 'Risen Land' or 'Exalted Earth', symbolising the fertile ground that emerged at creation. He is closely linked with religious traditions in Memphis, where creation is centred on Ptah, the chief god of Memphis. Tatenen may represent the underworld and creative aspect of the earth within this framework. His worship remains largely philosophical rather than cult based.

The First Intermediate Period: With political fragmentation, religious traditions at Memphis receive less state focus, but core ideas about the cosmos, including Tatenen, continuously remain through funerary texts and temple doctrine.

---

[373] The Egyptian Gods Archived 2009-05-03 at the Wayback Machine Retrieved 2008-10-21
[374] J. H. Breasted: Ancient Records of Egypt, Part Three, § 411
[375] C. J. Bleeker. Historia Religionum I: Religions of the Past, p.68
[376] The Egyptian Gods Archived 2009-05-03 at the Wayback Machine Retrieved 2008-10-21.
[377] Wilkinson, Richard H. (2003). The Complete Gods and Goddesses of Ancient Egypt. Thames & Hudson. p. 130

The Egyptian Gods   An Illustrated Introduction

Name, Wikipedia Creative Commons, Public Domain

The Middle Kingdom: Tatenen continues to be acknowledged as an aspect of the earth god and creation myths, particularly in literature. He remains tied to Ptah and Memphis, symbolising stability, rebirth, and the nurturing earth. Although there is little evidence of an independent cult, his role in the cosmos persists in religious texts.

The Second Intermediate Period: As with many deities, the period's political instability leads to limited new developments. Tatenen's presence endures in texts that preserve earlier traditions, especially with the elite and priesthoods.

The New Kingdom: Tatenen gains renewed significance, particularly under the 19th Dynasty. Pharaohs such as Ramesses II promote Tatenen as a creator god, often merged with Ptah in the composite form Ptah-Tatenen. In this form, he represents both the creative world (Ptah) and the life-giving earth (Tatenen). He is featured in temple inscriptions at Memphis, Luxor (Thebes), and other major sites, associated with divine kingship, renewal, and the hidden powers beneath the earth. He also becomes linked to the primeval gods and the Ogdoad.

The Third Intermediate Period: Tatenen retains relevance in religious thought at Memphis, especially in priestly circles. He continues to be mentioned in funerary texts and temple inscriptions, particularly in Memphis and Thebes.

The Late Period: Ptah-Tatenen remains a key religious figure in temples at Memphis. His attributes are expanded, and he is depicted as an androgynous, underworld creator who brings forth gods, minerals, and life from the depths of the earth. Iconography becomes more refined. He is shown with green skin (symbolising vegetation and rebirth), wearing a tall crown with two plumes, often holding a was-sceptre. He is revered as the latent creative force of the earth, bridging the worlds of the dead and the living.

The Ptolemaic Period: Tatenen continues to be venerated within the traditional priestly frameworks. At Memphis, his syncretic identity as Ptah-Tatenen is maintained in religious texts and temple rituals. Greek interpretations equate aspects of Tatenen with underworld or primordial deities, though his worship remains distinctively Egyptian in character. His role in the cosmos remains central, earth-born, generative, and mysterious.

The Roman Period: As Egyptian temple religion wanes, Ptah-Tatenen persists in religious iconography and inscriptions. His cult becomes more symbolic and limited to priestly and esoteric traditions. He continues to represent the earth's creative depths and the concept of rebirth.

The Byzantine Period: Tatenen, especially in the form of Ptah-Tatenen, fades from active worship with the decline of traditional Egyptian religion and the rise of Christianity. Modern knowledge of Tatenen comes primarily from theological texts and temple reliefs.

As a god of primordial earth and creation, Tatenen has some similarities with the Greek / Roman goddess Gaia / Terra Mater, as both represent the living earth that gives rise to life and stability. People could pray to Tatenen for fertile land, agricultural abundance, stability, wealth, creation, renewal, and life-giving energy.

Tefnut: Goddess of Moisture, Rain, and Humidity

Left: Two variations of 'Tefnut' in hieroglyphs

Tefnut is a goddess of moisture, rain, dew, humidity[378], and order. Her name is thought to mean 'that water' or may be linked to the root '*tef*', meaning 'to spit'[379], referencing her mythological creation. She is also known as the 'Lady of the Flame' in some texts as both a water deity and a solar goddess. She is the daughter of Atum along with her twin brother and consort Shu. She is the mother of Geb (earth god) and Nut (sky goddess). She is the grandmother of Osiris, Isis, Set, and Nephthys (children of Geb and Nut). Tefnut governs the vital moisture that sustains life, including rain and dew. She plays a crucial role in regulating the space between the earth and sky, maintaining physical and divine equilibrium. One story recounts her temporary departure to Nubia in anger, causing chaos and drought in Egypt. The gods send Thoth to persuade her to return[380], and her eventual reappearance restores balance and moisture to the land.

Tefnut is strongly linked with Ma'at. In some traditions she takes on fiery, protective aspects associated with the Eye of Ra[381], similar to goddesses like Sekhmet or Hathor. She is often depicted as a woman with the head of a lioness, sometimes crowned with a solar disk and uraeus (cobra). Occasionally, she appears in human form wearing a Feather of Ma'at or a tripartite wig. Her lion form reflects both her protective nature and divine retribution when order is threatened. Tefnut's main centres of worship include Heliopolis, where she is part of the Ennead[382], and Leontopolis, where she is venerated alongside other lion-headed deities.

The Early Dynastic Period: Early cosmological ideas that will later form the Heliopolitan Ennead are emerging. Tefnut is not yet clearly named, but concepts of elemental forces like moisture and atmosphere are developing.

The Old Kingdom: Tefnut appears in Heliopolitan religion as a goddess of moisture and humidity, sister and consort to Shu (god of air), and daughter of the creator god Atum. The Pyramid Texts refer to her role in the separation of sky and earth and the birth of the divine order. She is part of the Ennead, a system that underpins royal ideology.

---

[378] Hart, George (2005). The Routledge Dictionary of Egyptian Gods and Goddesses, Second Edition. Routledge. p. 156. ISBN 978-0-203-02362-4.
[379] Wilkinson, Richard H. (2003). The Complete Gods and Goddesses of Ancient Egypt. London: Thames & Hudson. p. 183. ISBN 0-500-05120-8. Retrieved 4 May 2022.
[380] Wilkinson, Richard H. (2003).
[381] Pinch, Geraldine (2002). Egyptian Mythology: A Guide to the Gods, Goddesses, and Traditions of Ancient Egypt. Oxford University Press. p. 197. ISBN 978-0-19-517024-5.
[382] Wilkinson, Richard H (2003).

Tefnut, Wikipedia Creative Commons, Public Domain

The First Intermediate Period: As with many deities, centralised worship is disrupted. However, the Ennead persists in religious traditions. Tefnut continues to feature in funerary and cosmological texts, though she is not the focus of personal devotion.

The Middle Kingdom: Tefnut's cosmological significance is reinforced in the Coffin Texts, where she plays a role in creation and the daily rebirth of the sun. She is described as both fierce and life-giving, embodying the dual nature of moisture, essential but potentially destructive. Her role within the Heliopolitan system remains central in priestly theology.

The Second Intermediate Period: Religious activity is more regionally varied during this fragmented period. Tefnut remains present in theological texts.

The New Kingdom: Tefnut gains more visibility, especially in royal and temple contexts. She appears in temple reliefs and cosmological scenes, often alongside Shu, supporting the sky or assisting in the rebirth of Ra. Her feline or leonine aspect becomes more pronounced; she is sometimes associated with the Eye of Ra, a violent, protective solar force also linked to Sekhmet, Bastet, and Hathor. In solar theology, she plays a key role in the myth of the Eye, where the goddess flees and must be returned to restore cosmic order.

The Third Intermediate Period: Tefnut's associations with solar and protective goddesses are emphasised. In some contexts, she is merged or linked with other lion-headed deities, reinforcing her role in state rituals, particularly those concerning kingship and cosmic balance.

The Late Period: Tefnut features more distinctly in religious iconography, often depicted with a lioness head or as a woman with a solar disk and uraeus. Her mythological role as part of the Eye of Ra complex is further ritualised. She is venerated as part of triads or divine families, often with Shu and Atum or Ra.

The Ptolemaic Period: Her functions are preserved in temple reliefs, especially at Edfu, Dendera, and Philae Island. Her identification with lion-headed goddesses becomes more explicit; she is often part of the 'Eye of Ra' narratives depicted in temple walls. Texts from this period treat her as both nurturing and wrathful, a divine force needing appeasement and control.

The Roman and Byzantine Periods: Tefnut remains represented in temples and religious texts, though public worship is increasingly overshadowed by the rise of Christianity. Final expressions of traditional Egyptian religion still acknowledge her place in the divine order. With the decline of ancient Egyptian religion, Tefnut's active worship ends. Her legacy survives in mythological texts, temple reliefs, and the preserved structure of the Ennead.

As a goddess of moisture, rain, and fertility, Tefnut perhaps has some similarity with the Greek / Roman goddesses Hera / Juno (as the rain-bringer) and Iris (personified the rainbow and moisture in the air). People could pray to Tefnut for rain, dew, fertility, balance, harmony, *ma'at*, protection and strength, emotional and spiritual renewal, and divine order and justice.

Thoth: God of Wisdom, Science, and Magic

Left: 'Thoth' in hieroglyphs

Thoth is a god of wisdom, writing, hieroglyphs, science, magic, judgment, and the moon. His name means 'He who is like the Ibis', referencing one of his sacred animals. He is also known as the 'Lord of Divine Words' and 'Scribe of the Gods'. He is the son of Ra in some traditions[383], Set, or Horus in others. In the religion of Hermopolis,

Thoth is self-created or born from the heart of Ra, or from the lips of Ra, making him a product of divine thought and speech. He is the husband of Ma'at[384] according to some traditions. In others, he is associated with Seshat, goddess of writing and wisdom, either as consort or female counterpart.

Thoth acts as the divine scribe and record-keeper, maintaining the order of the cosmos through language and knowledge. He oversees time, the lunar calendar, and sacred rituals, and is the patron of scribes and scholars. He also serves as a mediator between gods, and a judge in the afterlife, weighing the deeds of the dead alongside Osiris and Ma'at.

Thoth plays key roles in major myths, such as restoring the Eye of Ra after it flees, helping to pacify goddesses like Tefnut or Sekhmet. He is central in the Osirian myth, assisting Isis in reviving Osiris and protecting Horus. He acts as an impartial divine judge[385], healing Horus and recording the gods' decisions. He is also credited with creating the 365-day calendar by adding days to the year through a game with the moon goddess.

Thoth is most commonly depicted as a man with the head of an ibis, often holding a writing palette and stylus, symbolising his scribal duties. Alternatively, he may appear as a baboon, another sacred animal linked to wisdom and the moon. In both forms, he is sometimes shown with a lunar disk or crescent moon above his head, reinforcing his connection to time and cycles. His principal centre of worship is Hermopolis, where he is revered as the city's chief deity. Temples and shrines to Thoth also exist in Abydos and Thebes, and he is widely respected throughout ancient Egypt as a vital figure in religion, governance, and cosmic stability.

The Early Dynastic Period: Thoth's attributes, writing, measurement, and wisdom, begin to take shape. The intellectual and administrative role he would come to embody is already important in the emerging bureaucracy and temple record-keeping.

---

[383] Budge, E. A. Wallis (1969) [1904]. The Gods of the Egyptians. Vol. 1 of 2. New York: Dover Publications.
[384] Eric H Cline, David O'Connor (January 5, 2006), Thutmose III: A New Biography, University of Michigan Press, p. 127
[385] Budge, E. A. Wallis (1969) [1904].

The Old Kingdom: Thoth is fully established as a divine scribe, lunar deity, and messenger of the gods. He appears in the Pyramid Texts as a mediator in the afterlife and a recorder of the pharaoh's deeds. He is associated with Ma'at, often acting as the judge and keeper of divine balance. His cult centre at Hermopolis begins to rise in prominence. Iconography includes the ibis-headed man and the baboon, both sacred to him.

Name, Wikipedia Creative Commons, Public Domain

The First Intermediate Period: Political division affects state cults, but Thoth remains respected in funerary practices. Local priesthoods maintain devotion, and his intellectual and scribal roles ensure his continuity in elite circles.

The Middle Kingdom: Thoth's reputation as patron of scribes and god of wisdom becomes fully entrenched. The Coffin Texts invoke him as a protector of the dead and a judge in divine disputes. Hermopolis becomes a major religious centre and Thoth is described as a creator through speech and thought.

The Second Intermediate Period: Despite the disruption of central authority, Thoth's significance remains. Regional devotion continues, particularly in Hermopolis and Thebes. He is seen as guardian of sacred knowledge and mediator between gods.

The New Kingdom: Thoth enjoys widespread reverence across Egypt He plays a central role in the Judgement of the Dead, recording the results of the 'Weighing of the Heart' ceremony in the Book of the Dead. He is regarded as the inventor of writing, master of hieroglyphs, mathematics, astronomy, and ritual timing.

The Third Intermediate Period: Thoth continues to be venerated as a learned and just deity. He features prominently in funerary papyri, magical spells, and temple liturgies. His role as lunar god and divine arbitrator remains key in cosmological traditions.

The Late Period: Thoth's worship flourishes once again, especially in response to increased emphasis on intellectual and magical traditions. He is depicted in temples across Egypt, including Saqqara, Abydos, and Hermopolis. His identification with sacred knowledge leads to the development of esoteric traditions, influencing later Hellenistic beliefs.

The Ptolemaic and Roman Periods: Thoth is fully integrated into Greco-Egyptian religion. He is syncretised with the Greek / Roman god Hermes / Mercury. Temples honouring Thoth remain active with Thoth and Hermes / Mercury being worshipped side-by-side. Later this worship becomes increasingly symbolic as state support for traditional religion wanes. Hermetic texts inspired by Thoth's Greco-Egyptian form begin to circulate, merging Egyptian theology with Greek philosophy and mysticism.

The Byzantine Period: The worship of Thoth formally ends with the decline of Egyptian temple religion. However, his legacy thrives in Hermetic philosophy, Gnostic writings, alchemy, and early Western esotericism.

As a god of wisdom and intellect, Thoth is equated with the Greek / Roman god Hermes / Mercury, leading to the deity Hermes Trismegistus ('Hermes the Thrice-Greatest') or Mercurius Ter Maximus ('Mercury the Thrice-Greatest'), a foundational figure in Hermeticism, Hermetic Philosophy, Mercurianism, Mercurian Philosophy, and Western Esotericism.

Wadjet: Cobra Goddess and Protector

Left: 'Wadjet' in hieroglyphs

Wadjet is a goddess of protection, kingship, royal authority, and fertility. Her name means 'the green one', reflecting her connection to growth and the fertile Nile Delta. She is also known as the uraeus goddess, symbolising the royal cobra. Wadjet acts as a fierce protector, primarily guarding the pharaoh and Lower Egypt. She embodies the fiery Eye of Ra[386], defending divine order and punishing chaos. She safeguards women in childbirth and protects them from enemies that could do them harm.

Wadjet protects Horus while he hides in the Nile Delta marshes from his enemies[387]. Like other goddesses such as Sekhmet and Tefnut, she displays a wrathful nature that requires appeasement after unleashing her fury. She is frequently identified with other powerful protective goddesses, including Bastet, Sekhmet, and Mut, often merging aspects of their fierce and nurturing qualities. Wadjet is central to the concept of the Eye of Ra, a solar force of destruction and protection.

Wadjet is most commonly depicted as a rearing cobra, the uraeus, on the pharaoh's crown, ready to strike at enemies. She also appears as a cobra-headed woman, a lion-headed figure, or a winged serpent, often shown with the Deshret (red crown of Lower Egypt) or accompanied by a solar disk. Her main centre of worship is at Buto, located in the Nile Delta, an important site in prehistoric Egypt[388]. There, she is revered as a powerful local deity and, over time, as a symbol of national unity and royal authority.

The Pre-Dynastic Period: Wadjet emerges as a local goddess of Buto in the Nile Delta, closely associated with protection and fertility in this fertile region.

The Early Dynastic Period: Her role expands as the guardian of Lower Egypt, symbolised by the uraeus worn on the pharaoh's crown, marking her importance in royal authority.

The Old Kingdom: Wadjet becomes firmly entrenched in royal iconography, representing the divine protection of the king and the unity of the Two Lands (Upper and Lower Egypt).

The First Intermediate Period: Despite political fragmentation, worship of Wadjet continues in the Nile Delta, maintaining her status as protector of Lower Egypt.

---

[386] Wilkinson, Richard H. (2003) The Complete Gods and Goddesses of Ancient Egypt. Thames & Hudson. p. 227
[387] Pearson, Patricia O'Connell; Holdren, John (May 2021). World History: Our Human Story. Versailles, Kentucky: Sheridan Kentucky. p. 29. ISBN 978-1-60153-123-0.
[388] Morenz, Ludwig, "The Early Dynastic Period", in The Oxford Handbook of Egyptology (2020), p. 600

The Middle Kingdom: Her cult thrives in temples where she is honoured as both a fierce protector of the king and a guardian of women in childbirth.

Wadjet, Wikipedia Creative Commons, Public Domain

The Second Intermediate Period: During this time of foreign rule and instability, Wadjet's symbolic importance as a protector remains significant, especially in the Delta region.

The New Kingdom: Wadjet's identity merges with other goddesses like Bastet and Sekhmet, enhancing her role as the Eye of Ra, a divine force upholding order and punishing chaos.

The Third Intermediate Period: Although political power shifts, worship of Wadjet persists, particularly at her cult centre, as she continues to represent royal protection.

The Late Period: Her cult endures amidst foreign domination, with Buto remaining a key centre where Wadjet is revered as a symbol of Lower Egypt and kingship.

The Ptolemaic and Roman Periods: Greek rulers adopt traditional Egyptian deities, including Wadjet, preserving her worship and associating her with the legitimacy of their reign. Temples dedicated to Wadjet continue to operate, reflecting the persistence of ancient religious traditions under Roman governance.

The Byzantine Period: As Christianity spreads, the worship of Wadjet declines, yet some elements of her imagery survive in local customs before the cult ultimately fades away.

As a guardian of rulers and nations, there are perhaps some small similarities with the Greek / Roman goddess Athena / Minerva, as both are fierce protectors of cities and leaders. Wadjet defends the pharaoh as Athena / Minerva defends Athens. Wadjet could be prayed to for protection, victory, justice, fertility, health, renewal, and divine favour.

Wosret: Goddess of Power and Protection

Left: 'Wosret' in hieroglyphs

Wosret is a goddess of power, protection, and the city of Thebes. Her name means 'the powerful female one' or simply 'the powerful', and it is also the root of the ancient Egyptian name for Thebes (*Waset*). She is occasionally referred to as 'Mistress of Thebes' or 'She Who is Mighty'. She is the wife of Amun, the major Theban god (in early traditions). Wosret serves as a protective deity associated with strength, sovereignty, kingship, and divine authority. Her presence symbolises royal legitimacy and divine might, especially in relation to the Theban region during the Middle Kingdom.

There are few surviving myths involving Wosret, and she does not appear prominently in mythology. However, her significance is reflected in royal ideology. Wosret is not explicitly merged with other deities, though some scholars suggest she may have been an early aspect or precursor to the more prominent goddess Mut, who later takes her place as chief goddess of Thebes. It is also possible that Mut is simply a later name for Wosret[389].

Wosret is usually depicted as a woman wearing a tall, crown-like headdress, sometimes shaped like the ancient was-sceptre, a symbol of power, which may derive from her name. Occasionally she holds a was-sceptre and an ankh. Sometimes she is depicted carrying other weapons such as spears and a bow and arrow[390]. Unlike more widely-known goddesses, she does not have a widespread or standardised iconography.

Wosret's main centre of worship is Thebes, where she functions as a local goddess in the early Middle Kingdom. Her legacy persists in royal names and in the cultural memory of Theban religious history.

The Old Kingdom: Wosret's name is not widely attested in this period, but regional deities begin to emerge in Upper Egypt, especially around the Thebes region. The roots of her identity develop locally, connected to the city's name itself, Waset, which shares linguistic ties with her name.

The First Intermediate Period: During this politically fragmented time, Thebes gains local prominence, and Wosret becomes increasingly venerated as a local protectress and patron goddess of the city. She begins to be associated with political legitimacy and divine favour, particularly among rising Theban rulers.

---

[389] Ray, John Reflections of Osiris: lives from ancient Egypt p.28
[390] Richard H. Wilkinson (2003). The complete gods and goddesses of ancient Egypt. Internet Archive. Thames & Hudson. p. 169. ISBN 978-0-500-05120-7.

Wosret, Wikipedia Creative Commons, Public Domain

The Middle Kingdom: Wosret reaches the height of her prominence during the 12th Dynasty, as Theban rulers unify Egypt and elevate local deities. Pharaoh Senwosret I (also spelled Sesostris I) incorporates her name into his own, meaning 'Man of Wosret'[391]. Though she has no major temples surviving, textual and titular references suggest she was honoured as a powerful protective goddess. Wosret is seen as a consort or counterpart to Amun.

The Second Intermediate Period: As the central authority weakens again, Wosret remains a figure of regional importance in Thebes.

The New Kingdom: Wosret's influence declines considerably. As Amun rises to national prominence and Thebes becomes Egypt's religious capital, his consort is increasingly identified as Mut, who absorbs many functions of earlier local goddesses, including Wosret. Wosret's name and role fade from major religious texts and iconography; she is no longer actively worshipped as an independent deity.

The Third Intermediate Period: There is no evidence of active worship or revival of Wosret during this period. Theban religious traditions continue to be dominated by the Amun-Mut-Khonsu triad, leaving little space for the return of earlier local goddesses.

The Late Period: Wosret is not part of the religious revival movements seen during this time. She remains largely a historical and linguistic figure, known through royal names and earlier Theban associations.

The Ptolemaic Period: Wosret does not feature in temple reliefs or inscriptions from this era. Hellenistic religion focuses on established, syncretised deities like Isis, Hathor, and Mut. Her earlier identity is conflated or forgotten, with her characteristics fully absorbed into other more dominant goddesses.

The Roman Period: Wosret is no longer actively remembered or worshipped. She does not appear in temple inscriptions, religious texts, or visual iconography of the time. There is no evidence of a surviving cult, shrine, or priesthood dedicated to her, even in Thebes, where she once held local significance. By this period, the religious landscape is dominated by syncretic Greco-Egyptian deities such as Serapis, Isis, and Harpocrates, who are actively promoted by both Roman authorities and Egyptian priestly institutions.

The Byzantine Period: Wosret holds no place in the religious or cultural life of Egypt. Christianity is now firmly established as the dominant religion, and the old Egyptian pantheon is increasingly suppressed or forgotten. Pagan temples are either closed, repurposed, or left to decay, and the worship of traditional deities, particularly local or minor ones like Wosret, is no longer practiced.

As a goddess of royal power and authority, Wosret is perhaps comparable with the Greek / Roman goddess Hera / Juno, as both goddesses oversee kingship, marriage (alliances), and sovereignty, Wosret empowers rulers. Wosret could be prayed to for protection, royal authority, strength, courage, and divine favour.

---

[391] Richard H. Wilkinson (2003).

The Egyptian Gods   An Illustrated Introduction

Summary of Names in Hieroglyphs

Aker (Version 1)

Aker (Version 2)

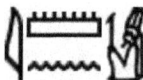
Amun

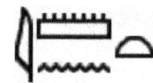
Amunet (Version 1)

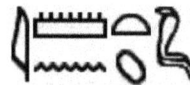
Amunet (Version 2)

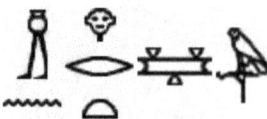
Anhur (Version 1)

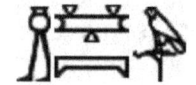
Anhur (Version 2)

Anput

Anubis

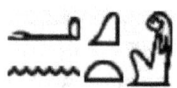
Anuket

Apis (Version 1)

Apis (Version 2)

Apis (Version 3)

Apis (Version 4)

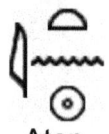
Aten

Atum

Bastet

Bat

Bennu (Version 1)

Bennu (Version 2)

Bes

Geb

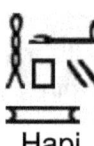
Hapi

Hathor

Hauhet

Heh (Version 1)

Heh (Version 2)

160

The Egyptian Gods — An Illustrated Introduction

Heqet

Heru-ur

Hesat (Version 1)

Hesat (Version 2)

Horus

Imentet

Imhotep (Version 1)

Imhotep (Version 2)

Imhotep (Version 3)

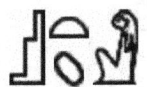
Isis (Version 1)

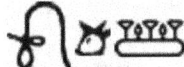
Isis (Version 2)

Kauket

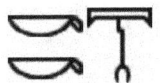
Kek (Version 1)

Kek (Version 2)

Kek (Version 3)

Khepri

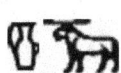
Khnum

Khonsu

Maahes

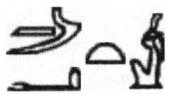
Ma'at (Version 1)

Ma'at (Version 2)

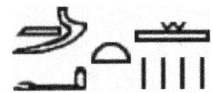
Ma'at (Version 3)

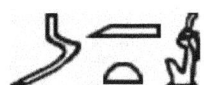
Ma'at (Version 4)

Ma'at (Version 5)

Ma'at (Version 6)

Ma'at (Version 7)

Ma'at (Version 8)

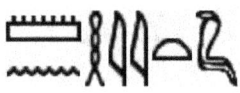		
Menhit	Min	Montu
	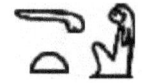	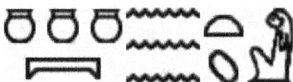
Mut (Version 1)	Mut (Version 2)	Naunet

Nefertem	Neith (Version 1)	Neith (Version 2)

Nekhbet	Neper (Version 1)	Neper (Version 2)
		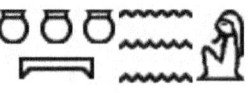
Nephthys	Nepit	Nu

Nut	Osiris	Pakhet
	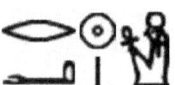	
Ptah	Ra (Version 1)	Ra (Version 2)
Ra (Version 3)	Ra (Version 4)	Ra (Version 5)
	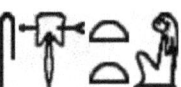	
Renenutet	Satis	Sekhmet

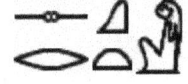 Serket (Version 1)	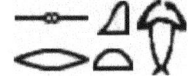 Serket (Version 2)	 Set
 Shu	 Sobek	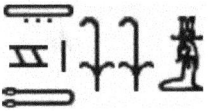 Tatenen
 Tefnut (Version 1)	Tefnut (Version 2)	 Thoth (Version 1)
 Thoth (Version 2)	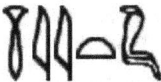 Wadjet	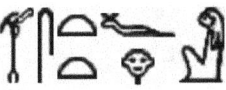 Wosret

Source Texts for Egyptian Mythology

Funerary and Afterlife Texts

These texts were designed to guide and protect the deceased through the afterlife, often inscribed on tomb walls, coffins, or papyri.

Royal Funerary Texts

Primarily reserved for kings (and sometimes queens), these texts describe the journey of the sun god and the deceased through the netherworld.

Pyramid Texts	The earliest religious texts, from the Old Kingdom, inscribed in royal pyramids.
Book of the Dead	A collection of spells to aid the dead in the afterlife, from the New Kingdom and later.
Amduat	Describes the sun god Ra's journey through the 12 hours of the night.
Book of Gates	Depicts the sun god Ra's passage through 12 gates in the underworld.
Book of Caverns	Describes how the enemies of the sun god are punished in the underworld.
Book of the Earth	Describes the sun's journey through the underworld.
Enigmatic Book of the Netherworld	An obscure and symbolic text found in the tomb of Tutankhamun.
Book of the Heavenly Cow	An explanation of the cosmos, suffering, and the afterlife, in royal tombs.
Spell of the Twelve Caves	Describes the soul's journey through 12 netherworld caverns.

Non-Royal Funerary Texts

These were used more widely, including by non-royal individuals, and often adapted from earlier royal texts.

Coffin Texts	An expanded collection of spells found in the coffins of non-royals, from the Middle Kingdom.
Books of Breathing	Texts designed to ensure continued existence in the afterlife, from the Late Period and Ptolemaic Period.
Book of Traversing Eternity	Describes a mystical journey of the soul through the sacred landscape of Egypt and beyond.

Liturgy and Hymn Texts

Texts meant for use in religious rituals or for praising deities.

Festival Songs of Isis and Nephthys	Ritual texts used in temple ceremonies, particularly for festivals of Osiris.

Great Hymn to the Aten	A hymn praising Aten, probably composed by the pharaoh Akhetaten.
Litany of Re	A chant recited in royal tombs to aid the king in uniting with the sun god.
Litany of the Eye of Horus	A ritual invocation and praise of the Eye of Horus, symbolic of protection and healing.

Mythology and Narrative Texts

Texts that convey mythic stories or moral/philosophical teachings through narrative.

The Contendings of Horus and Set	A mythological tale of the conflict between Horus and Set for the throne of Egypt.

www.ingramcontent.com/pod-product-compliance
Lightning Source LLC
Chambersburg PA
CBHW051409070526
44584CB00023B/3355